THE BATTLE OF THE WILDERNESS
IN MYTH AND MEMORY

THE BATTLE OF THE WILDERNESS IN MYTH AND MEMORY

Reconsidering Virginia's Most Notorious CIVIL WAR BATTLEFIELD

ADAM H. PETTY

LOUISIANA STATE UNIVERSITY PRESS
Baton Rouge

Published by Louisiana State University Press

Manufactured in the United States of America
First printing

Designer: Barbara Neely Bourgoyne
Typeface: MillerText
Printer and binder: Sheridan Books

Portions of chapter 4 first appeared, in different form, in "Reconsidering the Wilderness's Role in Battle, 4–6 May 1864," *Journal of Military History* 82 (April 2018): 413–38.

Library of Congress Cataloging-in-Publication Data
Names: Petty, Adam H., author.
Title: The Battle of the Wilderness in myth and memory : reconsidering Virginia's most notorious Civil War battlefield / Adam H. Petty.
Other titles: Reconsidering Virginia's most notorious Civil War battlefield
Description: Baton Rouge : Louisiana State University Press, [2019] | Includes bibliographical references and index.
Identifiers: LCCN 2019007993| ISBN 978-0-8071-7191-2 (cloth : alk. paper) | ISBN 978-0-8071-7213-1 (pdf) | ISBN 978-0-8071-7214-8 (epub)
Subjects: LCSH: Wilderness, Battle of the, Va., 1864. | Mine Run Campaign, Va., 1863. | Chancellorsville, Battle of, Chancellorsville, Va., 1863. | Spotsylvania County (Va.)—History—Civil War, 1861–1865. | Landscapes—Virginia—Spotsylvania County—History. | Forests—Virginia—Spotsylvania County—History. | Wilderness, Battle of the, Va., 1864—Historiography. | Collective memory—United States—History.
Classification: LCC E476.52 .P48 2019 | DDC 973.7/36—dc23
LC record available at https://lccn.loc.gov/2019007993

The paper in this book meets the guidelines for permanence and durability of the Committee on Production Guidelines for Book Longevity of the Council on Library Resources. ♾

To my dear wife Morgan,

who has always helped me find my way in the wilderness.

CONTENTS

PREFACE

The Wilderness of Spotsylvania was a forested region about halfway between Washington, DC, and Richmond, Virginia, which lay just to the west of Fredericksburg. It was, and remains, notorious for being a difficult battleground. From the spring of 1863 to the spring of 1864, the Federal Army of the Potomac and the Confederate Army of Northern Virginia conducted three campaigns, wholly or in part, within the Wilderness. Historians have hardly neglected these operations, which include Chancellorsville (April–May 1863), Mine Run (November–December 1863), and the Battle of the Wilderness (May 1864). The histories of these campaigns have usually included an obligatory paragraph describing the Wilderness and its origins as well as the havoc it could wreak. In addition, various geographical tidbits that shed some light on tactical issues often pepper these works. Beyond this commentary, however, these accounts have given little sustained attention to the forest itself. While a few works have provided some focused analysis on certain narrow aspects of the region, there is a conspicuous need for a broader treatment and a deeper understanding of the Wilderness.[1]

This study is a work of military history that concentrates on the interaction between the Wilderness landscape and the aforementioned campaigns. When I began this project, I intended it to be a contribution to the nascent field of Civil War environmental history. What resulted, however, was a thoroughly military history grounded in the venerable literature surrounding the three Wilderness campaigns rather than the newer environmental histories (as the notes bear out). While environmental history informs its arguments, the questions that drove this study were those of a military historian. That being said, chapters 1 and 3 address issues that environmental historians would recognize as familiar terrain, namely, how human actions contributed to the creation of the Wilderness and how ideas about wilderness landscapes and soldiers' experiences combined to shape the region's image.

Despite its foundation in military history, this book differs from preceding works on the Wilderness in two very important ways. First, instead of focusing on a single battle or campaign, its scope includes all three of the aforementioned operations. This gives an opportunity to observe change over time—especially regarding the attitudes and actions of generals and soldiers toward the Wilderness. That being said, the Battle of the Wilderness is the key event in the region's history. The myth that came to dominate the historical interpretation of the Wilderness formed in its aftermath, many of its elements being specific claims about that battle. As a result, this engagement receives more attention than the others. Second, this work is not a narrative history of the campaigns, but rather a reconsideration of the traditional interpretations surrounding the nature of the Wilderness, especially how it affected military operations and combat. It also differs from the existing Civil War environmental histories by analyzing not only the actual interaction between military and environmental factors but also the changing memory of this interaction over time.

There are five basic traditions that together form the Wilderness myth. First, the Wilderness was a distinctive and nearly unbroken forest made up of thick, second-growth trees and underbrush. This unique vegetation resulted from the local iron industry, which had cut down the original forest to provide fuel for furnaces, leaving the scrubby, thick woods to grow up in its place. Second, the Wilderness's extraordinary characteristics imposed certain conditions on military actions, namely the inability to see for any distance, properly maneuver or maintain a battle line, and use artillery or cavalry profitably. These limitations in turn created a unique and unprecedented combat experience. Third, the Wilderness exuded a mystique, for it was a wild, gloomy, weird, and woeful region associated with death and destruction, fire and hell, and even the supernatural. Fourth, because of the Confederates' superior knowledge of the region and the forest's ability to neutralize the Federals' superiority in numbers and artillery, the Rebels held an edge in any combat there. Fifth, Gen. Robert E. Lee trapped the Federals in these tangled thickets to exploit these advantages.

This Wilderness myth began to take shape during the war but truly blossomed in the postwar years. Union soldiers came away from the Battle of the Wilderness recounting the difficulty of fighting in the tangled landscape. The lingering question, though, was why they had failed to defeat Lee's army there. William Swinton, a wartime correspondent for the *New York Times,* sought to answer this question in a report published only days after the battle's conclusion. In it he, too, described the many natural obstacles the soldiers faced, but he also drew some conclusions that were to have a lasting influence on how historians portrayed the battle, as well as the Wilderness itself. Swinton argued that it was a unique engagement, citing the lack of visibility, the inability to maneuver, and the impossibility of employing artillery and cavalry effectively as reasons for the Federals' failure to obtain victory. He suggested that the possibility of fighting a battle in the Wilderness was a major drawback to Lt. Gen. Ulysses S. Grant's selected route of advance south, an option the Federals would have avoided had the Confederates not forced the issue. He then wondered whether Lee had meant only to delay the Union advance or had desired all along to engage in a decisive confrontation in the Wilderness. Swinton ultimately reasoned that the fierce nature of the fight as well as the advantages the Confederates enjoyed there—such as crowding the Union forces into unfamiliar woods to cancel out their strength in numbers—suggested that Lee meant to force a fight in the Wilderness.[2]

Swinton later perfected his interpretation in his 1866 *Campaigns of the Army of the Potomac,* which was not only one of the first histories of the war in Virginia but also the first to convey the Wilderness myth. Much of what he wrote echoed the sentiments of his wartime report, but Swinton made a few key additions. He emphasized that the Wilderness was an unusual if not unique forest, a byproduct of local mining operations. It was also a terrible place to fight a battle. Swinton no longer surmised but now affirmed that Lee had tried to trap the Union army there to benefit from the advantages it would give the Confederates. To these conclusions he added the element of mystique, calling the Wilderness "a region of gloom and the shadow of death," a "horrid thicket" where "lurid fires played" and in which "the crackle and roll of musketry like the noisy boiling of some hell-caldron . . . told the dread story of death."[3] Here, then, was the basic Wilderness myth fully formed within a year after the war's end.

The steady stream of historians and memoirists who followed then repeated, and often embellished, Swinton's interpretation, perpetuating the Wilderness myth to the present day. Take, for example, James McPherson's *Battle Cry of Freedom,* one of the most widely read modern accounts of the Civil War. McPherson painted the Wilderness as a "gloomy expanse of scrub oaks and pines," a place where Union "superiority in numbers . . . would count for less than in the open." For these reasons, Lee "hit the bluecoats in the flank as they marched through the Wilderness," while Grant had hoped to engage the Rebels "somewhere south of the Wilderness." Once the battle began, McPherson judged, the Confederates held the edge. They "knew the terrain and the Yankees' preponderance of troops produced only immobility in these dense, smoke-filled woods where soldiers could rarely see the enemy, units blundered the wrong way in the directionless jungle, friendly troops fired on each other by mistake, gaps in the opposing line went unexploited because unseen, while muzzle flashes and exploding shells set the underbrush on fire to threaten wounded men with a fiery death."[4] While McPherson's short sketch of the battle did not include every component of the Wilderness myth, it did include many of the most important elements. Each retelling of the engagement has provided its own mixture, but parts of the myth in one form or another are almost always present.

Like all myths, the one surrounding the Wilderness serves a purpose, and its various components contain some partial truths. The intention of this work is to sift through these venerable interpretations—

which, in some cases, have skewed our perception of the Wilderness and how it influenced combat and operations—in the hopes of sorting out truth from error and history from tradition.

Chapter 1 reconsiders the nature and origin of the Wilderness. It argues that, contrary to the traditional and more familiar descriptions, the Wilderness was not a monolithic forest of stunted trees and underbrush but had a patchwork character. Some of the region was the extra-thick forest of lore, while other parts contained thinner woods and even substantial clearings. In addition, the characteristic forest was not primarily the result of the local iron industry, although this economic activity certainly contributed to it. Other pursuits, namely the cultivation of tobacco and the building of plank roads, were also important and in some respects decisive in shaping the landscape. Finally, the Wilderness was not a unique landscape but simply one example of a Virginia phenomenon, for there were Wilderness-like forests in other parts of the state where exhausted and abandoned land was found.

The second chapter questions the oft-repeated notion that the Battle of the Wilderness was a unique engagement because of the environment in which it was fought. Comparing this action to Chancellorsville, which also was fought in the Wilderness, and Chickamauga (September 18–20, 1863), which was fought in northwestern Georgia, reveals several things about the nature of combat in the Wilderness. First, the Battles of the Wilderness and Chancellorsville were not the twins that many historians often imply them to be. Second, Chickamauga shared many of the characteristics of the Battle of the Wilderness despite being fought hundreds of miles from Virginia in a different type of forest. These findings suggest that the Battle of the Wilderness lay at one end of a spectrum of forest fights, having fewer open spaces, thus featuring less artillery and more infantry fighting, while having the lowest combat visibility. On the other end of this spectrum lay Chancellorsville, where larger open spaces allowed artillery to operate in a way that was unusual on a wooded battlefield. Chickamauga would fall somewhere in between these engagements. In the end, the Battle of the Wilderness was just one manifestation of the tactical problems that Civil War armies faced when operating in a forested region.

Chapter 3 analyzes the mystique surrounding the Wilderness. The term "wilderness" traditionally had negative connotations, indicating a forest that was beyond man's control and inhabited by savages. With time, the region's name came to set it apart as it fulfilled many of the expectations associated with the word. Many soldiers who campaigned in the Wilderness in May 1863 showed no awareness that they were in a peculiar expanse, but by the time of the Overland Campaign one year later, they recognized it as a distinct place with certain characteristics. Eventually, the Wilderness became notorious as a malevolent landscape associated with death, devastation, fire, and the supernatural.

The fourth chapter undermines the tradition that the Confederates held an edge in the Wilderness. In fact, as Earl Hess has argued, the Wilderness hampered both sides. Although many postwar writers claimed that the Confederates knew the region better, in reality, the two armies were more or less equally familiar with it. The Wilderness caused similar problems for each army. The one advantage the Confederates did enjoy was having access to a better road network allowing easier deployment of their forces initially. While the Wilderness disrupted Lee's flank attacks and limited their ultimate success, these strikes made the best use of the difficult landscape. Moreover, they demonstrate that the Confederates—through their initiative rather than any other factor—could turn the Wilderness to their advantage. Yet the Wilderness in and of itself did not prove innately beneficial to one side or the other. If it was a good place for the Confederates to fight, it was only because they made it so by aggressively taking advantage of the admittedly limited opportunities the landscape afforded.

Chapter 5 attacks the myth that the Federals sought to avoid fighting in the Wilderness at the outset of the Overland Campaign, while Lee sought to trap the Union army there. It tracks the plans pursued by both sides in all three campaigns in the Wilderness, providing a very different understanding of how the region figured into Confederate and Union thinking. Whatever reservations Federal commanders felt about the Wilderness at the time, they were not sufficient to override other concerns such as entrenchments, logistics, and safe river crossings. The commanders' reports, moreover, reveal little in the way of anxiety about the forest interfering with their plans. Lee, in contrast, showed a marked awareness of the Wilderness and the problems it caused his army, suggesting that he would not intentionally fight there unless forced by compelling circumstances, such as those presented at the opening of the Overland Campaign.

Ultimately, the Wilderness myth was the product of hindsight. The need to make sense of the May 1864 battle drove its formation, but the longevity of Swinton's interpretation depended upon the undeniable appeal of his creation. Not only did the Wilderness myth make a great story, but it also provided different constituencies with reasons to embrace and perpetuate it. Former Confederates used it to glorify Lee's generalship and his army's performance while denigrating Grant. Union critics employed it to excuse the Federal army's shortcomings while disparaging Grant's generalship. Friends of the Union general used it to explain away his failure to win a decisive victory at the outset of the Overland Campaign. All veterans of the war in Virginia, however, could glory in having fought on the worst battlefield of the war under the most trying conditions. Even well after the passing of these groups, Swinton's Wilderness myth remains compelling to both historians, who retell it, and to readers of Civil War history, who love the epic tale of a terrible battle between the two great generals of the war in a malevolent landscape. It is for these reasons that the Wilderness myth has endured. The Wilderness, however, was blamed for that which it was blameless and has since come down in history as a stumbling block of a battlefield craftily chosen by Lee. Here the Confederates could run roughshod over their Federal opponents in the dreadful and gloomy woods. In reality, the Wilderness was a battlefield that created very difficult combat conditions, but many of the claims of exceptionalism were unfounded, despite their wide-ranging influence in the annals of the war.

A NOTE ON TERMINOLOGY AND MAPS

In this book, the term "the Wilderness" refers to the entirety of that forested region of Virginia, while "the Wilderness battlefield" refers to the part of this region where the Battle of the Wilderness took place.

"The Chancellorsville battlefield" is another portion of the Wilderness, though it overlaps with the Wilderness battlefield to a small extent. To avoid confusion, I have referred to the clash on May 5–6, 1864, as "the Battle of the Wilderness" rather than simply "the Wilderness," as Civil War historians often do. I also at times refer to the three campaigns that took place either partly or entirely in the Wilderness as "the Wilderness campaigns." Finally, the Battle of the Wilderness was one action in the larger Overland Campaign, which traditionally extends from the Federal army's crossing of the Rapidan River in May 1864 to its initial assaults on Petersburg in mid-June 1864.

This volume contains one map of the Wilderness. Readers looking to follow the armies' movements during the various Wilderness campaigns would do well to consult the excellent maps produced by the National Park Service for Chancellorsville and the Battle of the Wilderness. John Bigelow's classic study of Chancellorsville has a number of wonderful maps in it that help explain that complex campaign. Martin Graham and George Skoch's study of Mine Run has useful maps, as does Gordon Rhea's work on the Battle of the Wilderness. The atlas that accompanies *The Official Records of the War of the Rebellion* is another essential resource.

ACKNOWLEDGMENTS

It is a distinct pleasure to acknowledge the many people who have helped me complete this book. First and foremost is George Rable, who gave enormous amounts of advice and feedback that fundamentally shaped this work and greatly improved its quality. I also want to recognize the assistance provided by Lawrence Kohl, whose sharp criticism and wise writing advice forced me to refine my work. He also deserves the credit for coining the phrase "wilderness mystique." Bart Elmore, John Giggie, and Lesley Gordon also assisted in this project, each in their own way. Rand Dotson and LSU Press were a pleasure to work with, and the anonymous reviewer they recruited provided excellent suggestions for refining this book.

John Hennessy and Eric Mink at Fredericksburg and Spotsylvania National Military Park also deserve thanks for providing space for me to work and for allowing access to the park's excellent collection of materials at Chatham. Hennessy also shared a rich cache of sources he has collected, which proved very valuable for my project, and read early drafts of some of the chapters. Jim Ogden was very helpful during my visit to the Chickamauga and Chattanooga National Military Park. He pointed me to many useful sources, and the conversation I had with him and a high school teacher from Oneonta, Alabama, proved very helpful in forming my thoughts about how soldiers react to battlefield environments. His tour of the battlefield for the Society of Civil War Historians in the summer of 2016 was a crucial moment that pushed me toward including Chickamauga material in this study. The many archivists I worked with at the US Army Heritage and Education Center at Carlisle Barracks, Pennsylvania, were all very helpful and accommodating despite my many requests and questions. The University of Alabama's history department and the College of Arts and Sciences provided three crucial research travel awards that proved instrumental for visiting the Wilderness battlefields and researching the Chatham materials. The US Army Heritage and Education Center awarded me a General and Mrs. Matthew B. Ridgway Research Grant, which allowed me to search their archives as well. Finally, the History Department of the Church of Jesus Christ of Latter-day Saints helped fund some of the costs associated with publishing this work. Many thanks to these institutions for supporting this project.

I would also like to thank friends and family for all the support they provided as I made my way through the early stages of my career. Daniel Burge, Katie Deale, and Marcus Witcher provided encouragement and helpful advice on the various challenges encountered while I was earning a PhD and navigating the publishing process. Extended family in South Carolina provided me with food, lodging, and good conversation on the way to Virginia. My parents and in-laws helped support our young family in many ways during the long years of working on this project, and I thank them for that. Special thanks goes to my mother and mother-in-law for helping out with the kids while I was away on research trips. My father, affectionately known as the Old Man, deserves acknowledgment for fostering my interest in history from an early age and for spending many hours discussing with me this project and the curiosities of the academy. He also accompanied me on several research trips and read over my manuscript. My daughters, Norah and June, were sources of much joy throughout this process. Many long walks, storytimes, piggyback rides, and cookie parties will forever be a part of our time in Tuscaloosa.

Finally, there is Morgan, my wife. Words are incapable of expressing all that this exceptional woman has done for me. It is no exaggeration to say that, without her, this project would not have come to fruition, although I suspect that she would be fine if she never heard of the Wilderness again. In the end, she is one of the main reasons why life is good.

THE BATTLE OF THE WILDERNESS IN MYTH AND MEMORY

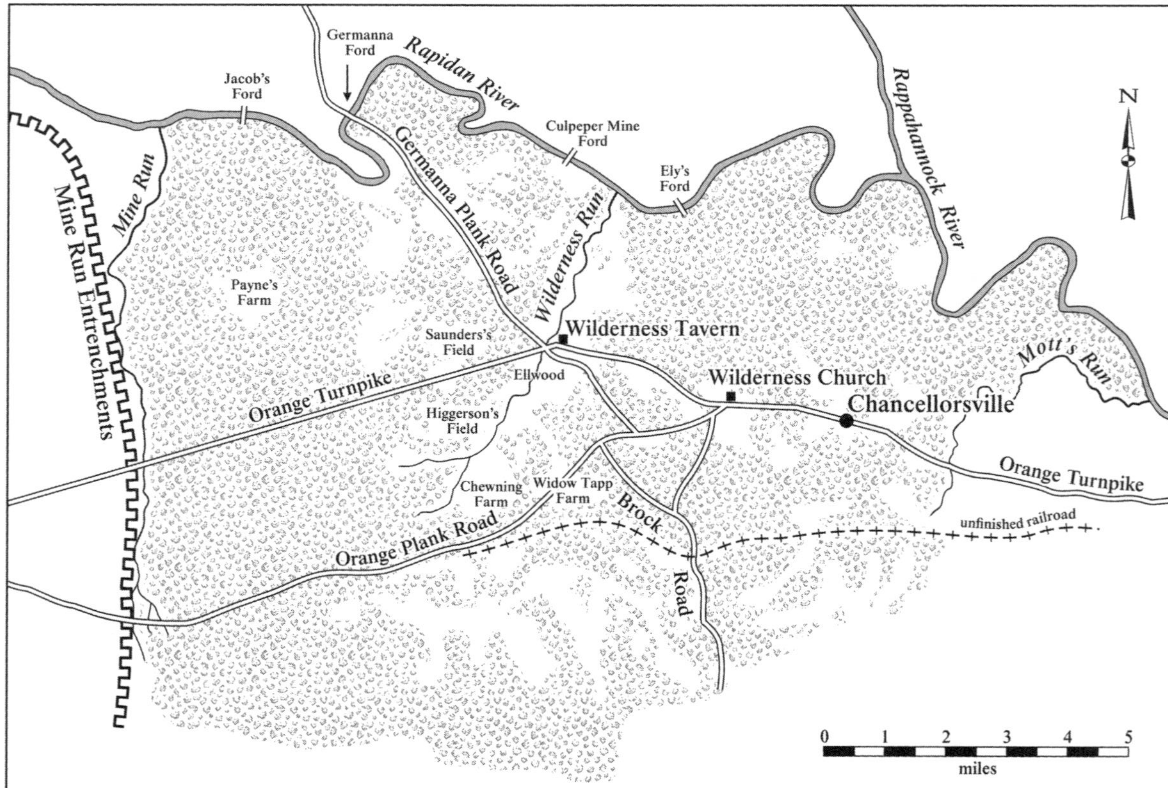

The Wilderness. *Map by Mary Lee Eggart.*

1

THE NATURE AND ORIGINS OF THE WILDERNESS

Most accounts of the various battles in the Wilderness include an obligatory paragraph, or perhaps just a quick aside, describing the region and its origins. Generally, they paint a picture of one vast forest full of thick vegetation resulting from the local iron industry. Armistead Long, a veteran of General Lee's Army of Northern Virginia, explained that the Wilderness "had been an extensive mining district, from which the timber had been cut to supply fuel for feeding the smelting-furnaces, and since then the young growth had sprung up ten times thicker than the primeval forest." Modern historians sound a similar note. Take Edward Steere's description of the region. He portrayed the Wilderness as "a dreary wasteland" in which "the primeval forest of stately pine and sturdy oak was felled . . . to provide fuel for smelting the iron ore torn from shallow pits." In time, "a second growth of scrub trees, interlaced with dense underbrush and thorny vines, rudely covered the ugly scars left by robbery of the subsoil."[1]

Often paired with this origin story is the idea that the Wilderness was a distinct, unusual, or even unique environment. William Swinton —a war correspondent turned historian—argued in his 1866 history that "the woods of the Wilderness have not the ordinary features of a forest." Later writers followed his interpretive lead. Adam Badeau, a member of Lieutenant General Grant's staff, also wrote about "the extraordinary character of the region." Even modern historians repeat this notion. Stephen Sears, for example, described the Wilderness as a "distinctive tract of Virginia woodland" and noted "its distinctive character."[2]

Some have gone further still, contending that the Wilderness stands out among the many battlefields of the war. Maj. Gen. Andrew Humphreys, who served as Maj. Gen. George Meade's chief of staff, claimed that, although certain features of the Wilderness "were found in other of the battle-grounds of the two armies," to his knowledge "no great battle ever took place before on such ground." In a similar vein Benson Lossing, in his 1912 history of the war, called the Wilderness battleground "one of the most remarkable battlefields ever known."[3]

This enduring origin story, with its accompanying notions about the nature of the Wilderness, constitutes one of the region's central and foundational myths. Upon it are based other myths, such as the Wilderness's menacing mystique and the unique battle conditions the forest caused, which allegedly favored the Confederates and shaped their military operations.

Only recently have historians begun to challenge the long-held ideas surrounding the nature and origin of the Wilderness. The best work on this topic has been done by Sean Adams, Noel Harrison, and John Hennessy, who have collectively undermined the traditional interpretation of a consistently dense woodland created by iron manufacturing. Instead, they have argued that the Wilderness landscape was already present in the eighteenth century as a consequence of tobacco cultivation, with various waves of deforestation in the Wilderness creating a patchwork of woods of different density.[4]

Indeed, a close analysis shows that the Wilderness was far from uniform. Rather, it was a patchwork of open areas and forest of varying density that reflected a long collaboration between man and nature. Its topography was not uniform either, some areas being flat and some hilly, with runs and swamps thrown in for good measure. It was also a changing landscape, although it might well appear timeless to anyone first encountering it. The Wilderness was a poor, sparsely populated region in which nearly everything—from the soil, to the vegetation, to the buildings, to the roads—was in decay. Its origins were also more complex than the traditional interpretation suggests. While mining enterprises and iron works certainly caused some deforestation, they were not the only culprits. Tobacco cultivation stripped the region early on and sapped the soil's fertility. The planters then abandoned the exhausted fields, allowing the forest to reclaim the land. Abandoned fields covered in stunted trees, like those in the Wilderness, were hardly unique, although they might seem so to the uninitiated. In fact, they were present in various parts of Virginia, even on other Civil War battlefields. With the tobacco fields exhausted, enterprising men then turned to mining and iron works to squeeze a profit from the worn-out land, clearing additional land in the process. The construction of several plank roads during the 1850s resulted in another, smaller measure of deforestation and subsequent second-growth woodlands. This last round of cutting probably gave the Orange Plank Road corridor, where much of the heaviest fighting took place during the Battle of the Wilderness, the extra-thick covering of saplings that the troops so often described. The combination of these activities—tobacco cultivation, mining, and road building—left the land forested on the whole, but with thickets in various stages of maturity and density.

To have a proper understanding of the events that took place in the Wilderness, as well as the soldiers' reactions to them, it is necessary to have a clear picture of what this region was actually like. For contemporary witnesses, the Wilderness seemed to be one vast, interminable forest, a notion reinforced by the fact that they only saw a small slice of a large region. "We are in a dence wilderness nuthing but woods all round," as one Federal soldier, Albert Reid, described it, stating further, "sins we have crossed the river I think we have marched fifteen miles in woods without coming to a cleering." Another Union soldier agreed, concluding that it was "one continuation of forest, with occasional small islands of clearing," while William Randall of the 1st

Michigan Sharpshooters called it "a Wilderness of Pines extending for many miles." Perhaps Edwin Groff of the 143rd Pennsylvania captured the reactions of Union soldiers best, explaining to his parents that he could not "give [them] any idea of the country through here" but advised them to "just think of woods. Nothing but woods of scrub oak, stunted pines, and vines with here and there a small farm and a cleared field with ravines and hollows and a stream of water here and there."[5]

Many Confederates concurred with their opponents, portraying the Wilderness as one vast forest. One Southerner described it as "a very continuously and densely wooded poverty stricken section" that was "densely wooded and grown up with underbrush." Another found it to have "very few 'clearings'" as it "consists almost wholly of a forest of dense undergrowth." Alexander Boteler, a member of Maj. Gen. J. E. B. Stuart's staff, went further, claiming that "for miles along the road the forests are unbroken by a single clearing and the traveller may journey on for hours without seeing a sign of . . . habitations." Moreover, "there is . . . on both sides a tangled mass of undergrowth apparently interminable" and "densely intricate."[6]

While contemporary witnesses commonly portrayed the Wilderness as a largely unbroken forest, an alternative—as well as more accurate—depiction would be a "patchwork" landscape.[7] This term suggests that the Wilderness, rather than being one mass of thick trees with a few small openings, was a more varied landscape, with patches of vegetation of varying density, a shifting topography, open areas, and runs and swamps.

Some, however, recognized the variety within the Wilderness landscape. Although to Vermont native Wilbur Fisk "it [appeared] to be one uninterrupted wilderness," his description of the region during the Mine Run Campaign included small clearings; land "covered with small second-growth pine" that "looks as if it had been under cultivation once, but probably worn out and abandoned"; and other parts "grown up to oak and other solid timber of all sizes," which had "probably been forest from time immemorial." Of special interest is Theodore Lyman's account. As an aide for General Meade, Lyman traveled to various parts of the region and probably saw far more of it than most soldiers. He claimed that the Wilderness was "a more or less dense growth of pine or of oak," implying that the vegetation was not consistent. He then specified that "the very worst of it is parallel [to the] Orange plank and upper part of the Brock road," where it was "mostly a low, continuous, thick growth of small saplings, fifteen to thirty feet high and seldom larger than one's arm."[8] This last statement again suggests that the Wilderness was far from uniform, a fact not always apparent to soldiers with more limited views of the region.

Even when the soldiers did not make these sorts of distinctions, historians can discern them by comparing the testimony of groups of witnesses from different parts of the Wilderness. The Wilderness battlefield provides a good example of how the variety of topography and vegetation becomes apparent by using this method. Men fighting on the northern part of the battlefield encountered hilly terrain with a fairly diverse covering of vegetation. Milton Myers, a soldier in the 110th Ohio, found that "the surface here is quite hilly, or uneven," and described the area as "thickly overgrown with trees of all sizes," with "small trees and shoots" and bushes, along with "larger ones" such as "oaks 3 feet in diameter, some hickory, and plenty of little dogwood trees." Many complained of the thick underbrush. John R. Adams, a chaplain for the 5th Maine, described the area north of the Orange Turnpike as being "filled with low bushes" and "covered with thick underbrush." Likewise, Washington Roebling, a staff officer in the V Corps, recalled seeing "an exceedingly thick growth of small pines and underbrush." Others described a greater variety of obstacles. One North Carolinian in Lee's army complained that it was "almost impossible for a man to walk, as the woods are thick with an underbrush growth and all kinds of shrubbery, old logs, grapevines, and goodness knows what." Daniel Holt, a surgeon in the VI Corps, had similar observations about the ground his unit occupied. "Swampy, hilly, bushes thick as dog's hair, grape vines, rotten logs and fallen trees, make up this pretty picture," he sarcastically concluded.[9]

In contrast, those fighting farther to the south near the Orange Plank Road found a flat or gently rolling landscape whose dominant feature was dense growths of saplings. Philip Powers, a Confederate, described the part of the Wilderness he saw as "perfectly flat," while Union chaplain A. M. Stewart noted how the land was "undulating with occasional swamps, . . . through which, if a man attempts to walk, he sinks leg deep." As always with the Wilderness, though, it was the trees that made the biggest impression. Rhode Islander Daniel Handy simply stated that "it is all young woods," while a chaplain with the 10th Massachusetts provided a more detailed description, finding "a thick growth of small oak trees from one to three inches in diameter and with the branches so interlaced as to render passage through them extremely difficult and to render any but the most limited view impossible." Peter Alexander, a Confederate news correspondent, had similar complaints about the "dense and almost impenetrable growth of stunted bushes, pines, and black jacks."[10]

Not only were the Wilderness's woods not uniform, but they also were marked by open areas that contained farms of varying size and productivity. These included places like Saunders's field, the Widow Tapp farm, the Chewning farm, Higgerson's field, Payne's farm, and Ellwood. Most of these local farms were not particularly large or productive. Fisk observed during the Mine Run Campaign that "once in a while, a small clearing with a log house in the center, and a high fence all around it, and with some signs of the land having been cultivated in modern times" was visible, but he decided that "these places have strayed away so far from all civilization that it will be hardly worth while to take them into account." Boteler provided a more specific example, describing the Widow Tapp farm as "an old field, scantily covered with sedge grass and a scattered growth of stunted pines." While the Tapp farm was hardly a model of good agriculture, Ellwood, in contrast, was a substantial estate and apparently well maintained. During the Chancellorsville Campaign, Brig. Gen. Alpheus Williams found himself "near Old Wilderness," not far from Ellwood, and concluded that it was "no wilderness but the best-cultivated part of Virginia I have seen outside the valley."[11]

Other open spaces housed a variety of decaying structures. Numerous taverns dotted the area, including Wilderness Tavern, Robertson's Tavern, Todd's Tavern, and most famously Chancellorsville. One traveler passing through the Wilderness in 1846 observed that before the railroads opened up in Virginia, "all the traveling was done either in stage coaches or in private conveyances," and these taverns benefited from this traffic. For instance, Chancellorsville, which opened for business by 1816, was but ten miles from Fredericksburg and consequently received the stagecoaches for breakfast, "which was a source of great profit to the Inn keeper."[12] Yet by the time the traveler was writing, the railroads had "entirely broken up all the Taverns which formerly did a great business but which do nothing now," a fact of which "the Inn keepers complain bitterly." By the time of the Civil War, the region's stores had likewise seen better days. Maps of the Wilderness show several places of worship, including the Wilderness Church, New Hope Church, and Piney Branch Church. Private dwellings, with some exceptions, were modest. Charles Brewster, a Massachusetts soldier, remarked during the Mine Run Campaign that "the houses were mostly mere huts in the woods." Compared to Chancellorsville, which was "an old fashioned brick house," or Ellwood, most of the residences in the Wilderness were indeed humble.[13]

There was also a network of roads that crisscrossed the Wilderness. These varied in quality but constituted the only other open areas of note in the region. Most were primitive, being little more than trails through the forest. Lyman referred to them as "narrow roads" that were "mere farmers' or woodcutters' thoroughfares" connecting the various open spaces in the Wilderness. But there were also more substantial roads passing through that connected Fredericksburg with Orange Court House. The two main east–west routes were the Orange Turnpike and the Orange Plank Road. The former, incorporated by the Virginia legislature in 1810, was originally a macadamized road made up of crushed stone. By the time of the Civil War, it had become a plain dirt road and was in disrepair.[14] The Orange Plank Road was of more recent construction and lay to the south of the Orange Turnpike. Completed sometime in the 1850s, only "the right-hand side coming eastward," which is where "the more heavily loaded wagons" would travel, was actually planked. Like the Turnpike, the Orange Plank Road was in poor condition. At Wilderness Church the two roads merged until they reached

Chancellorsville, where they again diverged. Another plank road made its way from Culpeper to Germanna Ford before eventually merging with the Orange Plank Road. Often called the Germanna Plank Road, predictably, it too was in disrepair. The final major addition to the Wilderness's transportation network was a railroad, unfinished at the time of the Civil War, which lay to the south of the Orange Plank Road. Thomas Mann, a Massachusetts soldier writing about his experience during the Mine Run Campaign, saw the "old RR there that had been graded" but found that "the track [was] never laid."[15]

In addition to the varied woods, open areas, and roads, several creeks—including Mine Run, Wilderness Run, Flat Run, Mott's Run, and Scott's Run, to name but a few—cut the Wilderness landscape and formed swamps in low-lying areas. A watershed, upon which the Orange Plank Road was built, separated the runs feeding the Rapidan River to the north from those that fed rivers, such as the Ny and Po, to the south. Together these various elements combined to create the patchwork that was the Wilderness.

Both depictions of the Wilderness have something to offer. The interminable-forest portrayal reveals the Wilderness's ability to awe those who entered the region with its vastness and monotony. It is easy to see how a soldier could come away with such an impression. Marching along a narrow road and seeing nothing but trees and maybe a small clearing or two for miles could be memorable, if not exciting, scenery. The fact that most of those who fought or traveled through the Wilderness did so along a narrow slice of what was a large forest would have limited their vision and might have encouraged such a uniform interpretation. This portrayal also demonstrates how a dominant characteristic of an environment can crowd out the finer details. For a soldier explaining the terrain to the folks back home, it was much easier to write a simple depiction of its central features rather than its various particulars. This interpretation also goes a way toward explaining why the troops found the Wilderness so noteworthy and so menacing. During the Civil War, men marched and fought through many different woodlands. Moreover, some of these woods had characteristics very similar to those encountered in the Wilderness, though not on such an unprecedented and intimidating scale, at least as the soldiers perceived it. This may have been especially the case for Northerners from urban areas or more settled rural regions, where open farmland had long since replaced primeval forest. Added to all this were the soldiers' recurring encounters with the area and the harrowing nature of combat during the Battle of the Wilderness, which left one feeling blind and vulnerable against an oft-unseen enemy. Also, the sheer number of dead and wounded that soon littered the forest floor surely played some role in how participants recalled their physical environment, no doubt making the seemingly endless Wilderness all the more menacing.

On the other hand, the patchwork interpretation is a more accurate portrayal of the actual Wilderness than the simpler depiction provided by many veterans as well as modern historians. Although to some degree it robs the Wilderness of its menacing character, what it takes away in feeling it returns in information, providing a much more detailed look of what the region was like and showing how the various ingredients combined to create the whole. This interpretation emphasizes the differences within the Wilderness, which then helps explain why familiarity with the landscape was not as helpful as one might suspect and why a soldier might experience the Wilderness differently depending on what part he was in.

Whatever merits a patchwork interpretation has, the image of a vast, unyielding Wilderness persisted to become the dominant interpretation in the postwar literature. Swinton found that "the whole face of the country is thickly wooded, with only an occasional opening, and intersected by a few narrow wood-roads." In like manner, Grant's aide and biographer Badeau depicted the Wilderness as "a wild and rugged area . . . with hardly a wood-road passing through; here and there is a ravine or a brook, and one or two houses are visible, with a bit of open land around them; all the rest is one tangled mass of stunted evergreen, dwarf chestnut, oak, and hazel, with an undergrowth of low-limbed bristling shrubs, making the forest almost impenetrable."[16]

Some postwar writers offered patchwork depictions of the Wilderness, but nuanced descriptions of the region were the exception rather than the rule. Morris Schaff, a Union veteran turned historian, described the Wilderness as "a vast sea . . . of dense forest . . . , a second growth" in which "the trees are noticeably stunted, and so close together, and their lower limbs so intermingled with a thick underbrush, that it is very difficult indeed to make one's way through them." Mixed in with these small trees were more substantial ones, along with swamps; dead trees; worn-out roads and winding paths; dilapidated buildings; "old fields preempted by briars, sassafras, dwarf young pines, and broom"; and a few larger openings. He also recognized the area's varying topography, noting that the "southern half . . . may be designated as low or gently rolling," while the "northern half, along the rivers, is marked by irregularly swelling ridges." Federal veteran George T. Stevens's memoir also noted the woods' varying density. During the Wilderness Campaign, he watched his line moving through "a thick growth of oak and walnut, densely filled with a smaller growth of pines and other brushwood; and in many places so thickly was this undergrowth interwoven among the large trees, that one could not see five yards in front of the line." As the troops continued to advance, however, he noticed that "the thick tangle in a measure disappeared, and the woods were more open." Even there, however, the "infantry found great difficulty in advancing, and at length" they found themselves "again in the midst of the thick undergrowth."[17]

A third depiction that Union veterans put forth after the war portrayed the Wilderness as possessing a core, or heart, of very thick woods and an outer ring of common woods. Usually, the Wilderness battlefield constituted this core, while the other parts of the region made up the surrounding ring of normal woods. Francis Walker, historian of the II Corps, talked about the area around Robertson's Tavern, near where the armies operated during the Mine Run Campaign, as being "vastly better than the Wilderness, in which our troops had been smothered the previous May, and were to be smothered again this May," despite not being "altogether paradisiacal in character." In this instance the "Wilderness" included both the Wilderness and the Chancellorsville battlefields, while the Mine Run area was not considered part of the Wilderness proper but instead part of a thinner periphery. Humphreys's history of the Overland Campaign suggested that the 1864 Wilderness battlefield formed the thick core. He found the Mine Run battlefield to be "more open and better ground," noting "still more open country" in the area around Lee's Mine Run line. Moreover, "the ground occupied by the Army of the Potomac in the vicinity of Chancellorsville in the Spring of 1863 was either open or in woods chiefly of ordinary character with but little undergrowth." Sartell Prentice also depicted the Wilderness battlefield as the core of the Wilderness, observing that the "densest part, its heart of hearts, was about eight by six miles, with the Wilderness Tavern for its centre." Likewise, Schaff affirmed that the 1864 battlefield was "at about the heart of the Wilderness."[18]

Modern historians tend to perpetuate the interminable-forest understanding of the Wilderness. The limitations on space in their narratives and their larger purpose of conveying the events that happened in the Wilderness lead to concise descriptions of the region, a situation that lends itself to a simpler interpretation. For example, Gordon Rhea described the Wilderness as "a densely wooded tract," "a broad stretch of impenetrable thickets and dense second growth," and a region having "few negotiable roads" where "clearings were scarce" and "visibility rarely exceeded a few hundred feet."[19]

While the veterans and historians have all agreed that the Wilderness was a large forested region, they have been less sure about where exactly it began and ended, consequently causing some confusion about its limits. The general consensus, however, has been that the Wilderness's boundaries were the Rapidan River on the north and Spotsylvania Court House on the south. During the Overland Campaign, Lyman observed that the Wilderness constituted "a very large part of this region, extending east and west along the plank and pike, and the south, nearly to Spotsylvania." The western border was generally placed at Mine Run by postwar authors. Swinton explained that the "region known as the Wilderness . . . extends a considerable distance southward from the river, and westward as far as Mine Run."[20] The eastern limit was less definite. Lyman included "the field of Chancellorsville" within the Wilderness's bounds but did not pin down an exact line. Brig. Gen. Gouverneur K. Warren, who served as the chief of topographical engineers in the Army of the Potomac during the Chancellorsville Campaign, provided a good description of the hazily defined eastern boundary, explaining that "between Chancellorsville and Fredericksburg the country becomes more open and clear as you approach the latter place" but otherwise giving no definite line.[21]

Contemporary estimates of how many square miles the Wilderness covered could vary considerably. Jacob Raymer, a soldier in the 4th North Carolina, described the Wilderness as "a scope of country some ten miles square," or one hundred square miles. In contrast, Myers of the 110th Ohio reported that the Wilderness "is said to be some thirty miles long, by ten wide," which would put it at three hundred square miles.[22]

Postwar writers also tried to compute its area, but their conclusions were just as inconsistent. Edward Porter Alexander, an artillery officer in the Army of Northern Virginia, explained that "Chancellorsville was situated about a mile within the limits of a tract called the Wilderness . . . , [which] stretched some 12 or 14 miles westward along the Rapidan and was some 8 or 10 miles in breadth," making it 96–140 square miles in size. Holman Melcher, a Federal veteran, asserted that the Wilderness was "about fifteen miles square," or 225 square miles. More recently, Stephen Sears and Daniel Sutherland, in their works on Chancellorsville, have put the area of the Wilderness at a mere 70 square miles, a much more conservative estimate. Based on my own calculations, the Wilderness could have had a maximum area of 132–156 square miles, though there is no way to verify its actual size.[23]

Having a correct understanding of the Wilderness's nature is certainly important for studying the campaigns that took place there. It is equally vital, however, to have a proper understanding of the Wilderness's origin. Many postwar writers claimed that its thick vegetation constituted a distinct, if not a unique, landscape caused by local iron-mining and smelting operations. This in turn allowed them to claim that the Wilderness caused unique battlefield conditions favoring the Confederates and thus leading them to trap the Union army in the forest at the start of the 1864 campaign. In short, this origin story is a key piece of the Wilderness myth. In reality, the area's thick vegetation was not caused solely by the iron industry. Rather, a variety of economic activities, including tobacco cultivation, iron and gold mining, and road building, all contributed to the creation of the dense woodlands. Tobacco cultivation was the prime culprit, sapping the land's fertility and causing erosion, leading to the abandonment of the land and its reclamation by stunted vegetation. Not surprisingly, there were other areas of Virginia that could boast of similarly thick, Wilderness-like vegetation. The Wilderness, then, was just one notorious example of a statewide phenomenon. While the character of the region as a whole probably originated from the effects of tobacco cultivation, the construction of the Orange Plank Road in the 1850s probably accounts for the especially dense thickets that Lyman encountered on that part of the Wilderness battlefield.

Tobacco cultivation was the first economic activity that affected the Wilderness and was primarily responsible for creating its thick vegetation. It is difficult to overestimate the importance of tobacco to colonial Virginia's economy. Despite efforts to diversify, tobacco remained a force to be reckoned with—as historian Avery Craven has noted, "the very conditions which made it the dominant crop, determined that its production should be at the expense of the soil." At one point over 90 percent of Virginians who paid taxes were growing tobacco. This reliance on a single crop was clearly visible in Spotsylvania County, which (along with neighboring Orange County) was the home of the Wilderness. Here, a 1726 census revealed that, during a two-year span, the amount of tobacco raised in the county had increased roughly twofold. Such cultivation meant clearing the land of its virgin forest. The Wilderness's soil originally supported a mixture of hickories and oaks, though by the 1720s predominantly oaks due to planned burns by American Indians. These trees were later cleared by farmers through girdling, a practice that "strips a layer of bark around a tree, leaving it to die and making it easier to chop down." Tobacco could then be planted among the remaining stumps.[24]

At this point the tobacco plant and Virginia's notoriously hard rains combined to sap the soil's vitality. Since soil quality declined with each successive crop, planters needed virgin land to produce the best tobacco. After a few years, the land was given over to growing corn and wheat before finally being left for the forest to reclaim. Moreover, the intensive care that tobacco plants required meant that planters had little time or labor for rehabilitating or sustaining the land's fertility. The methods of cultivation also damaged the soil, for the cleared fields with their loose soil were very susceptible to erosion. After the lands were abandoned or planted instead with corn and wheat, conditions only got worse. The land could quickly become scarred with "deep gullies," and the shallow furrows made by Virginian plows when planting corn "ran straight up and down the hillsides to become veritable watercourses in time of rainfall," carrying away the loose soil and its nutrients.[25]

In 1732 William Byrd wrote about the fruits of Virginia's agricultural practices in what became the Wilderness. On "either side" while traversing the region, Byrd saw "continual poisoned fields, with nothing but saplings growing on them." In addition, he noted that "a great deal of land," owned by the proprietor of a local iron mine, was "exceedingly barren, and the growth of trees upon it [was] hardly big enough for coaling." Writing in the 1850s, Frederick Law Olmsted observed a similar pattern throughout eastern Virginia. "Not more than a third of the country, visible," he noted, "is cleared; the rest is mainly a pine forest." Of the land that had been previously cleared, "not more than one-quarter seems to have been lately in cultivation," while the remainder "is grown over with briars and bushes, and a long, coarse grass of no value." The only crops grown by the 1850s, he reported, were corn and wheat. Near Petersburg, where farmers had more recently grown tobacco on their land and then abandoned it some years before, Olmsted came upon "old fields" full of "pine trees and broom-sedge" in which, "for acres, the pines would not be above five feet high," while in other parts "there were patches of every age," with trees at times reaching a hundred feet in height.[26]

Even after the Civil War, a similar pattern held true. John Trowbridge, who visited Virginia in the immediate aftermath of the war, found the "striking feature of the country" to be its "'old fields,'" which he implied were the consequence of growing tobacco, "the devouring enemy of the country." Initially, these old fields were "covered with briers, weeds, and broom-sedge," but these soon gave way to a "thick growth" of pines. "In two or three years," explained Trowbridge, these pines could be five to six feet in height, and with the passage of a decade, one might expect to see a fledgling forest. Moreover, "in some of the oldest of the old fields, now heavily timbered, the ridges of the ancient tobacco lands are traceable among the trees." Robert Somers traveled from the Potomac River to Richmond in the early 1870s, and his observations reinforced Trowbridge's conclusions. Somers found that "the soil has . . . at one time been nearly all cultivated" and noticed that "the marks of the plough are everywhere seen." Nevertheless, he saw how "thousands of acres are rapidly returning to a state of nature, and little forests of young pines are springing where Indian corn and even wheat may have recently grown." He concluded that "when the soil has been exhausted by bad cultivation, and is left to take its own way, it is prolific of pines," a pattern he witnessed "in many fields, over which the furrows were still traceable, [now] covered with little pine-shoots, thick as if planted in a nursery." While Union observers often found the characteristics of the Wilderness to be unusual and even unique, its landscape was, in truth, just the most famous example of a longstanding and widespread Virginia phenomenon.[27]

That being the case, it should come as no surprise that Union soldiers found Wilderness-like woods in other parts of Virginia. General Warren described Stafford County, which lay north of Spotsylvania County, as having "a lack of fertility in the soil," with "dense woods and thickets of black-jack oak and pine [covering] most of the ground." Little wonder, then, that he concluded, "the general character of the country is that of a wilderness, and it forms part of that distinguishing belt of country which continues through Orange and Spotsylvania Counties and southwesterly in a general direction parallel with the Blue Ridge," of which the Wilderness was a part. One Union soldier thought the Wilderness and Spotsylvania battlefields similar enough to lump them together, calling them "the meanest part of Virginia, properly called the Wilderness." Upon leaving Spotsylvania, he found it "quite refreshing to get where civilization can be seen, after being hemmed in by woods for so long a time."[28] Charles A. Dana, the assistant secretary of war, reported later during the North Anna phase of the Overland Campaign that the Union army passed through a region "densely wooded with pine, much like the Wilderness region." Still later, while in the area between the Pamunkey and Chickahominy Rivers, Dana found "the country . . . thickly wooded with pines, with few good openings," a description that was certainly reminiscent of the Wilderness. Near Petersburg, Lyman found a battlefield that "beggars description," as "it is a wood, with a tangled thick undergrowth that almost stops the passage of a man." Grant likewise remarked in his memoirs that "most of the country" over which the Overland Campaign was fought was "covered with a dense forest, in places, like the Wilderness and along the Chickahominy, almost impenetrable even for infantry except along the roads."[29] The fact that none of these other thickly wooded areas gained sinister reputations suggests that other factors—not just the character of its woods—played an important role in setting the Wilderness apart.

During the war, some soldiers noted the ties between the Wilderness and Virginia's agricultural practices.[30] Wilbur Fisk, writing during the Mine Run Campaign, described the area as "covered with small second-growth pine, and looks as if it had been under cultivation once, but probably worn out and abandoned for more fertile regions." Furthermore, he claimed that the Wilderness "has the appearance of being good soil" and that he "should call it just such land as would tempt the eyes of almost any practical farmer, if it was up in our Northern States, instead of being here in decayed Virginia." During the Overland Campaign, an Ohio soldier contrasted "the primitive forests of Virginia," which "are truly beautiful; the different kinds of oak predominating, with hickory and pine," with the "thickets of shrub pine and cedar" that "cover the original farms of the old Commonwealth." For these blights he blamed "the effects of slavery in old Virginia." Confederate journalist, Peter Alexander, similarly observed some of the effects of tobacco cultivation. "Producing little for the subsistence of either man or beast," he called the Wilderness "a blasted region, adjoining the district known as the 'poisoned fields of Orange.'" Alexander found "the soil destitute of fertility, the supply of water scant, [and] the ground broken and covered with a dense and almost impenetrable growth of stunted bushes, pines, and black jacks."[31]

In the postwar years some writers still pointed to soil exhaustion as a factor in the creation of the Wilderness, often coupling this with the traditional iron-mining explanation. Edwin C. Mason, a former Federal soldier, did just that. While he mentioned the region's mining ventures, he explained that "the soil in places had also been found adapted to the cultivation of tobacco." Yet in time "the mines became unproductive and the soil unfit for the profitable raising of the tobacco-plant," and consequently "the territory was abandoned to nature," becoming "so thickly overgrown with pine and scrub-oak, interlaced with brambles and trailing vines, that a dog could scarce force his way through." Sartell Prentice explained that the region was "once a garden-spot in favored Virginia,—one of its most fertile, productive, and choice of highly cultivated and valued sections," which was also the site of gold and silver mining, until it "had been in process of time exhausted, both as to soil and mines, and finally abandoned." He concluded that with the passage of time, "nature had picked up this exhausted and abandoned land, and planted it with lavish hand to a growth, that in time became immense, of tree and vine." Another Federal claimed that the Wilderness "was in years past a flourishing section of the country, but the soil becoming exhausted it was abandoned and allowed to become what it really is—a wilderness." Likewise, Norton C. Shepard, a veteran of the 146th New York, found that "in the South . . . most especially in Virginia, most of the land has been cleared off and cultivated," and "after many years of cultivation it has become worn out and has been abandoned as useless." In place of the original forest grew "pine and scrub oak to become a wilderness," with trees that were "usually about six inches in diameter with branches growing thick from the ground to the top." Other writers took note of the Wilderness's poor soil but made no connection between that infertility and tobacco cultivation, apparently suggesting that it was sterile by nature. The historian for the 7th Rhode Island Infantry simply noted that "the clayey soil is so barren as to have attracted but few settlers."[32]

Although agricultural practices substantially changed Virginia's landscape, in the Wilderness there were additional factors at work, such as mining and ironmaking. Iron deposits lay scattered across the Wilderness, and the region's forests provided the fuel to transform the raw ore into pig iron. Alexander Spotswood, while not the first to note the area's potential, was certainly the first to exploit it. He gained title to vast tracts of land throughout Spotsylvania County in 1716, 1719, and 1722 totaling more than 60,000 acres, among which was the Wilderness Tract, from which the Wilderness possibly derives its name. His Tubal Furnace became operational during this period, and by 1723 he had already shipped tons of iron back to Britain. When Byrd visited the area in 1732, he found Spotswood still engaged in mining iron and refining the ore. After Spotswood's death in 1740, his ironworks declined. By the time the Revolution swept the colonies, it stood abandoned. Later, the iron industry would revive at the Catharine Furnace, built by John Wellford. This furnace operated from 1837 to 1847 and from 1862 to 1865 but never thrived, surviving on contracts from the Federal and then the Confederate government.[33]

During the war, some soldiers pointed to this iron industry as the source of the Wilderness's distinctive characteristics. A Union chaplain commented that "a dozen or more years since, the timber had all been cut off this section for the supply of an iron furnace in the neighborhood," noting that "a thick young growth of oak and hickory has sprung up." Later this origin story made its way into the flood of soldier memoirs and war histories to become the dominant explanation for the region's character. Swinton asserted that "the woods of the Wilderness have not the ordinary features of a forest" because "the region rests on a belt of mineral rocks, and, for above a hundred years, extensive mining has here been carried on. To feed the mines the timber of the country for many miles around had been cut down, and in its place there had arisen a dense undergrowth of low-limbed and scraggy pines, stiff and bristling chinkapins, scrub-oaks, and hazel." Writing after the turn of the century, Schaff repeated more or less the same story but emphasized the local iron furnaces as primarily responsible for shaping the landscape. He noted that "this whole mystery-wrapped country is a mineral region, holding pockets of iron ore and streaked with . . .

veins of gold-bearing quartz." Schaff, like Swinton, located the origin of the Wilderness in the eighteenth century. In his telling Spotswood, for whom Spotsylvania County was named, "uncovered the ore-beds, built iron furnaces, and converted the primeval forest into charcoal to feed them." Schaff blamed this activity for the Wilderness's thick vegetation, noting that "the present timber aspect is due entirely to the iron furnaces and their complete destruction of the first noble growth."[34]

This traditional interpretation has seeped into modern accounts as well. Sears, in his book on the Chancellorsville Campaign, notes that the Wilderness region, "since colonial times . . . , had been the site of a nascent iron industry." He explains that "it was this iron industry that gave the Wilderness its distinctive character." Similarly, Rhea, in his campaign history, states that the Wilderness woodlands the armies encountered in 1864 "had replaced forests cut down to fuel local iron and gold furnaces." More recently, Aaron Sachs has repeated this same interpretation, noting that Spotswood "needed a vast supply of wood . . . to fuel his blast furnaces." Later, when the iron industry declined, the forest rebounded "because Virginians found the local soil to be too acidic and too poorly drained for extensive farming." In place of the original forest, "a second-growth 'Wilderness' developed, dominated by tangles of scrub and brush amid stunted trees that struggled to soak up enough nutrients from the ground."[35] Suffice it to say that this venerable theory remains alive and well.

While these historians have argued that the activities of the local iron industry explain the Wilderness's thick vegetation, others such as Adams, Harrison, and Hennessy have recently suggested that these works did not consume enough wood to create the Wilderness. Adams, in his study of the Catharine Furnace, explains that "a steady flow of charcoal from the surrounding forests was required to keep the operation going." But how much wood was consumed? While he admits that historians have offered a variety of estimates, Adams suggests that the ironworks would need "roughly between 300 and 400 acres per year for charcoal." This estimate means that "the impact of Catharine Furnace's charcoaling operation would have clear-cut less than a square mile per year of operation," for a total of perhaps, "at the most, nine or ten of

Spotsylvania County's more than 400 square miles of territory." Even if we use Sears's and Sutherland's conservative estimates of the Wilderness being only 70 square miles, the local iron industry still cannot account for the majority of the area's woods. Adams concludes that, although iron mining and manufacturing, among other things, "certainly contributed to the environmental conditions that created the Wilderness by 1863–1864, . . . it was by no means solely responsible for it."[36]

In addition to the iron operations, gold mining took place in the Wilderness at several different points. Nearer Chancellorsville was the United States Gold Mine, while closer to the Wilderness battlefield lay the Culpeper Gold Mine. By the time war came, both operations, like most things in the Wilderness, were idle. Landon of the 14th Indiana claimed that "these gold mines were worked up to within about twelve months since," observing that "on the river bank there is quite an extensive establishment for washing, &c., with all the washers and other mining implements scattered around." Mann of the 18th Massachusetts, however, concluded that the war had brought the "pretty extensive mining operations" to a halt. Though one Union soldier thought that the mines "have long since ceased to be worked," another suggested that the war was to blame as "Conscription Acts and Emancipation Proclamations have exhausted manual mining material." While some "five hundred men were employed in digging for the precious metal" before the shooting started, now "no work is performed."[37] How much these mines contributed to deforestation in the Wilderness is unclear. It does, however, seem safe to assume that, while they probably used some timber in their operations, they were not major culprits behind the creation of the second-growth landscape.

The construction of the Wilderness's transportation network, particularly the Orange and Germanna Plank Roads, also altered the landscape significantly. Hennessy has provided estimates of how much timber both the Orange Plank Road and the connecting Germanna Plank Road would require. He suggests that one "mile of road required about 147 cords," while an acre of woods provided "between 15 and 20 cords." From this reckoning, "each acre could plank between 540 and 720 linear feet of road," thus "each mile required between 7.33 and 9.8 acres of timber." By Hennessy's estimates then, assuming that there were "22 miles of plank roads through the Wilderness," they would require "160–215 acres of timber" for materials, or less than one square mile.[38] This is a significantly smaller amount of deforestation than that caused by iron mining and manufacturing (estimated at nine to ten square miles), which in turn is much smaller than that probably caused by growing tobacco.

Yet this relatively small amount of newer deforestation might have had a disproportionate influence on how Civil War soldiers experienced the Wilderness. Hennessy and Harrison have argued that the Wilderness had an exterior layer of very thick vegetation along the roadways, with more-open sections away from the roads. The construction of the plank roads in the 1850s probably caused the builders to cut down nearby trees. This being the case, the trees along the outer rim of the roads would have been smaller and thicker than those farther away, having been more recently cut. Thus, most of the soldiers would have described the thick vegetation that they marched by or fought in near the roads, not the more-open centers.[39] This also might account for Lyman's observation that the areas along the Orange Plank Road and the Brock Road were the very thickest part of the Wilderness.

Contemporary witnesses did not connect the construction of plank roads with the Wilderness's vegetation, though McHenry Howard, a Confederate writing after the war, made an oblique reference to the possibility. "In many places," observed Howard, "the large trees had been cut down in years past,—whether for the construction of plank roads or for furnaces I do not know,—and a jungle of switch had sprung up ten or twenty feet high, more impenetrable, if possible than the pine."[40]

Taken as a whole, these activities created the Wilderness's characteristic vegetation. Early on, tobacco cultivation deforested the greatest portion of the region, sapped the soil's fertility, and gave the Wilderness its stunted, second-growth woodlands. With time, these trees and shrubs should have matured to present a more or less typical Virginia forest. Meanwhile, the iron industry, gold mining, and plank-road construction would have each contributed to deforestation on a smaller scale, creating newer areas of stunted, second-growth forest, a process that gave the region its patchwork character.

The myths surrounding the character and the origin of the Wilderness have had a long life, spanning from the war itself up to the present day. Nevertheless, these obscure the region's true nature. The Wilderness was not one vast, thick forest, although it might have seemed that way to those who entered it, but a patchwork of open areas and vegetation of varying density. Given that its landscape was more complex than what postwar writers presented, it should come as no surprise that its origins were also more complex than the traditional telling suggests. The Wilderness was a creation of tobacco cultivation, iron mining, and road building. Considering that these activities were not unique to the region, it is only natural that other Wilderness-like areas should exist in Virginia, even on other battlefields where the same armies fought. Taken together, this reinterpretation of the Wilderness not only provides a better picture of what the region was actually like, but also helps unravel other Wilderness myths that are as tangled as the forest they describe.

2

BATTLE IN THE WILDERNESS

Postwar writers often claimed that the Battle of the Wilderness was an exceptional engagement. In his 1866 history of the Army of the Potomac, William Swinton warned his readers that "the battle of the Wilderness is scarcely to be judged as an ordinary battle." During the 1880s and 1890s, others repeated this interpretation. Regis de Trobriand, a brigadier general in the II Corps, thought it important to "bear in mind that it was in no respect like any other battle." Horace Porter, a member of Grant's staff, largely agreed. He claimed that "there were features of the battle which have never been matched in the annals of warfare." An important corollary that accompanied this claim—often implicitly and at times explicitly—was that the special environment in which the battle took place caused these distinct characteristics. Major General Humphreys, Meade's chief of staff, complained of the many tactical problems stemming from "the character of the field on which [the battle] took place." He argued that "some of its features were found in other of the battle-grounds of the two armies; but so far as [he knew], no great battle ever took place before on such ground." Fitzhugh Lee, a Confederate major general, went further. The cavalryman contended that "it was like a huge Indian fight, and different from any other battle," that the "contest on this unique ground can be compared to nothing in military records, ancient or modern." This sense of the Battle of the Wilderness being exceptional because of the extraordinary place in which it was fought has even continued in more modern works, the most striking example being Bruce Catton's *A Stillness at Appomattox*.[1]

Two important questions arise. First, what type of combat conditions did the Wilderness create? In order to answer this, it is necessary to look at both the Battle of Chancellorsville and the Battle of the Wilderness. On the surface, these engagements look like twins, and often historians treat them as such. They were fought about a year apart in May 1863 and 1864. Both took place, in whole or part, within the Wilderness. The Confederates in both instances used the landscape to screen successful flanking maneuvers. In each battle a triumphant Confederate flank attack was seemingly robbed of its momentum by the accidental shooting of one of Lee's most important lieutenants—Lt. Gen. Thomas J. "Stonewall" Jackson in 1863 and Lt. Gen. James Longstreet in 1864. In both campaigns forest fires raged, burning alive many of the wounded.

A closer look at how the Wilderness affected combat conditions, however, reveals that these battles were not the twins they are often purported to be. It is crucial to remember that the Wilderness was a patchwork, not a uniform forest. While there are certain similarities and some shared tactical problems, on the whole they were two very different engagements because of their distinct fields of battle. The telling differences suggest that combat in the Wilderness did not follow a set formula. They also serve as a warning to historians who might be tempted to lump these two battlefields together—as if they were the same place—and assume that the same tactical problems would result, something often implied with Chancellorsville and the Battle of the Wilderness.

Second, were the fighting conditions at the Battle of the Wilderness unique, or could they be found in other engagements in heavily wooded areas? Obviously, combat in the Wilderness was vastly different from fighting in more open terrain such as at Antietam or Gettysburg. A more apt comparison would be with another engagement fought in mostly wooded terrain. Thick and tangled Wilderness-like woods could be found on other battlefields, after all. Earl Hess, in his work on Civil War infantry tactics, has observed that "thick woods . . . often filled half the ground of any given battlefield of the Civil War," while "in some engagements, such as Chancellorsville and the Wilderness, tangled vegetation dominated the landscape."[2] One battlefield where vegetation was the dominant feature was Chickamauga. Although located in northern Georgia, Chickamauga's landscape was in some ways similar to that of the Wilderness and provides a good point of comparison, affording an opportunity to demonstrate that many of the battle conditions created by the Wilderness battlefield were not unique but instead were common to other engagements fought in forests.

While postwar commentators employed many colorful phrases to explain what made combat during the Battle of the Wilderness so distinct, the challenges the armies faced can be boiled down into two key factors. First, a lack of open space within the Wilderness prevented the armies from using much artillery and made maneuvering a challenge. Swinton explained, "it is impossible to conceive a field worse adapted to the movements of a grand army" as "artillery was wholly ruled out of use" and "manoeuvring here was necessarily out of the question." Humphreys in turn noted that "it was very difficult for even small bodies of men to move in" the thick vegetation there. "To handle large bodies of troops in battle in such a field was exceedingly difficult," and except in a few places, "artillery would be of little use." Others agreed with these conclusions. Robert Stiles, a Confederate gunner, described the Battle of the Wilderness as "almost exclusively, an infantry fight, and we of the artillery saw, in fact, next to nothing of it, but hovered around its edge."[3]

Troop formations were disrupted—or at times disintegrated altogether—making it necessary to stop and reform units. The historian of McGowan's Brigade noted that his South Carolina unit "was greatly impeded by the matted growth of saplings and bushes" and claimed that, in the Wilderness, "it is impossible to keep even a regiment well dressed." Likewise, Moxley Sorrel, a member of Longstreet's staff, explained how, after the general's May 6 flank attack, the Confederates "were . . . so disorganized by the chase through the woods that a halt was necessary to reform." Maj. Gen. Winfield S. Hancock's May 6 attack was plagued by similar problems. "The Union columns had become terribly mixed and disordered in their forward movement," explained Francis Walker, the II Corps historian. "Under the excitement and bewilderment of battle, through woods so dense that at the best no body of troops could possibly preserve their alignment," the Union troops "in some cases . . . were heaped up in unnecessary strength," while "elsewhere great gaps appeared" as "men, and . . . officers, . . . lost their regiments in the jungles."[4]

Second, the forest limited visibility. The men in the ranks often could not see friend or foe, and the commanders had difficulty directing their troops, knew little about their own position or the enemy's, and found it difficult to judge the course of battle. William H. Powell described how "the peculiar nature of the ground fought over made this a weird uncanny contest—a battle of invisibles with invisibles." While admitting that "there had been wood-fights before," he thought there had been "none in which the contestants were so completely concealed as in this." In the Wilderness "nothing could be seen of the enemy or his doings but the white smoke that belched out of the bushes." Hazard Stevens of the VI Corps observed that commanders were "unable to see but a hundred yards" and "unable to fix or direct the movement of troops but through this narrow range of vision." As a result they "could only form and deploy properly and make the right connections on the flank at the outset, and then start them forward with the certainty that the lines would soon become crooked and disordered." Soldiers meanwhile had to direct their fire by sound or the direction of enemy fire. Porter explained how "it was the sense of sound and of touch rather than the sense of sight which guided the movements. It was a battle fought with the ear, and not with the eyes." Humphreys agreed, observing that "but little of the combatants could be seen" and that the battle's "progress was known to the senses chiefly by the rising and falling sounds of a vast musketry fire that continually swept along the lines of battle." Evander Law, a brigadier general in Lee's army, similarly recalled that "officers could not see the whole length of their commands, and could tell whether the troops on their right and left were driving or being driven only by the sound of the firing."[5]

Because of the limited visibility, the opposing forces often stumbled into each other, resulting in heavy and continuous musketry at close range. Trobriand commented on how "the adversaries came upon each other twenty or thirty paces apart," firing "desperately until they saw no one in front of them." Stevens explained it this way: "Usually when infantry meets infantry the clash of arms is brief," as "one side or the other speedily gives way." In the Wilderness, though, "neither side would give way, and the steady firing rolled and crackled from end to end of the contending lines, as if it would never cease." These close-quarter infantry fights then degenerated into a "heavy pounding match between masses of brave and determined men" in which "the lines did not move much" and "both sides hugged the ground, or whenever possible sought the partial shelter of a ridge, and kept up a steady fire."[6]

Besides these tactical challenges, several other factors influenced the nature of combat during the Battle of the Wilderness. First, casualties were high. While the nature of the Overland Campaign made it difficult to compile accurate statistics, estimates of Confederate casualties at the battle have numbered between 7,750 and 11,000 men, while the Union tally reached 17,666. Second, the intense combat did great damage to the forest. Frank Wilkeson, a private in the II Corps, "noticed that small limbs of trees were falling in a feeble shower in advance of me . . . as though an army of squirrels were at work." Another Union soldier asserted that "on every side, [he] could see the effects of the previous day's severe fighting." On many saplings "the bark was so much peeled, that they had the appearance of being painted," while "broken branches and stout little trees had been completely cut off by the bullets." The forest was not only mangled but also set ablaze. Andrew McBride of the 10th Georgia testified that "the woods took fire . . . , and many of the poor fellows burned to death." Likewise, Isaac O. Best of the 16th New

York witnessed one of the Wilderness fires and also thought that "many wounded were burned to death." The next day "corpses were found with the clothing burned off them, and their flesh horribly charred."[7]

Many soldiers also constructed makeshift field fortifications to protect themselves. One Confederate noticed that the Wilderness battlefield was "filled with fallen trees of moderate size, which formed admirable material for the rapid construction of breastworks." He thought that "it was surprising to see how rapid the fellows would erect a good protection against minnies with the fallen timbre and dirt thrown up with tin plates, shingles, by hand, etc.' the earth having been first loosened with the bayonett or knives." He was not alone in marveling at the speed of the entrenching or in the hodgepodge of materials employed. A II Corps signal officer "found the 6th Corps throwing up temporary breastworks of timber and rails and the plank of the road," and once the II Corps had joined them, "there were three or four miles of these works" built in what he deemed "an incredible short time." Similarly, a Union correspondent observed how soldiers "with instinctive haste . . . commenced throwing up entrenchments, using for the purpose, old logs, planks from the road, in fact anything that would stop a bullet." Frederic Swift, a Federal soldier, even reported the Confederates employing "several of [their] dead . . . in their rifle pits," with the corpses "thrown in among the logs and *only partly covered.*"[8]

Since both the Battles of the Wilderness and Chancellorsville were fought in the same forested region, one might be tempted to assume that similar tactical limitations affected the armies in these engagements. A closer look, however, reveals that this was not necessarily the case because of environmental differences between the two battlefields. Too often historians lump the two fights together as if they took place on the same ground, when in reality the two locations were distinct. Not only were they miles apart from one another, but they also were diverse in terms of topography and vegetation. These variations, while seemingly small, made for two very different engagements.

While the Chancellorsville battlefield had the thick woods and underbrush so characteristic of the Wilderness, it also contained an unusually large open space around the Chancellor house and notable open elevations, such as Hazel Grove and Fairview. These features allowed artillery to dominate the battle on May 3, 1863, in a way it could never do on the Wilderness battlefield a year later, although cannon admittedly played only a limited role during Jackson's flank attack the previous day. The infantry also played an important part at Chancellorsville. May 2 saw Jackson's legions hit the unprepared XI Corps, sending those troops scurrying through the woods, just as Longstreet's and Brig. Gen. John Gordon's attacks would do to the Federals in May 1864. While there was little sustained combat as at the Battle of the Wilderness, the thick woods and underbrush of the Chancellorsville battlefield disrupted Confederate formations during Jackson's advance. On May 3 the style of fighting was very different from that at the Battle of the Wilderness. Instead of static firefights at close range with a seemingly never-ending stream of musketry, the Chancellorsville fighting was dominated by repeated Confederate assaults on entrenched Federal positions, with each side benefiting from artillery support. Again, Confederate formations became disordered and broke apart, but visibility was apparently not an issue, resulting in a type of combat distinct from that associated with the Battle of the Wilderness.

In contrast, the Wilderness battlefield's terrain was flatter along the Orange Plank Road corridor, where much of the heaviest fighting took place. The few open spaces available, such as Saunders's field or the Widow Tapp farm, were also much smaller than the clearings around Chancellorsville, so it should come as no surprise that the use of artillery was limited and that musketry dominated. It is also crucial to understand that the Orange Plank Road corridor was considered by some to be the thickest part of the Wilderness, while the woodlands of the Chancellorsville battlefield were seen as comparatively thinner, with less dense vegetation and more open spaces.[9] This goes a long way toward explaining why Battle of the Wilderness veterans complained about visibility more frequently than did those writing about Chancellorsville. These environmental factors and the different types of battles they caused also point to why soldiers looking back at the Battle of the Wilderness would set it apart as a unique engagement in ways they never did with Chancellorsville. They also suggest why veterans might have had little to say about the Wilderness at Chancellorsville, while they might have a great deal to say about the region a year later. The Wilderness's complex nature helps explain these differences in the soldiers' experiences.

The fighting on May 2 was in some ways similar to what later took place in the Battle of the Wilderness. While soldiers at Chancellorsville did not usually complain about visibility, some Union commanders grumbled about the woods screening Confederate movements. Carl Schurz, a major general in the star-crossed XI Corps, reported that the Wilderness's woods were "thick enough not to permit any view to the front, flank, or rear, but not thick enough to prevent the approach of the enemy's troops."[10] In a similar vein Maj. Gen. O. O. Howard, the corps commander, listed the blindingly thick forest as one of the causes for the calamity that befell his command. "Though constantly threatened and apprised of the moving of the enemy," stated Howard, "the woods was so dense that he was able to mass a large force, whose exact whereabouts neither patrols, reconnaissances, nor scouts ascertained."[11]

The artillery's role on May 2 affords another good example of similarities between Chancellorsville and the Battle of the Wilderness, as few Confederate guns were able to come into play during Jackson's flank attack. Edward Porter Alexander, an artillery officer attached to Jackson's column, found that during the initial flank attack, there was "no opportunity to use artillery." Similarly, the commander of an artillery battalion concluded that the thick forest "afforded no ground for artillery" until the Confederates found an opening nearer Chancellorsville, and even then only a few cannon could be placed. The Federals, meanwhile, used artillery to defend fixed positions at close range, a role the big guns would play again during the Battle of the Wilderness. A member of the 44th Georgia described how, after the initial success of Jackson's flank attack, the men kept advancing through field and forest until they came upon an opening where "a battery open[ed] upon" them, unleashing "a perfect storm of grape, canister, shot, and shell."[12]

Infantry combat at Chancellorsville on May 2 also shared certain similarities with the fighting a year later. Jackson's flank attack was just as successful as those made by Longstreet or Gordon on May 6, 1864, yet also suffered from the same shortcomings. Using the woods to screen their movements, the Confederates surprised their opponents and drove them for some distance. Maj. Gen. Robert Rodes, who commanded a Confederate division at Chancellorsville, summarized Jackson's triumph: "So complete was the success of the whole maneuver, and such was the surprise of the enemy, that scarcely any organized resistance was met with after the first volley was fired," and the enemy "fled in the wildest confusion." Brig. Gen. R. E. Colston, another Confederate division commander, gave a similar appraisal. He remarked that "notwithstanding the tangled and very difficult character of the woods and the resistance of the enemy, our troops advanced with great rapidity, driving the enemy like chaff before them."[13]

As later at the Battle of the Wilderness, though, woods, darkness, and the accidental shooting of their leader limited what the Confederates could achieve with Jackson's flank attack. Colston commented on this as well. "Owing to the very difficult and tangled nature of the ground over which the troops had advanced, and the mingling of the first and second lines of battle," he found that "the formation of the troops had become very much confused, and different regiments, brigades, and divisions were mixed up together."[14] The colonel of the 40th Virginia also gave a sense of the problems the advancing Rebels faced. He reported that "the rapid flight of the enemy, the eagerness of our pursuit, the tangled wilderness through which we had marched, and the darkness of the night, created much confusion in our ranks." There were also problems with units being torn apart. In one case the 5th North Carolina became "separated from [its] brigade in the tangled wilderness," a problem aggravated by the inability "to see any portion of the brigade over 50 yards" away.[15] Just like at the Battle of the Wilderness, commanders took the opportunity to reform their lines when given a chance. Rodes, for instance, recalled taking advantage of an open space to bring some order to his intermingled units.[16]

While the experience of the Chancellorsville flank attack showed many of the same characteristics as the Battle of the Wilderness, the bloody combat on May 3 was very different from the blind, close-range musketry exchanges that were so typical a year later. Robert E. Lee's report revealed a series of assaults on Union entrenchments. "Three times were these works carried, and as often were the brave assailants compelled to abandon them," noted Lee. It was not until the Confederate artillery combined with several converging infantry assaults that the Federals finally broke. These Rebel attacks were made against positions they could see. Col. D. H. Hamilton, who commanded a Confederate brigade at Chancellorsville, noted that as his men "cleared the woods the fire of the enemy was opened upon us," then "with a shout of defiance we rushed forward, cleared the Yankee breastworks at a bound, and, pushing 100 yards or so to the front, engaged the enemy" stationed behind entrenchments.[17] In a similar vein Brig. Gen. Carnot Posey, another Confederate brigade commander, noted that his attack was "made in fine order, under heavy fire of shell and grape as each regiment attained its position," then his men "pushed forward gallantly and irresistibly through a dense wood and over a wide abatis and into the trenches of the enemy, driving him off with much slaughter and capturing many prisoners." This was a far cry from the indecisive but equally deadly musketry affairs at the Battle of the Wilderness. Even at Chancellorsville, though, Posey found his troops "somewhat scattered on account of the dense woods and vigorous pursuit," forcing him to pause and repair his lines.[18]

During the Confederates' May 3 assaults, their lines not only tended to merge but also became disjointed or broke apart. Col. J. M. Hall, who led a Rebel brigade during the battle, explained how his command's line split in two and moved in diverging directions, a fact that, "owing to the dense forest," was not initially discovered. The havoc the Wilderness played on the Rebel lines is readily apparent in the frequent descriptions of the unusual depth of Confederate formations. This was accidental, as successive lines became merged during the advance as one line caught up with another, giving the appearance of unusually deep lines or columns. For instance, one Union sharpshooter saw the Confederates "six ranks deep," while a New Jersey soldier observed the

Rebels advancing four deep.[19] It was simply difficult for the Confederates to control their forces on the Chancellorsville battlefield. General Rodes admitted that "on account of the dense forest, the undulating character of the ground, and the want of an adequate staff, it was not in [his] power during the subsequent movements, to give a great deal of personal attention to the actions of any of my command," with the exception of a few brigades enjoying easy access to a road.[20]

Both armies' artillery in many ways dominated the fighting. Union guns took a terrible toll on the repeated and determined Confederate assaults. A New Yorker observed that "the Rebels made the most desperate attempts to capture our entrenched batteries, but were driven back repeatedly with great slaughter." An artilleryman from Rhode Island agreed, noting that "the enemy brought forward large masses of troops"; although "the concentrated fire of our artillery and infantry was terrific, yet he hurled brigade after brigade against our line with a prodigality of lives I have never seen equaled." Confederate witnesses also testified to the slaughter. A soldier from the 48th Georgia described his unit coming "under the fire of heavy batteries of the enemy posted around Chancellorsville, which were pouring a storm of iron missiles in every direction." The Rebels found the going tough as "a murderous fire was opened on us from the rifle pits," and the Union cannon "swept every approach to them—and poured through the woods through which our advance was to be made, shot, shell and shrapnel in one continuous storm." A member of the 4th North Carolina told a similar tale. His regiment "advanced in solid column" through the woods and to the enemy's entrenchments, all the while enduring "the shower of shells, grape, canister, solid shot and minnie balls," which "was trully appalling," with "men . . . falling on all sides." He marveled that "sometimes whole ranks were swept away, around them."[21]

This artillery fire ripped through the woods, just as it did the Rebel ranks, and the falling debris further hindered the Confederate advance. Noah Collins, a North Carolina soldier, recalled that the movement forward was "greatly retarded or hindered by the trees and tree tops that were cut off by the shells, grape and cannister shot," and he recoiled at the "limbs and chunks" that the artillery fire "knocked off the green trees," which were "constantly falling" on him. This "so intensely alarmed" Collins that he fled as best he could.[22] There was nothing at the Battle of the Wilderness approaching the intensity and scale of this Federal artillery fire at Chancellorsville.

It is also important to note that the Confederates used large numbers of cannon offensively at Chancellorsville—a situation unheard of in the Battle of the Wilderness—which played a crucial role in their attacks on May 3. Stationing their artillery on the Orange Plank Road and at Hazel Grove and later at Fairview, the Rebels shelled the Union positions, making the Yankees very uncomfortable. Alexander, the Rebel officer in charge of the bombardment, explained that his guns had "a fine field of fire" and observed that "the magnificent fire of our guns . . . and the steady advance of our infantry . . . proved too much for the enemy's nerve." Union observers later tried to convey the intensity of this bombardment. Robert McAllister, an officer in the III Corps, recalled that "the enemy's shells were bursting by hundreds around us," claiming at the time that "this was the hottest artillery fire [he had] ever been under." Brig. Gen. Alpheus Williams of the XII Corps marveled "that anything could live on that slope and hill-brow in front of Fairview," where the Union lines were stationed at the time, for "shot and shell and musketry swept it from end to end and side to side, and the columns of destructive missiles seemed to increase every moment."[23] It is not surprising, then, that the unsupported Federals, pounded and hounded as they were by this artillery fire and repeated infantry assaults, felt compelled to withdraw to a new position.

Although the fighting at Chancellorsville was in many ways distinct from the combat of May 5–6, 1864, some of its features paralleled this later clash. Like the Battle of the Wilderness, Chancellorsville was an engagement with a remarkably high butcher's bill. Federal forces sustained losses totaling 12,294 men, while the Confederates suffered 10,705 casualties.[24] The battle also saw the forest shot to pieces, just as it was a year later. "The iron hail," remembered Robert McAllister, was such that "trees fall before the terable storm." Jacob Raymer of the 4th North Carolina likewise explained how "the woods through which they had charged was torn up with shot and shell most frightfully." He reckoned “a hurricane could not have slashed down the timber worse,” with “scarce a shrub or sapling . . . left standing, all . . . shot away.” The intense artillery and musketry not only ripped through the forest but also, as during the later battle, set it aflame. Jedediah Hotchkiss, a member of Stonewall Jackson’s staff, recorded that “the woods were on fire in many places and some of the wounded must have been burnt up.” Aaron DeArmond of the 30th North Carolina likewise saw that “the woods cot on fire and it burnt the leave[s] of the ground and it burnt up a many a man.” While the timber provided fuel for the fires, it also supplied the material for making field fortifications, just as it would in 1864. Charles T. Bowen of the 12th US Infantry recalled that his unit “fell to work & formed a breastwork of logs & earth along our line, & in front we slashed the woods & are now ready for the rebels in any number.”[25]

While Chancellorsville shared some traits with the Battle of the Wilderness, they are not the twins that they are often taken to be, a fact explained by the differences in the two battlefields. At Chancellorsville, artillery played a commanding role, and visibility never seemed to cause the problems that it did at the subsequent battle, suggesting that the lack of uniformity in the Wilderness’s landscape could create a variety of combat conditions. If the Battle of the Wilderness had been fought farther to the east, which would have included the open areas around Ellwood, then conditions similar to Chancellorsville might have easily prevailed. Similarly, if the Confederate flank attack at Chancellorsville had failed to drive the Union forces toward more-open areas, then it seems likely that it might have degenerated into the inconclusive musketry fighting so typical of the Battle of the Wilderness. In short, the Wilderness did not always produce the unique type of combat that postwar writers attributed to it.

While the Wilderness could create a variety of combat conditions, battlefields outside of this region could pose tactical challenges like those experienced during the Battle of the Wilderness. An excellent example of this is the Battle of Chickamauga (September 18–20, 1863). Here the Union Army of the Cumberland, commanded by Maj. Gen. William S. Rosecrans, and the Confederate Army of Tennessee, led by Gen. Braxton Bragg and bolstered with units on loan from Lee's Army of Northern Virginia, engaged in an epic contest in the forests and hills of northern Georgia. The Chickamauga battlefield, rather like the Wilderness, was a patchwork of thick forest with underbrush, open woods, and cleared fields. Maj. Gen. George Thomas, who commanded the XIV Corps, provided a general description: "the surface of the country is undulating and covered with original forest timber, interspersed with undergrowth, in many places so dense that it is difficult to see 50 paces ahead." Other writers have provided more nuanced portrayals. The historian of the 38th Indiana noted that "for a mile east of the La Fayette and Chattanooga road the woods were almost entirely free from underbrush, but nearer the Chickamauga river the growth was quite dense." Archer Anderson, a Confederate veteran, provided a description of the Chickamauga battlefield that could have easily applied to the Wilderness. He found it to be a "rather flat country, not rough or even rolling till you approach the spurs of the low mountains, thickly wooded, with here and there a field of Indian corn, then just ripe, and occasionally an opening of gladelike, treeless land not under any crop." For Anderson, "the impression is of almost unbroken forest, of a rather flat, thinly peopled, poorly tilled, wooded region." Perhaps most interesting was the description provided by Alpheus Williams, who had previously fought at Chancellorsville. He looked over the Chickamauga battlefield and "was surprised to find the battleground so level and almost wholly covered by dense forests," a strange reaction for someone who had been in the Wilderness, a supposedly unique and terrible forest.[26]

Although its forests were generally more mature than the thick, scrubby trees so characteristic of the Wilderness battlefield, many of the same tactical limitations prevailed at Chickamauga. Limited visibility presented many obstacles to the commanders, officers, and soldiers of both sides. Smoke and thick woods combined to hide the enemy and screen his movements, although visibility was better in the open areas. Commanders could not see their own soldiers, had a difficult time controlling their units, and relied on sound rather than sight to guide their actions and comprehend the course of combat. As a result, Chickamauga was a disorienting engagement, not unlike the Battle of the Wilderness. The Georgia battlefield's thick woods also hampered soldiers' movements and formations. Furthermore, the artillery's role was limited by the forest, as batteries were often forced onto the defensive in the few open areas. Sudden encounters with the enemy were common at Chickamauga, just as they were at the Battle of the Wilderness, and in some ways the fighting at Chickamauga was reminiscent of that contest. Makeshift entrenchments were present during the battle, fires swept parts of the Chickamauga battlefield, and casualties were staggering. In short, many of the supposedly unique characteristics of the Battle of the Wilderness, allegedly caused by the region's unique landscape, could also be found at Chickamauga in ordinary woodlands.[27]

Like at the Battle of the Wilderness, Chickamauga's forests and underbrush combined with smoke from forest fires, musketry, and artillery fire to produce very reduced visibility. Many Confederates testified to this effect. "The nature of the country," explained Anderson, was "a tangled forest, through which you could not see the enemy a hundred yards off, and with no elevated points from which even his distant movements could be observed." Likewise, J. B. Polley, the historian of the Texas Brigade of Longstreet's First Corps of the Army of Northern Virginia, recalled that at one point it took the Confederates "almost a minute" to find the enemy's line, only to find out that "they were lying down, and shooting from behind trees, fallen logs and other cover." The thick smoke, common to Civil War battlefields, aggravated this tactical challenge. Brig. Gen. John C. Brown reported running into "the enemy in an unbroken forest, rendered the more difficult of passage by the dense undergrowth which for more than 200 yards extended along my entire line; and the difficulties were still further enhanced by the smoke of battle and the burning of the woods, rendering it impossible to distinguish objects 20 paces in advance." The terrible consequences of fighting blind were all too apparent to veterans of the contest. N. J. Hampton recalled that "there was such a volume of smoke that we could not distinguish the enemy from our own men ten steps away," a fact that his regiment proved when it fired into fellow Confederates, "killing and wounding thirty or forty."[28]

Union observers voiced similar complaints. "Beneath the cover of the thick woods and dense underbrush," explained one veteran, "the Rebel lines advanced often within a few feet of the Federal troops ere they could be seen." Maj. Gen. James Negley, who commanded a division in Thomas's XIV Corps, recalled that at one point "the smoke was so dense and the firing so heavy that I failed to see the enemy on the crest until I confronted his line within 100 feet of him." Charles G. Harker, the colonel of the 65th Ohio, reported that "the ground on [his] immediate front was slightly rising, and covered with a dense thicket and undergrowth. The enemy, therefore, had every advantage over us, as he could perceive our own movements, though his were concealed from us." Like at the Battle of the Wilderness, there were open areas at Chickamauga where visibility was much better, and "on the borders of these glades the contending forces were in plain view of each other except when obscured by the thick smoke of battle."[29]

In addition to the limited combat visibility for soldiers, the commanding generals and the many officers in the armies struggled to see what was happening, a situation often repeated during the Battle of the Wilderness. Longstreet, who commanded half of the Confederate army on September 20, remarked that "on the most open parts of the Confederate side of the field one's vision could not reach farther than the length of a brigade." The historian of the Texas Brigade likewise explained that "it was difficult for an officer on horseback to get an extended view in any direction, and to footmen it was simply impossible," a point emphasized by the fact that, as "short as was the line occupied by the Texas Brigade, neither flank of it could be seen from the other."[30]

Given this limited visibility, it should come as no surprise that commanders struggled to maintain control of their forces at Chickamauga. Anderson thought that there were "extraordinary difficulties surrounding the commander on that obscure and tangled field," for "he could see nothing with his own eyes" and "very little through the eyes of others." Richard W. Johnson, a Union veteran of Chickamauga, claimed that on such a field "no one commander could see the flanks of his regiment even, and so division commanders could only learn how the battle progressed through their orderlies, staff officers, and occasional wounded men brought from the various parts of the line." Like Hancock at the Battle of the Wilderness on May 6, the Confederates at Chickamauga on September 20 had difficulty recognizing the scope of their victory. The fact that Federal forces "were not overwhelmed or at once vigorously pursued by the victorious enemy," observed Arba Waterman, a Union veteran, "was due to the fact that in the broken and heavily timbered country the Rebels did not fully understand what they had accomplished, and hence proceeded with more hesitation and caution than the real facts demanded."[31]

As with the fighting in the Wilderness in 1864, Chickamauga was a battle whose course was tracked by sound rather than by sight. The historians of the 36th Illinois commented on this feature of the engagement. "The army lines extended over nearly three miles of ground, and only by the smoke that rose above the heights, the dust that ascended above the forest trees in the valley, or as the cannon's roar and the rattling discharges of musketry were heard upon surrounding hills, could the observer note the ebb and flow of the tide of battle." Commanders resorted to using sound to judge where to station their troops. One Union veteran noted how "the firing was very heavy to our right and rear," information that his corps commander used to determine where to send his reserve brigades. Colonel Harker also had to use sound to direct his troops: "There was very great confusion among the troops which had been engaged, and no one seemed to have any definite idea of our own lines or the position of the enemy. I was compelled therefore, to resort to my own judgment alone and be guided by the general direction of the firing."[32]

Given the limited visibility and the difficulties the commanders faced in understanding what was taking place and where friend and foe were located, it is no surprise that Chickamauga was a confusing and disorienting fight. "There was very little system about the fighting," recalled the chronicler of the 38th Indiana. "There was no general alignment of the forces on either side, and detachments of brigades and divisions seemed to strike each other by accident." He was not alone in this opinion. The historians of the 36th Illinois explained that "besides the beginning of the conflict, being on the part of both Generals [Rosecrans and Bragg] rather accidental than intentional, the lines had a great deal of an extempore character, and on our side the different divisions were arranged without any reference to their place in the corps, each being thrown in where it was most needed." Absalom Baird, a brigadier general in the XIV Corps, recalled how this disorientation could afflict the soldiers. "We had, during the day, been fired into from every point of the compass, and when we fell back, no other portions of our troops being in sight, it was impossible to tell where they could be found or when we would encounter the enemy." Given these challenges, it is only natural that General Williams deemed it "a poor spot for a great battle." He for one was "not astonished that the reports show a series of defenses and isolated combats of which the rest of the army seem to have been in ignorance."[33]

As at Chancellorsville and the Battle of the Wilderness, the vegetation at Chickamauga hampered troop formations and limited the ability to maneuver. One Union veteran called the Georgia battlefield "the worst possible region in which to maneuver an army, being without landmarks or regular slopes, and so thickly wooded that it was impossible to preserve any alignment." He concluded that "even companies became broken in the thickets, and taking different directions were lost to each other." R. T. Coles, a soldier in the 4th Alabama, recalled similar problems maintaining a formation. The Texas Brigade was on the left of Coles's brigade but was forced to change its front when a large Federal force suddenly appeared on the Texans' left flank. This movement split the Confederate line, creating a potentially dangerous gap. Even brigades could not keep together, as Coles's own showed during a "rapid rush through the timber" during which the other regiments lost connection with the 44th Alabama.[34]

Like at the Battle of the Wilderness, the armies at Chickamauga could only employ artillery as open spaces in the forest permitted. The rugged forests and small fields of northern Georgia, according to several observers, were hardly the ideal setting for these big guns. General Longstreet stated that "the field, so far as it could be surveyed . . . , was not a field, proper, but a heavy woodland, not adapted to the practice of artillery." His Federal opponents arrived at this same conclusion. Negley reported that "the character of the ground" where his men were operating on September 20 "prevented the effective use of all the batteries." Harker agreed with Negley but provided a richer description of the obstacles the Union artillery faced. He claimed to have "at once perceived that we would be compelled to fight in a perfect jungle, and that artillery could not be used to advantage; but, on the contrary, would be subject to capture should our troops meet with a sudden reverse." Experience in battle confirmed his initial impression. "In many instances batteries . . . were placed in positions where artillery could not be effectively used, and, from the nature of the country, could not easily be extricated." Harker concluded that "it was in this way that most of our artillery was lost in the late engagement," while in some cases the Union artillery struck its own men "from a want of judgment and knowledge of our lines."[35]

Officers often complained about the inability of the artillery to penetrate Chickamauga's thickets. General Baird recalled, "we were then in a thick wood interspersed with thickets and openings," and "the artillery could not advance in line with the infantry, nor, indeed, could it have been used except at rare intervals. It could not, at the same time, be left behind for want of protection, and it was directed to follow closely the brigades, making its way through the trees." Marco B. Gary, who commanded Battery C of the 1st Ohio Light Artillery, encountered the same problem. He found "the ground on which" his battery "maneuvered on the 19th . . . so densely covered with timber and underbrush as to render rapid movements of artillery exceedingly difficult and uncertain." While Baird and Gary tried to precariously push Union artillery through the woods, others did not even make the attempt. The colonel of the 8th Kentucky recounted, "the artillery moved along the road until within the vicinity of the enemy, when it became necessary to move the brigade to the right of the road over rough ground and into thick timber." When "a suitable position for the battery" could not be located, the guns were "not moved into the timber, but halted in rear, near the road."[36]

Given that "the ground on which the battle was fought" was "undulating and thickly timbered," and "therefore unfavorable for the use of artillery," it is hardly surprising that musketry dominated the fighting and accounted for more than its fair share of casualties. Glover Perin, the medical director for the Army of the Cumberland, gave evidence to this effect. While "the wounds received were inflicted by a variety of missiles," he believed that "those from the rifled-musket were perhaps more numerous in proportion than usual for so great a battle." Maj. Gen. John Palmer, commanding a division in the XXI Corps, likewise concluded that "few positions could be found for the effective use of artillery," reporting that "the work was confined mainly to the musketry."[37]

Like their counterparts at the Battle of the Wilderness, soldiers at Chickamauga reported sudden and deadly encounters with the enemy. Coles of the 4th Alabama remembered "advancing blindly and rapidly through a dense undergrowth" when his unit "ran unexpectedly right into a column of infantry, which poured a deadly fire into our ranks." He recalled that "for a moment the regiment was stunned and dazed from the suddenness of the fire," but then the Confederates charged the Federals and drove them from their position. In a similar fashion the 101st Ohio moved "cautiously, but steadily, through the dense woods" but "soon struck a strong rebel force advancing obliquely across our front toward our left. Instantly the two lines became engaged in a most desperate conflict."[38]

Makeshift breastworks also played a prominent role in the fighting at Chickamauga as they had during Chancellorsville and would during the Battle of the Wilderness. Several Union divisions at Chickamauga constructed "rough barricades of logs, rails, stumps and stones along their front," although there "were no rifle pits, nor any defensive works on any other part of the line." William G. G. Shanks, a newspaper correspondent, described the Federal fortifications in greater detail. These were "rude works about breast-high . . . using rails and logs for the purpose. The logs and rails ran at right angles to each other, the logs keeping parallel to the proposed line of battle and lying upon the rails until the proper height was reached. The spaces between these logs were filled with rails, which served to add to their security and strength." Unlike other campaigns, in which earthworks were conspicuous, at Chickamauga "the spade had not been used."[39] Instead, the troops turned to the materials at hand to provide themselves with sufficient cover.

There were also repeated, furious attacks on entrenched positions reminiscent of Chancellorsville. One Union veteran remembered that "our men held their fire until the front line was within a hundred yards, and then opened up with a volley which staggered the enemy." The Confederates reformed their lines and attacked again and again, resulting in a "heavy [loss] on the part of the enemy, while ours was insignificant." Overall, casualties at Chickamauga were very heavy, with Confederate losses estimated at between 14,328 and 20,950 men, while the Union forces reported 16,179 casualties.[40]

The intense fighting at Chickamauga proved as destructive to vegetation as the struggles in Virginia's Wilderness. One Union soldier commented on how "the Trees in some places are cut down so much by the artillery that it looks as if a tornado had swept over the field."[41] In a similar vein, the historian of the 38th Indiana noted how the "treetops, limbs and twigs were clipped off over our heads and fell all around us." As in the Wilderness, the trees remained scarred for some time. General Williams, who visited Chickamauga months after the battle had taken place, still found "torn trees" that marked "the scenes of the heaviest fighting."[42]

Fires also broke out during the fighting at Chickamauga. Some started in open fields. David W. Magee's 86th Illinois had to cross a field that "had been fired by . . . shells" earlier in the day, and "a more desolate sight never met the eye" as "the entire country seemed to be one smoking, burning sea of ruin." Fires also plagued the 36th Illinois, which was stationed "in an old field where the ground was covered with dry grass and old logs," which proved ready fuel for flames ignited by "bursting shells." Other fires broke out in Chickamauga's woods. Hampton saw how "the woods caught fire, burning our wounded men before we could take them up." Like at the Battle of the Wilderness and Chancellorsville, men would try to save themselves, but to no avail. He recalled seeing "numbers of wounded soldiers who in some way would get a stick or dead limb, and in an attempt to save their lives would rake the ground around them perfectly clean so that the fire could not reach them." Despite "their hard struggles, many of them were scorched to death with the sticks in their hands." As did many of the witnesses of such scenes at the battles in the Wilderness, Hampton concluded that "this was one of the most terrible sights man ever witnessed."[43] William Preston, a Confederate brigadier general who commanded a division at Chickamauga, also recorded instances of men suffering fiery deaths. He reported that "the musketry from the low breastworks of the enemy . . . had set fire to the dry foliage, and scorched and blackened corpses gave fearful proof of the heroism and suffering of the brave men who had stormed the hill." As at the Battle of the Wilderness, the Union breastworks at Chickamauga sometimes caught fire. The historian of the 38th Indiana remembered such a scene, noting how the men "who had only a few drops of water in their canteens, passed them up until the fire was extinguished."[44]

While many postwar writers claimed that the Battle of the Wilderness had unique characteristics because of where it was fought, in reality it shared certain features with both Chancellorsville and Chickamauga. High casualties, forest fires, trees torn by bullets and shells, and the use of makeshift field fortifications marked all three engagements. Each also furnished numerous examples of how trees and underbrush could hamper movement, disorient troops, and disrupt formations. These problems seem to have been common to all battles fought in the woods. Meade's aide Lyman observed as much during the Overland Campaign. He explained that "there are several chronic troubles" that armies encountered when fighting in the woods: "The divisions have lost connection; they cannot cover the ground designated, their wing is in the air, their skirmish line has lost its direction, etc."[45]

These three clashes differed from each other, however, in battlefield visibility. There were two types of challenges that a wooded battlefield produced. First, the forest screened movements. Second, it made it difficult, if not impossible, to see the enemy in the middle of combat. All three wooded battlefields in this study provided excellent screens for troop movements, but anecdotal evidence suggests that the Battle of the Wilderness had the worst combat visibility, followed by Chickamauga, then Chancellorsville. Much of this had to do initially with the thickness of the woods, although the introduction of smoke from the musketry, artillery fire, and burning woods would have certainly aggravated this problem.

The battles in question also were distinct in the use of artillery and infantry. Chancellorsville had the largest open spaces of the three battlefields, and naturally artillery was able to shape that contest in a way that was simply not possible at Chickamauga or the Battle of the Wilderness. At Chancellorsville cannon in fairly large numbers were used offensively, while at the other two battles the big guns were largely confined to the defensive in the few, small open areas available on those battlefields. In contrast, at Chickamauga and especially at the Battle of the Wilderness, infantry tended to dominate the fighting.

These findings suggest that the Battle of the Wilderness lay at one end of a spectrum of forest fights, featuring fewer open spaces, using less artillery and more infantry, and having the lowest combat visibility. On the other end of this spectrum lay Chancellorsville, where larger open spaces allowed artillery to dominate in a way that was unusual in a wooded battlefield. Somewhere in between these engagements lay Chickamauga. Although fought in a different type of forest hundreds of miles from the Wilderness, it displayed many of the same tactical challenges that supposedly made the Battle of the Wilderness an engagement unlike any other.

It is also worth pointing out that the Wilderness battlefield, for all the challenges it presented, was not necessarily the most difficult landscape a Civil War soldier might encounter. The experience of John Henry Otto of the 21st Wisconsin underscores this point. His unit, which had fought in the western theater, marched past the Wilderness on its way to Washington in 1865. He reported that a "good many of the Officers and soldiers wished to see the grounds and the lay of the memorable battleground where Grant and Lee's armies fought so desperate without any decisive result, and of which so much has been talked and written about." What they beheld disappointed them. While Otto observed that "everything denoted that a fearfull struggle had taken place here," he "found the battlefield no more of a wilderness" than what his unit had encountered "in numbers of battles out west and south." In fact, Otto claimed that he "would rather fight on the wilderness battlefield, than in the Cedarswamps at Stone river, or in the swamps and briars below Kenesaw Mountain, Georgia, or in the swamps of the Pocotaligo and Tullafinny rivers in South Carolina."[46] In the end, the Battle of the Wilderness was not so much a unique engagement as just one manifestation of the tactical problems that Civil War armies faced when operating in a forested region.

3

THE WILDERNESS MYSTIQUE

There is no question that the Wilderness has a mystique about it. Historians have often conveyed it, even if they have never put a name to it. Yet no historian has systematically analyzed this characteristic or sought to explain its origins. Obviously, the nature of combat during the Battle of the Wilderness was an important component of the aura surrounding the region. Yet this mystique—which no other battlefield of the war could match—went beyond combat conditions and was actually an amalgamation of multiple elements that created something that none of its individual parts could have produced.

It began with the name. Unlike many battlefields, the Wilderness has an appellation that carries specific negative connotations, indicating a forest empty of man and beyond his control. The name also sets it apart as a distinct region. Many Union and Confederate soldiers who entered the Wilderness in the spring of 1863 had no inkling that they had stepped into a place marked by a special name and physical characteristics. By the time of the Overland Campaign, however, the men in both armies were calling it "the Wilderness" and attributing certain features to this forested region. Over time, and especially during the postwar years, descriptions of the Wilderness became images of a malevolent landscape. First in the contemporary accounts of the 1864 battle and later in postwar writings, the Wilderness became increasingly associated with death and destruction. The remains of the 1863 Chancellorsville battleground, the high casualties, the destruction of vegetation, and the corpses, skeletons, and graves that littered the Wilderness combined to cast the region as a place where the shadow of death lingered. It also became connected to the fires that ravaged the battlefield and engulfed the wounded. Such scenes caused some postwar writers to compare the Wilderness to hell itself. These images of death and destruction, fire and hell, formed important elements in the Wilderness mystique. The supernatural also found its way into the legend, as postwar writers portrayed the Wilderness as haunted or even as a spirit itself that could lash out and change the course of battle—and with it, the destiny of the nation.

While most Civil War engagements derived their names from a nearby town, landmark, or body of water, the Battle of the Wilderness took its appellation from a region. It is with this name—the Wilderness—that any investigation should commence, for it was not a neutral term. In order to understand a place bestowed with such an evocative name, it is necessary to investigate the term's origin as well as the contemporary meaning it held for Civil War soldiers. Roderick Nash, in his trailblazing book *Wilderness and the American Mind,* argued, "although later extensions of its meaning obscured the word's original precision, the initial image wilderness generally evokes is that of a forest primeval." The term also "implied the absence of men, and the wilderness was conceived as a region where a person was likely to get into a disordered, confused, or 'wild' condition." Nash's definition of "wilderness," then, conjured "the image . . . of a man in an alien environment where the civilization that normally orders and controls his life is absent."[1]

When soldiers encountered the Wilderness, they often remarked that the name fit perfectly. Moreover, they agreed with Nash's definition and pointed to the lack of cultivation, the vast unbroken forest, and the absence of inhabitants as the region's defining characteristics. "It may well be called the Wilderness," explained Union colonel Robert McAllister, "for there is not one acre of land in a hundred that is cleared." Likewise, a Rhode Island infantryman remarked that "this place is called the Wilderness" and judged that "it is rightly named for ten square miles there is not a dozen acres of cleared land." Wilbur Fisk, a Vermont soldier, concluded that "it would be hard to conceive of a name more appropriate" for the area as "it appears to be one uninterrupted wilderness, extending fifteen or twenty miles either way, without any other inhabitants than owls, buzzards, and such like animals." Confederates, too, noted these same characteristics. Philip H. Powers complained that "this is a dreary dismal country . . . most fitly called the Wilderness," explaining that "for many miles not a house and not an open field" was present but instead "a wilderness of tree and underbrush and marsh," all of which was "perfectly flat."[2] In short, the Wilderness was a wilderness to these soldiers because it was a region full of trees, empty of men, and seemingly beyond human control.

Nash also noted the traditions linking the Wilderness with "wild men" and argued that savages "sweeping out of the forest to strike, and then melting back into it . . . were almost always associated with wilderness." With such notions as these embedded in American culture, it is no surprise that veterans of the Battle of the Wilderness at times associated combat there with Indian fighting. A. M. Stewart, a Federal chaplain, found that the fighting at the Battles of the Wilderness and Spotsylvania "much more resembles the old back-woods' contests with the Indians, than modern, or what may be termed 'civilized' warfare." Orlando B. Wilcox similarly thought that "the fighting reminded [him] of stories of Indian fighting in the northwest," while Fitzhugh Lee simply compared the Battle of the Wilderness to "a huge Indian fight." One postwar article went even further, arguing that the battle "was not even Indian-fighting." At least "the scalp locks of the Aborigines were . . . occasionally exposed" in that sort of combat, whereas in the Battle of the Wilderness "nothing could be seen of the enemy."[3]

This same association of wilderness with wild men led some Federals to liken their enemies to savages. Just as others did, William Swinton concluded that "only Indian tactics told" when it came to fighting the Battle of the Wilderness. Yet he also claimed that the Confederates had "an almost Indian skill in woodcraft." Mason Whiting Tyler, a veteran of the 37th Massachusetts, recalled the stress that fighting in the Wilderness against an unseen and supposedly savage enemy could exert on the men. "In recesses of the forest," remembered Tyler, "lurked our foes, using all the tricks and devices of savage warfare, crawling through the brush, shooting at us from concealed thickets, springing at us from trees and bushes, while the bullets from unseen guns and masked batteries prostrated our soldiers by the thousand." He concluded that "human nerves were not made to stand the strain of such a warfare as this," claiming that "a man can be brave as long as he can see his foe, but will quail and tremble in the presence of darkness and the goblins of the air."[4]

While the name was meaningful in itself, the Wilderness's mystique was more than just a catchy label. Over time the region developed a reputation as a malevolent landscape, a process that culminated in the war's aftermath. At Chancellorsville many, if not most, soldiers failed to recognize the Wilderness as a distinct place and merely commented on some of its features, such as dense woods and underbrush. Moreover, the feelings expressed toward the Wilderness were usually neutral. During the Mine Run Campaign, however, an increasing number of Union soldiers began to recognize the Wilderness as a special and seemingly hostile environment. They tended to focus on the vast forest as a perfect incarnation of a wild country. By early May 1864, soldiers in both blue and gray were calling the battleground the Wilderness and continued to marvel at how fittingly it was named. It was also after this battle that descriptions of the region really began to take a serious negative turn. This pattern then continued into the postwar years, when visitors and writers set the Wilderness apart as a strange and hostile environment.

The Chancellorsville Campaign was the first encounter the two armies had with the Wilderness, and the soldiers' reactions were mixed. Many witnesses gave no indication that they knew the name of the place or that there was anything special or distinct about the region. They might have noticed certain environmental characteristics such as thick woods, swampy areas, and vegetation, but there was no effort to make these local observations apply to the entire region. Their comments at this time gave little indication that the place was especially haunting. Alpheus Williams, a brigadier general in the XII Corps, was typical in this respect. He found around himself "the densest kind of pine thickets and underbrush" along with "thick woods, mostly of stunted pines," and mud holes. Others offered similarly straightforward assessments. The piece of the Wilderness through which Jacob Raymer's 4th North Carolina charged on May 3 "was thickly set with trees of ordinary size, saplings and underbrush," while later his unit "entered a dense pine thicket." In a similar vein the 27th Virginia was stationed in "very thick bushes and small timber," while the 44th Georgia was "in a dense oak forest." Lemuel Jefferies provided one of the more negative assessments. He described the area as covered in "a jungle of scrub and bun oaks and brambles" that "in places . . . is almost impregnable." The soldiers who tried to "force their way through" would find "their faces cut, clothes torn, and knapsack jerked off."[5] For many Union and Confederate soldiers, though, the Wilderness at this point was just an undefined forest in which they happened to be fighting.

There were, however, some men who did recognize the Wilderness as a distinct region during the Chancellorsville Campaign. On the Federal side, generals such as Gouverneur K. Warren, Winfield Scott Hancock, Daniel Sickles, and Henry W. Slocum used the term "the Wilderness" in their reports, although what they were referring to was not always clear.[6] Some Confederate officers likewise showed a similar awareness. Maj. Gen. J. E. B. Stuart, Lee's cavalry commander, commented in his after-action report that "this region of country is known as the 'Wilderness.'" In addition, a handful of men in both armies made observations about the area. Warren B. Person of the 64th New York recalled "turning into a piece of woods which proved to be a vast forest called 'The Wilderness.'" Likewise, a Confederate described the Wilderness as "a dense skirt of woods running for several miles . . . 'with occasional openings of cleared and cultivated fields.'" He found the woods to be "principally black jack, and to the eye presented almost an impenetrable thicket."[7] Warren, then the chief of topographical engineers for the Army of the Potomac, made similar observations, commenting on the "dense woods and thickets of black-jack oak and pine [that] cover most of the ground," declaring that "no one can conceive a more unfavorable field for the movements of a grand army than it presents."[8]

By the time of the Mine Run Campaign, an increasing number of Union soldiers showed an awareness that they were in a distinct region known as the Wilderness, a marked change from Chancellorsville. Examples of this recognition abound, often coupled with commentary on the density and breadth of the forest. A soldier from the 13th Massachusetts told the folks back home that the regiment was "now in the portion of Virginia known as the Wilderness, it being almost impenetrable, and extending for miles, in front, rear, and on both flanks." Many Union soldiers at Mine Run claimed that the region was the very incarnation of the word "wilderness." An artilleryman remarked that "the nature of the whole country from the Rapidan is a perfect 'Wilderness,' and as the country is covered with an almost impassable jungle, you can imagine the difficulties under which we labored." Of special interest is the description offered by a soldier from the 65th New York. He reported, "we entered the Wilderness, and for six miles saw nothing but forests on either hand; dense, black, mysterious, the abode of hydras and goblins."[9] This last remark hints at the fearful images already developing in the minds of Union soldiers, even before the Battle of the Wilderness.

In contrast to their Union foes, Confederate soldiers during the Mine Run Campaign generally did not identify the Wilderness as a specific place, although they did comment on some of its salient features. For instance, Lee did not name the region but did describe "the country in that vicinity" as "being almost an unbroken forest." Oscar Hinrichs, a staff officer, followed the same pattern, recalling that "the country is thinly settled, and heavily wooded; [its] undergrowth [is] very much on the style of the Chancell[or]sville woods," while failing to identify it as the Wilderness.[10] One notable exception to this trend was General Stuart, who having called the area the Wilderness during the Chancellorsville Campaign, naturally identified it again at Mine Run. He noted that "the ground on either side" of the Orange Plank Road was "covered with the dense scrub-oak characteristic of that wilderness region." Others provided descriptions of the immediate areas in which they operated rather than of the region as a whole. Charles F. Bahnson, for one, found himself "in an old field, in which pine trees had grown up to a considerable size," remarking on the thickness of their trunks.[11] One of Lee's division commanders, Maj. Gen. Edward Johnson, ordered his men "to drive the enemy out of the tangled wilderness in which he had sheltered himself."[12] But there was nothing here to indicate that any of these men—with the exception of Stuart—set the Wilderness apart in their minds, and certainly none of them implied that it was a particularly frightening place.

During the Overland Campaign, negative portrayals of the Wilderness by Union soldiers grew in frequency and intensity. Some were reminiscent of the descriptions from the Mine Run Campaign that focused on the perfect wilderness landscape. A member of the 143rd Pennsylvania wrote home that he could hardly "give . . . any idea of the country through here" but encouraged his parents to "just think of . . . nothing but woods of scrub oak, stunted pines, and vines with here and there a small farm and a cleared field with ravines and hollows and a stream of water here and there." The Wilderness elicited grumbling responses from others. Henry Keiser complained about having to make his way "for two miles through the awfullest brush, briars, grapevines, etc. I ever was in." Daniel Holt, a Union surgeon, called the Wilderness "the raggedest hole I about ever saw. . . . Swampy, hilly, bushes thick as dog's hair, grape vines, rotten logs and fallen trees, make up this pretty picture. A fine place to fight in surely: a perfect quag mire." Fisk heard his fellow Vermonters call it simply "'a wilderness of woe.'" Perhaps a Pennsylvania soldier best captured the prevailing sentiment, saying that the Wilderness's name was "a word which expressed much of the toil and pain to any one who has experienced its brushy and swampy and somber realities."[13]

Meanwhile, during this same campaign, many Confederates showed a newfound awareness of the Wilderness, recognizing the woods as a distinct place for the first time. One Rebel remarked that they "fought in the woods of the Wilderness (a very continuously and densely wooded poverty stricken section in Spotsylvania Co. in which the Battle of Chancellorsville was fought).” Raymer called it “the renowned Wilderness,” suggesting that the region had obtained some notoriety, and the North Carolinian’s description was comparable to those that Union soldiers had provided. He observed that “the face of the country is broken into gentle hills, interspersed with many swamps and marshes; the soil sterile, few farms or habitations are to be seen—large timber is scarce, but the underbrush, brambles and such like, are so dense as to be almost impenetrable.” One of the richest portrayals of the Wilderness was by Alexander Boteler, a member of Stuart’s staff. He agreed with his Union opponents that its name “fitly applies to the locality it designates, for a gloomier, wilder and more forbidding region can hardly be found this side of the Alleghanies.” He added, “for miles . . . the forests are unbroken by a single clearing and the traveller may journey on for hours without seeing a sign of . . . habitations. Not only do over-arching trees on either hand hem in the road and hide the sky, making it at high noon there seem more like twilight gray, but there is also on both sides a tangled mass of undergrowth apparently interminable as so densely intricate that it would be difficult for a dog to get through it.”[14] The stark contrast between these descriptions and those provided by Confederates at Chancellorsville and Mine Run suggest a sea change in their understanding of the Wilderness.

What would cause soldiers’ descriptions of the Wilderness to evolve over the course of the three campaigns? One possible explanation is the far from uniform vegetation. Some Union veterans argued that there was a core, or heart, of the Wilderness, where the forest was supposedly thicker than the woods around Chancellorsville or the woodlands stretching toward Mine Run. This postwar interpretation might go a good way toward explaining why the men who participated in the Wilderness Campaign seemed to react harshly against the environment. It also would account for why more Union soldiers mentioned the Wilderness sooner than their Confederate counterparts. The Federals had marched through this core during the Mine Run Campaign, after which many of them first began to mention the Wilderness as a specific place with special features. This would also explain why the Confederates suddenly started mentioning the Wilderness in greater numbers and with more vivid detail in May 1864, when they campaigned in this extrathick forest for the first time. The Wilderness battlefield might have been simply a more difficult, thicker, and less open tract of woods than what Lee's men had experienced previously.

It is also conceivable that the Union forces had simply developed an aversion to the Wilderness through experience. Repeated frustrations only compounded with each failure, leading men to view the forest south of the Rapidan as a place of misfortune.[15] It seems likely, however, that if the armies had not met for a third time in the Wilderness in May 1864, then its name might have little meaning to modern historians.

Another possibility is that Union soldiers might have found the woods in the Wilderness more noteworthy. For example, when writing his memoir, Norton C. Shepard of the 146th New York felt obliged to clarify the different meanings "wilderness" had in the North and South. "In the North," he explained, "a wilderness is a wood in a state of nature with great trees that have stood for ages, with other trees uprooted and fallen, with old logs lying prone upon the ground, with dry stubs and dead trees ready to fall at the first storm, so that in places it is almost impossible to travel." To this primeval, northern notion of wilderness, Shepard contrasted the southern, manmade version. He found that "in the South, . . . especially in Virginia, most of the land has been cleared off and cultivated," and "after many years of cultivation it has become worn out and has been abandoned as useless." In the place of the original forest "grows up . . . pine and scrub oak to become a wilderness," with trees that "are usually about six inches in diameter with branches growing thick from the ground to the top." Shepard's explanation, then, suggests that Union soldiers were unaccustomed to seeing these sorts of wasted and abandoned areas in the North, while Southerners might have found them more familiar and thus less worthy of remark.[16]

There is also the influence of newspapers. Soldiers were avid consumers of the press, and reading correspondents' descriptions of the Wilderness certainly had the potential to shape their own views on the region, though the men also could have influenced what the reporters wrote. While the relationship is not clear, there is no question that journalists were identifying the Wilderness and describing its characteristics from early on. A Richmond newspaper, for instance, published a report after Chancellorsville that gave the region's name and called it "a country of gravelly clay soil, and a black-jack growth, presenting in many places an almost impenetrable thicket." Likewise, during the Mine Run Campaign, a correspondent for the *New York Times* labeled "the country hereabouts . . . one of the worst conceivable for field operations," arguing that "it is truly named the 'Wilderness,' for a wilderness of small growth wood covers nine-tenths of the whole surface of the country." In another report the same writer suggested that "no one unacquainted with this section of the country can conceive of the difficulties this army has to surmount" while operating there.[17] Suffice it to say that newspapers had the potential to spread these perceptions of the Wilderness, if they needed spreading, and shape the soldiers' attitudes toward the region. Whatever the cause, by the time of the Overland Campaign, soldiers in both armies recognized the Wilderness as a distinct place.

The increasingly negative descriptions of the Wilderness actually gained strength in postwar memoirs and histories. One Confederate veteran noted, "what I have read—& more particularly from northern writers[—]raises a mistery or horror about the name of that part of Spottsylvania Co," an observation that other postwar writings bear out. Some of the descriptions were brief. Hazard Stevens called the forest "dense, gloomy, and monotonous," while another Union veteran, Thomas Hyde, portrayed the Wilderness as a "bushy, briery, labyrinth." Others provided more elaborate portraits. The historian of the 118th Pennsylvania recalled that "it was a wild, weird region. Everywhere was dense and trackless forest. The piercing cry of the whip-poor-will rang through the somber pines and the screech owl echoed from the tree tops."[18]

Not only was the Wilderness a strange place but also, for some Federals, an enemy. Sartell Prentice portrayed nature as having refurbished the exploited land only to wreak vengeance on man when he returned in 1864: "Nature's obstacles hindered and hurt the invading thousands in such way as history tells no like of in all its hundreds of years of memory." Likewise, the historian of the 146th New York recalled the "sense of ominous dread which many of us found almost impossible to shake off" as the sounds of birds, insects, and hushed men combined, "seeming to forebode evil to those who had invaded this solitude." Morris Schaff took a slightly different approach. Like others, he described the Wilderness as a "mystery-wrapped country," a "lonely region" with confusing roads, but contended that the woodlands seemed to sap Union commanders of their reason and strength. Hooker, he explained, "no sooner was . . . there than he became mentally numb and purposeless as though he had breathed some deep, stagnating fumes." At the Battle of the Wilderness, Schaff claimed, "the lotus in the fateful region's gloom was again at work."[19]

Postwar travel accounts continued to portray the Wilderness as a malevolent landscape. An article for *Metropolitan Magazine* published in 1907 tried to explain the feeling of traversing the Wilderness, where the "path is narrow, dense foliage meets overhead, and the traveler is completely hemmed in." The "solitude is awesome, broken only by the disturbance of the dry leaves as the lizards and creeping things flee before approaching hoofbeats. It is boundless!" Visitors seemed to expect such feelings when they entered the region. An 1879 narrative betrayed the anticipation one traveler had of finding "'the dark lugubrious, somber, impenetrable jungles of the Wilderness.'" In obvious disillusionment he "saw nothing particularly 'wild,' 'weird,' or 'howling,' about the Wilderness" and contented himself with observing, "it was not the most interesting country to be sure." The ruins of "the far-famed Chancellorsville" proved equally disappointing, as the traveler "rather expected to see a neat little village" but found only "the remains of a large and pretentiously built tavern." The generous hospitality he received at the well-kept Ellwood estate, "situated in a beautiful valley and extending in some directions as far as the eye could reach," also seemed to ill fit his idea of the "'weird shadows and the awful gloom of the Wilderness.'"[20] While this account suggests a failure to visit many of the important parts of the battlefields, the expectations are very telling.

Some modern accounts of the Battle of the Wilderness continue to reflect similar themes. In *A Stillness at Appomattox,* Bruce Catton's

Wilderness "was a mean gloomy woodland . . . lying silent and forbidding." Edward Steere's study of the Wilderness Campaign called the Wilderness "a dreary wasteland" and a "brooding jungle" that set "eternal shadows over stagnant pools and marshy creek bottoms" and "imposed the conditions of combat in its gloomy depths." While James McPherson's *Battle Cry of Freedom* was more subdued, portraying the Wilderness as "that gloomy expanse of scrub oaks and pines," Mark Grimsley's history of the Overland Campaign painted the Wilderness as a "country [that] seemed to hate every man who dared walk through it." Grimsley concluded, "it was less a patch of vegetation than a force of nature."[21] Such depictions suggest that while the region's image evolved during the war years, becoming increasingly negative, the postwar interpretation became a static, if not exaggerated, rendition—the malevolent Wilderness—that received the sanction of tradition while losing none of the image's appeal.

Just as the Wilderness morphed into a malevolent landscape, it also became associated with death and destruction.[22] This is not particularly astonishing considering that it was a battlefield, but all the same, the association is a key element in its mystique. This process began with the Overland Campaign of 1864 as the Union soldiers began the march south. After the Battle of the Wilderness, the men remarked on the carnage as well as the destruction of the vegetation during that engagement and were amazed that anyone could have survived. Burial parties also collected the remains of the killed. Later visitors to the battlefield remarked on the ruined vegetation and the shadow of death over the land. Those who wrote about the Wilderness in postwar histories and memoirs continued this association with death and brought it to its highest form.

At the start, as well as the conclusion, of the Battle of the Wilderness, Federal soldiers passed through the old Chancellorsville battleground of 1863 and saw the ruins, the debris, and especially the dead. William D. Landon of the 14th Indiana made such a visit and noted that "strange feelings crept over me as we marched along the same road and over the same ground where one year and a day before I had stood up with my comrades in line of battle," seeing also "the old white house occupied as headquarters by Gen. Couch during the fight, shattered and torn with hostile shot and shell, still standing, a refuge for bats and owls (ghosts, too, for aught I know)." Cornelius Moore, a soldier with the 57th New York, had a similar reaction. He came upon the Chancellor house, "now a mass of ruins," which appeared in his "mind's eye spectre-like, reminding me of the horrors of a scene witnessed with-in their site, but one short year ago." Albert Reid of the 77th New York succinctly concluded, "It looks prety rough around there." While these soldiers focused on the ruins, others dwelt upon different reminders of the earlier battle. One Federal soldier discovered that "over the whole field was scattered the usual *debris* of a battle field." In contrast, soldiers from the 86th New York focused on the graves. They found the old battlefield "covered with" them, and during one night they "slept among the graves of their comrades who fell just one year ago to-day." Bedding down in such a place, "the scenes of that fearful conflict [remained] fresh in their recollection and they retired for the night knowing that but a few hours would elapse before they would be repeated with all its horrors of blood and carnage."[23]

Perhaps most unnerving of all were the skeletons of troops killed a year earlier. One Union soldier explained that these men had been buried, but "only a few inches of dirt was thrown over them and now their bones lie bleaching in the sun, scattered about where the beasts of the forest left them." Many soldiers recorded seeing those grisly reminders as they passed through the old battlefield. Moore observed "one of the boys [pick] up, at our feet, a man's foot, incased in a stocking and shoe, just as it was when shot from the leg." Indeed, the bones were not hard to find. "The woods were strewn with the skeletons of comrades killed here one year ago," remarked Landon. Charles Brewster also found that "there were lots of human skulls and bones lying top of the ground and we left plenty more dead bodies to decay and bleach to keep their grim company."[24] If there was a perfect place to rehearse the graveyard scene from *Hamlet,* this was it.

During the Battle of the Wilderness, this association with death continued as soldiers witnessed the terrible toll exacted by an unseen foe. Andrew J. McBride, a soldier in the 10th Georgia, observed, "the woods . . . is riddled with bullets . . . and is tonight thickly strewn with dead and wounded Yankees." Others testified to the same effect. A Federal signal officer saw 450 dead Rebels in front of the II Corps's line, which he called "only one instance of the terrible slaughters and encounters of the Wilderness battle." Wilbur Fisk, a Vermont soldier, wrote home that his regiment had suffered 264 casualties and thought that "had the rebels fired a little lower, they would have annihilated the whole line; they nearly did it as it was." Fisk then lamented, "there was so many men missing from our number that it hardly seemed like the same regiment." Likewise, a Confederate in the Texas Brigade mourned losses in his regiment. "At sun-up two hundred and seven strong men stand in line of battle; half an hour afterward all but seventy-seven of them are dead or wounded—mangled, torn, and dismembered." In these descriptions the Wilderness became a terrible place where soldiers went in whole and came out wounded or lifeless. Theodore Lyman attested to this. He was present as Col. Samuel Carroll's brigade "disappeared in the woods," arousing "the musketry with double violence," only to see Carroll "brought back wounded." Then Brig. Gen. Alexander Hays's brigade followed, and "in a few minutes, General Hays was carried past . . . covered with blood, shot through the head."[25]

Soldiers often paired their remarks about high casualties with comments on the destruction of vegetation and marveled that anyone could have survived such a maelstrom. Landon saw a "thick undergrowth of black-jacks . . . literally mowed down with balls," came upon "trunks splintered, bruised and torn by rifle balls and cannon shot," and found "saplings . . . split into matches by the storm of bullets." Meanwhile, Fisk spotted a place along his Vermont unit's line where "every bush and twig was cut and splintered by the leaden balls" and wondered "if a single tree could have been found that had not been pierced several times with bullets, and all . . . hit about breast high." Confederates, too, recorded nature's doom. "Every sapling and every twig," declared one soldier, "were—some many times—pierced with balls," and another commented on the trees being "literally torn into splinters." Jacob Raymer concluded, "that a single soul should come out living is truly a wonder."[26]

By the end of the fight, the Wilderness battlefield was covered with casualties, and in time it would be pocked with graves and littered with bones. Brewster remarked that "the woods we have fought over both there and here are strewn with the dead bodies of both parties who lay as they fell unburied." Later, a Union soldier who returned after the battle to bury the dead observed that those who were farther than a mile away from the hospital "remain as death found them, with the exception of their clothing," which had been removed. "It is estimated," he went on, "that 15,000 of our men, and as many, or more, of Rebels lie here unburied; and as six weeks have passed since the battle, imagination in its wildest fancies cannot begin to paint the spectacle." It is little wonder that he called the field of battle "this wilderness of death" and "this wilderness and shadow of death." Another Federal returning to collect the wounded remarked on the newest round of burials: "Hastily dug graves could be seen everywhere; some with head-boards; some with nothing to tell whether the men below were rebel or patriot." Moving toward Parker's Store, he stumbled upon "large numbers of rebel graves" on one side of an entrenchment and a "great many" Union graves on the other.[27]

In other instances, the dead remained where they fell, unsheltered by even the shallowest of graves. John Trowbridge, a reporter who visited the battlefield after the war, discovered "the unburied remains of two soldiers" while making his way through the Wilderness's thickets. While such an encounter was disturbing, the sight of skeletons in the Wilderness was becoming increasingly rare. As Drew Faust has pointed out, the US government took steps in the war's immediate aftermath to account for the Union dead, especially to identify and inter those who had not received a decent burial. One of the first efforts was at the Wilderness and Spotsylvania.[28]

In June 1865, soldiers came back to the Wilderness to inter "the remains of Union soldiers yet unburied" while "marking their burial places for future identification." Landon, an Indiana veteran involved in this effort, found that “very few had been buried” on the Union right around the Orange Plank Road. With “every fourth man carrying a sack, [they] commenced the search for skeletons through woods, thickets, fields and swamps.” He discovered that “bodies of our soldiers were thickly strewn through woods and fields in all directions,” and they had “no difficulty in ascertaining where those lay who fell in the open field, as the rank growth of weeds marked each spot.” Several days of labor produced “a huge pile of grinning, ghastly skulls—the frames of three hundred and fifty Union soldiers.” It was summer, and “many had to be buried where they lay in the swamps and marshes, their remains being too offensive to handle under the circumstances.” Along the Orange Plank Road they “gathered . . . six hundred and fifty of the bleaching bones of [the] gallant dead,” many of which the soldiers “were compelled to bury as they lay.” In front of the Brock Road works, the Rebel dead “were piled in heaps.” Landon claimed that “had our search been made early in the spring before vegetation was so far advanced, many more remains would have been discovered.” Nevertheless, long after these efforts, an 1884 travel account warned those who would tour the Wilderness that “even now a straggler through the tangled and scrubby woods will occasionally come suddenly upon a skeleton with a few tattered threads of blue or gray clinging to the bones—a ghastly reminder of war’s grim horrors.”[29]

Postwar visitors to the Wilderness understandably continued to connect the place with death. The region seemed to evoke a palpable feeling in many who visited it. At the Wilderness battlefield, Trowbridge observed in typically overwrought language that “a cloud passed over the sun,” and “all the scene became somber, and hushed with a strange brooding stillness, broken only by the noise of twigs crackling under my feet, and distant growls of thunder. A shadow fell upon my heart also, as from the wing of the Death-Angel, as I wandered through the woods, meditating upon what I saw.” Writing about a visit to the Chancellorsville battlefield, David McIntosh, a former Confederate artillery officer, sensed that “the spirit of death seemed still to brood over the place. Not a sound could be heard through all the forest, not the note of a bird. The silence and the gloom was painful.”[30]

The ruinous state of the Wilderness also linked it to destruction, as attested to by both witnesses and contemporary photographs. The vegetation long remained scarred. In 1865 Trowbridge noted how "the marks of hard fighting were visible from afar off" at the Chancellorsville battlefield. Of particular interest was the "growth of saplings edging the woods on the south [which] had been killed by volleys of musketry" and that "looked like thickets of bean-poles." West of the Chancellor house, Trowbridge found "the tree-trunks pierced by balls, the boughs lopped off by shells, the strips of timber cut to pieces by artillery and musketry fire." Lyman found similar destruction on the Wilderness battlefield. In 1866 he saw along the Orange Plank Road "the noted spot where every tree (they are saplings all) was cut down by the musketry," something that he was reluctant to believe "without [his] own observation." East of the Widow Tapp farm he discovered "every tree with two, three, even half a dozen bullet marks on its lower trunk and many cut in two by the rebel shells." Some five hundred yards in front of the Brock Road, Lyman noticed that not one tree "was standing for a distance of some hundred yards in length," like "a whirlwind had twisted off each trunk and left the top hanging by the torn fibres." One postwar account, published in 1884, claimed that "the woods still bear the marks of the fierce struggling . . . , and although the lapse of time and nature's softening touches have to a great extent obliterated the traces of battle, yet the larger trees are scarred and torn with bullets and here and there a shell-mark shows itself."[31]

Postwar writers cemented this association of the Wilderness with death and destruction. William Swinton wrote of "a region of gloom and the shadow of death." Here in this "horrid thicket there lurked two hundred thousand men . . . ; and, though no array of battle could be seen, there came out of its depths the crackle and roll of musketry like the noisy boiling of some hell-caldron that told the dread story of death." Here again were tales of visiting Chancellorsville on the eve of the Battle of the Wilderness. Frank Wilkeson, a Union veteran, recalled scenes of walking the old battlefield, where "many polished skulls lay on the ground." Later, as the soldiers spoke of the previous year's battle, "the dead were all around," and "their eyeless skulls seemed to stare steadily at us." After a sobering talk about the obstacles that would face them if they fought in the Wilderness, one soldier, "who had . . . been prying into the shallow grave he sat on with his bayonet, suddenly rolled a skull on the ground before us, and said in a deep, low voice: 'That is what you are all coming to, and some of you will start toward it to-morrow.'" The fearful carnage of the Battle of the Wilderness again took center stage. William J. Seymour, a member of Lt. Gen. Richard S. Ewell's Second Corps, thought that "never was there a more grim and ghastly spectacle of the horrors and terrible destructiveness of War than was presented under the deep and solemn shades of the Wilderness; while the atmosphere for miles around was filled with the noisome odors that came up from the putrifying corpses." The common connection between the high casualties and the destruction of nature also persisted in the postwar literature. "Thousands of men," observed one regimental history, "lay scattered through the woods," and "trees were riddled with bullets from their roots to the top, and the brush was cut away as if mowed with a scythe. Walking over the ground after the battle it seemed almost impossible that any one should have escaped."[32]

For the soldiers who fought in the Wilderness, the forest was a place where death held sway. It was everywhere to be found, from the remnants of Chancellorsville to the terrible toll in killed and wounded, from the toppled trees to the buried bodies and bleaching bones. For this reason, Union veterans like Horace Porter almost seemed compelled to connect the two. For him, the Wilderness would always be "a tangled forest the impenetrable gloom of which could be likened only to the shadow of death"—and thus the Wilderness and death became one and inseparable, a legacy that lives on.[33]

Alongside death and destruction, the fires that had raged during the Battle of the Wilderness also formed an important element in the Wilderness mystique. Contemporary witnesses and images focused on two aspects of the fires: the burning of the wounded, often described as the worst part of the battle, and the combat amid the flames along the Brock Road on May 6, 1864. Postwar writers perpetuated and, some would say, embellished these accounts, which became standard fare in any history of the battle. It was in the postwar histories and memoirs that the Wilderness became associated not just with fire, but with hell itself.

The connection between the Wilderness and fire actually began during the Battle of Chancellorsville in May 1863. There, on May 3, fires broke out, consuming wounded soldiers from both sides and leaving those who witnessed such scenes deeply disturbed. John Tiffany of the 27th Virginia called the burning of the wounded "one of the most horrible sights I ever witnessed in my life," observing that when his unit got to the Chancellor house, "bodies were singeing and frying among the burning fragments of the house." Francis S. Johnson, a soldier in the 45th Georgia, similarly expressed the strong reaction that witnessing such awful deaths could elicit. "One of the most horrible and heart rending things," he explained, occurred when the fires caught the wounded. "The poor fellows tried to get out of the way but could not do it." Johnson declared, "it was the worst thing I ever saw in my life and I have seen many bad sights." The Rebels were not alone in their revulsion. Union colonel Robert McAllister confessed that "it is horrible to think of" the wounded burning but suspected that "some will no doubt survive to tell the particulars of these sad and painful stories." Charles Wainwright, a Federal artillery officer, found his only comfort in the hope "that many of them crawled, or were got off before the fire reached them, and that it made quick work with the others."[34]

Roughly a year later, the Battle of the Wilderness left the woods both ablaze and littered with dead and wounded men. Like at Chancellorsville, many contemporary witnesses dwelt upon the fires because of the dangers they posed to the wounded and helpless men. This situation greatly troubled soldiers on both sides, even if they never actually saw anyone burn to death. Alexander Boteler found it "horrible to think of hundreds of wounded men [being] in danger of being roasted alive." Others, however, had a more direct experience. William W. Williamson, an officer in the 8th Georgia, saw that the "dead and wounded were burned and scorched until they looked as black as negroes." Likewise,

Landon of the 14th Indiana observed "all the horrors of a battlefield, including the charred and blackened remains of those who were burned and smothered in the blazing leaves and underbrush."[35] Yet there was literally more to the Wilderness fires than met the eye. Williamson agreed that "it was a most horrible sight" but found "the smell that the burnt corpses emitted extremely shocking and sickening to the senses." The cries of the wounded could also be awful, especially when accompanied by the sounds that burning bodies make. Raymer of the 4th North Carolina discovered that the "bodies burned with a crackling noise," and "the screams, the unearthly shrieks [of the burning wounded] made the night hideous." Given the strong emotions such sights and sounds evoked, it is not surprising that some witnesses thought the burning of the wounded to be the most dreadful aspect of combat in the Wilderness. Raymer concluded that the wounded men burning to death "in one awful funeral pile" infused "untold horrors to the scene of carnage."[36]

Combat amid the flaming forest, especially along the Brock Road, proved to be another problem altogether. George A. Bowen of the 12th New Jersey wrote of how "the heat and smoke [were] almost suffocating." There was also the danger of explosions when fires found the black powder the men carried. In his after-action report, Edwin Dow of the 6th Maine Artillery gave a good example of this hazard. He complained that during Lee's May 6 attack along the Brock Road, his unit's fortifications, "composed of dry logs, caught fire," and, despite this, some of his inexperienced men brought up cartridges to a gun near the blazing works. "The cartridges took fire . . . and exploded, burning 5 of the cannoneers severely." Josiah Murphey, a sergeant in the 20th Massachusetts, explained how Union soldiers were obliged to let any flaming breastworks burn on until the fighting concluded. Once the shooting stopped, the men then felt at liberty to tear down the works near the burning portion and simply "built around it letting the fire burn itself out."[37]

The fires that swept the Wilderness were not only hazardous but also had the potential to change the course of battle. The best example occurred during the Confederate attacks on the Union works along the

Brock Road on May 6. Fires that had begun in the woods earlier in the day had spread and reached the Union breastworks. Thomas Galwey, a Union soldier in the II Corps, painted the scene graphically. "Some of the brush had taken fire and the flames, smoke, and heat had driven many of the men out of the works," during which time the Confederates pressed their attack "in heavy masses," and "some of them got in through the burnt-out sections of the log parapets and were subjecting our first lines to attacks simultaneously in front and flank." They soon had control of a portion of the Union breastworks, above which flew "their little red flags." Despite this stroke of luck, the Federals were able to expel the Confederates from the burning entrenchments through a one-two punch of close-range canister and an infantry charge.[38]

The postwar accounts of the Wilderness fires repeated much of what the contemporary sources had to say. The familiar themes of the horror of the wounded burning alive and the battle amid the flames along the Brock Road appear time and again in memoir after memoir, so much so that the absence of these themes becomes more notable than their presence. Individual memoirs, however, diverge from the standard recitation, providing interesting details that elaborate, or some might say embellish, these fiery episodes.

One contribution that the memoirs make is providing accounts of those who were in peril of being consumed by the merciless flames. Wilkeson, for example, emphasized the fear the soldiers felt during the Battle of the Wilderness at the thought of burning alive. Before the battle, a crusty veteran warned the men of the fires that were likely to break out and expressed his own fear of roasting in the flames. Once the combat commenced, Wilkeson reported that "the wounded were haunted with the dread of fire." He recalled that "they conjured the scenes of the previous year, when some wounded men were burned to death, and their hearts well-nigh ceased to beat when they thought they detected the smell of burning wood in the air." Once wounded, "the bare prospect of fire running through the woods where they lay helpless, unnerved the most courageous of men, and made them call aloud for help" while clinging to their rifles, in case they needed to put themselves out of their misery. One instance in particular stuck with

Wilkeson, when he saw a wounded soldier whom he knew "meant to kill himself in case of fire—knew it as surely as though [he] could read [the man's] thoughts."[39]

The postwar memoirs also recounted moments when the sight of the dead and the fires combined to create terrifying experiences. Abner R. Small of the 16th Maine recalled Confederate shells exploding on the ground from time to time, which "would start a blaze in dry leaves." The dark night would be illuminated for a moment, then the blackness would set in again. Under such circumstances, Small at one point was trying to make his way through the darkness when he lost his footing, and his "outflung hands pushed up a smolder of leaves" from which a fire ignited and "caught in the hair and beard of a dead sergeant." The effect of this "ghastly face and wide-open eyes" illuminated by the sudden spurt of flame was too much, and Small "rushed away in horror."[40]

Like many contemporary accounts, memoirs often focused on the fires as the culmination of the horror that was fighting in the Wilderness. Yet their descriptions achieved new levels of hyperbole by comparing combat in the flames to a battle in hell. The historian of the 106th Pennsylvania depicted the Confederates, who attacked the fiery Brock Road fortifications on May 6, as pressing forward "like so many devils through the flames, charging over the burning works upon our retreating lines." Others compared the burning of the wounded to some terrible, hellish vision. "To add to the horrors of the scene," recalled Channing M. Smith, a Confederate, "the woods caught fire, and many of the wounded of Grant's army were burned alive." Smith doubted whether "the scenes depicted in 'Dante's inferno'" could top what he saw in the Wilderness. Of all the memoirists, perhaps Horace Porter, a member of Grant's staff, best captured the spirit of how the Wilderness fires came to be remembered. "All circumstances seemed to combine to make the scene one of unutterable horror," reported Porter, as "forest fires raged; ammunition-trains exploded; the dead were roasted in the conflagration; the wounded, roused by its hot breath, dragged themselves along, with their torn and mangled limbs, in the mad energy of despair, to escape the ravages of the flames; and every bush seemed hung with shreds of blood-stained clothing. It was as though Christian men had turned to fiends, and hell itself had usurped the place of earth." Later historians echoed this theme. Douglas Southall Freeman called fighting amid the flames "war in Inferno," while Jeffry D. Wert contended that "the horror of the unfortunate men's screams and the smell of burning flesh could only have elicited images of hell."[41]

If the Wilderness was a place of death akin to hell, then it is only natural that some postwar authors portrayed the region as a haunt of ghosts and spirits.[42] One Federal, returning to the Wilderness battlefield to look for his fallen brother, found partially exposed bones. He tried to pull on one of them but found that "something at the other end seemed to detain it, and . . . stopped suddenly as if the dead man himself had put his scrawny hand on my shoulder and said 'Don't disturb my bones with such rude hands.'" The notion "that lifeless bones should make resistance as though still animated by an unwilling spirit, filled [him] with dread and [he] hurried away." Others saw the Wilderness as a land where spirits ambled about. Channing Smith, a Confederate veteran, called it "a place of gloom, the home of the snake, the bat, and the owl," claiming that "if the souls of departed heroes are permitted to visit the spot where their bodies lie, it is surely visited by specters who wander in the gloom of the forest until cockcrow." While the locals never claimed that the Wilderness was haunted, they certainly acted as if it was. A 1907 article for *Metropolitan Magazine* reported how "the natives shake their heads and look puzzled when one, of his own free will, accepts the challenge of that nigh boundless tract." One person preferred to lose some of his hogs rather than chase after them in the Wilderness. So, too, "the negroes and simple folks thereabouts pass" the derelict Chancellor house "quickly and quietly in broad daylight," and "after nightfall they avoid it entirely."[43]

One of the more imaginative interpretations of the Wilderness as a haunted region came from Morris Schaff. He portrayed the region itself as an avenging spirit that intervened in the Battle of the Wilderness to defeat the Confederates and strike down slavery. In his telling, the slaves who had tended the iron furnaces and cut down the original forest had suffered great wrongs, injustices that the Wilderness observed and for which the forest set out to exact revenge. After Schaff laid out Lee's hopes for victory in the Wilderness, he observed that the Rebel general had not "reckoned upon a second intervention of Fate: that the spirit of the Wilderness would strike Longstreet just as victory was in his grasp as it had struck Stonewall." Later in this account, the ghost of Stonewall Jackson appears, wandering the old battleground at Chancellorsville while the "Spirit of the Wilderness," described as a "cowled figure," stalks him in the brush. Apparently, the Spirit of the Wilderness was haunting others as well, for Jackson's ghost runs into "a gaunt, hollow-breasted, wicked eyed, sunken-cheeked being" who beseeched him, saying: "Stonewall, I am Slavery and sorely wounded. Can you do nothing to stay the Spirit of the Wilderness that, in striking at me, struck you down?" As the fighting progressed and Longstreet's May 6 flank attack reached the height of its success, Slavery rejoiced. "Frenzied with delight over her prospective reprieve, [she] snatches a cap from a dead . . . Confederate soldier, and clapping it on her coarse, rusty, gray-streaked mane, begins to dance in hideous glee." Schaff subsequently warned Slavery to "dance on, repugnant and doomed creature! The inexorable eye of the Spirit of the Wilderness is on you! . . . For in a moment Longstreet, like 'Stonewall,' will be struck down by the same mysterious hand, by the fire of his own men, and the clock in the steeple of the Confederacy will strike twelve."[44] Schaff's interpretation nicely combined the idea of the Wilderness as a malevolent landscape with the Wilderness as a haunted region. Yet in contrast to the traditional interpretation, which argues that the Confederates benefited from fighting in the Wilderness, Schaff portrayed the region, or at least the Spirit of the Wilderness, as an enemy to the South's cause.

What, then, constitutes the Wilderness mystique? Part of it was certainly the combat conditions at the Battle of the Wilderness, but there was more to it than that. The name itself evoked negative connotations of an area uninhabited and beyond the control of man's favorite tool for taming nature—agriculture. The soldiers' reactions to the Wilderness also changed over the course of time. At first the area was just a forest like any other, but then soldiers began to attach the name to the place and certain conditions to the name. By the time of the Overland Campaign, men in both armies called it the Wilderness, and from that campaign and into the postwar years, the region became increasingly portrayed as a woebegone, gloomy, malevolent labyrinth of a forest. The Battle of the Wilderness was the key event that defined the region's mystique. It was in the immediate aftermath of this battle that the Wilderness became closely associated with death, destruction, and fire. This was only magnified in the years following Appomattox until it had become a land of the shadow of death and a region compared to hell itself. The postwar literature also saw the Wilderness become a land of ghosts and a haunt of specters, and at least in one account, a spirit itself that could strike down those it deemed deserving.

This, then, was the aura that came to surround the Wilderness, a mystique that has continued from the war to the present day. There were many woodlands in which Civil War soldiers fought, even ones similar to the Wilderness, yet there was only one Wilderness. Only one carried the name. Only one became the malevolent woods where soldiers would find death and hell with accompanying spirits. Why was this the case? It is undeniable that terrible things happened in the Wilderness—thousands of men died there, not a few of them at the hands of the merciless flames. Yet there were other battlefields noted for slaughter and still others in which forest fires took their toll among the wounded. What made the Wilderness different?

The size of the seemingly interminable Wilderness unquestionably set it apart and awed those who entered it. Moreover, repeated visits led the soldiers' understanding of the region to evolve. The very name of the Wilderness evoked the animus between man and untamed nature, while its decayed landscape provided a gloomy backdrop for the fighting that occurred. Any analysis of why the soldiers set the Wilderness apart in their minds and memories would be incomplete, though, without acknowledging the supreme importance of the Battle of the Wilderness in this process. Without that bloody engagement, it is doubtful that the region would have received the notoriety it did. Depictions of the Wilderness became decidedly negative in the battle's aftermath, and through these travails, the mystique was born. The Wilderness's wounds have healed, the armies have left, and the dead have returned to mother earth. But the Wilderness mystique lives on, and will do so as long as men remember what happened in that Virginia forest so long ago.

The Wilderness, on the Brock Road, 2nd Corps—May 11th 1864, by Edwin Forbes (1864). Union fieldworks along the Brock Road. This area was considered one of the worst parts of the Wilderness. In the background is a mixture of saplings and mature trees. *Morgan Collection of Civil War Drawings, Prints and Photographs Division, Library of Congress, Washington, DC.*

Makeshift fortification along the Orange Plank Road. The thick vegetation, so typical of the Wilderness, makes it difficult to see the man behind the breastworks. *Stanford Collection, Prints and Photographs Division, Library of Congress, Washington, DC.*

Bones to the north of the Orange Plank Road. Notice the relatively thinner woods when compared to some of the other images of the Wilderness, testimony to the patchwork character of the forest. *Civil War Photograph Collection, Prints and Photographs Division, Library of Congress, Washington, DC.*

Wounded Escaping from the Burning Woods of the Wilderness, by Alfred R. Waud (1864). This image conveys some of the fear soldiers must have felt when confronted with this deadly element in the tangled Wilderness. *Morgan Collection of Civil War Drawings, Prints and Photographs Division, Library of Congress, Washington, DC.*

Ripped trees and scattered bones tell the story of destruction and death in the Wilderness. *Stanford Collection, Prints and Photographs Division, Library of Congress, Washington, DC.*

Graves of soldiers from the V Corps killed during the Battle of the Wilderness. *Stanford Collection, Prints and Photographs Division, Library of Congress, Washington, DC.*

Veterans on the Orange Plank Road showing the position of the First Division of the IX Corps on May 6, 1864. This photograph emphasizes how the Wilderness could overwhelm someone with its monotony and vastness as the soldiers marched along one of its narrow roadways. *MOLLUS—Massachusetts Civil War Photograph Collection, US Army Heritage and Education Center, Carlisle, PA.*

4

THE CONFEDERATE EDGE IN THE WILDERNESS

On May 4, 1864, Frank Wilkeson, a private in the II Corps of the Army of the Potomac, "walked to and fro over the old battle-field" at Chancellorsville. While the afternoon light lasted, he and his comrades tarried to inspect the "bullet-scarred and canister-riven trees," but what really caught their eye were the bones. Last spring's dead, carelessly interred, were there for one final viewing. "Many polished skulls lay on the ground," and Wilkeson observed that "leg bones, arm bones, and ribs could be found without trouble." Perhaps even more unsettling was the "grinning, bony, fleshless face" which now and again "peered through the low mound that had been hastily thrown over" a slain soldier. With the sun setting, the men, now seated on the burial mounds, gathered around a fire. There with "the dead . . . all around," Wilkeson and his comrades "talked of the battle of the preceding year." A soldier recounted how many of the wounded had burned when the woods had caught fire. He concluded with a warning that this was "an awful place to fight in." Once Union troops were within the thick woods, they would barely be able to see, their artillery would be next to useless, and, as at Chancellorsville, the wounded were "liable to be burned to death." The prospect of breaking a leg and being unable to escape the flames terrified the crusty veteran, and he wished that the army would "get through this chapparal without fighting." His hope was in vain, however, as the following day a battle opened in the very heart of the Wilderness.[1]

Most, if not all, historians have agreed with this veteran's grim assessment of the Wilderness. Traditionally, scholars have argued that, during the Battle of the Wilderness, the landscape handicapped the Union army while helping the Confederate Army of Northern Virginia. Typical of this perspective is William Swinton's 1866 account, remarkable not only because it was one of the first widely referenced interpretations of the battle, but also because most memoirists and historians repeated its conclusions in part or in whole. Swinton argued that the Confederates held a decided advantage over their Federal adversaries in the Wilderness for several reasons: Lee knew the area better than Grant; artillery could not be used; Grant's numerical superiority could not be wielded effectively; and the Confederates had "an almost Indian skill in woodcraft."[2] Over time, other writers simplified Swinton's explanation into two main points: First, the Confederates knew the area better than the Federals. Second, the Wilderness prevented the Federals from taking advantage of their greater strength in both infantry and artillery.

Yet the assertion that the Wilderness favored the Confederates tactically is largely unsubstantiated. Recently, Earl Hess has challenged this traditional historiography, asserting that the Wilderness hindered Lee's army just as much as it did Grant's, prevented either army from gaining a decisive victory, and hampered Confederate flank attacks. In short, Hess concluded that "Lee's offensive tactics were muffled by his choice of battlefield."[3] Union and Confederate accounts suggest that Hess is mostly right. First, the two armies were more or less equally familiar with the Wilderness. Second, the landscape caused similar problems for both armies, except that the Confederates had access to a better road network that initially made it easier for them to deploy their forces. Hess is also correct about the Wilderness disrupting both Confederate flank attacks and limiting their ultimate success.

Hess's assessment, however, loses sight of the fact that the only advantage the Wilderness offered for an attacking force was that it could screen movements and allow troops to advance on the enemy unexpectedly. As Hess has pointed out, direct attacks tended to bog down in close-range fighting. While the Wilderness would disorder any attack eventually, a flank attack was the Confederates' best choice given the circumstances, and in many ways the effectiveness of such assaults was enhanced by the forest's screening power. Certainly, those attacks show that, despite the difficult landscape, the Confederates, through their initiative, could turn the Wilderness to their advantage. In the end, however, the Wilderness in and of itself did not prove innately beneficial to one side over the other. If it was a good place for the Confederates to fight, it was because they made it so by aggressively taking advantage of the limited opportunities the Wilderness afforded.

Traditionally, historians have argued that the Confederates enjoyed an advantage over their Union foes because of their superior knowledge of the Wilderness. Swinton asserted that while the Wilderness was "well known" to Lee, to Grant it was "pure *terra incognita.*" Many memoirists and historians have repeated these assertions and claimed that not just Lee but also his army was intimately acquainted with the Wilderness—or at the very least more familiar with it than the Federals—and therefore the Rebels held a distinct advantage during the battle. For instance, Wilkeson claimed that "the Confederates knew the region thoroughly," that "many of their soldiers had worked in the region," and that "they knew where the roads led to, where the water was, [and] where the natural line of defence was." Francis Walker, the historian of the II Corps, arrived at a comparable conclusion. He pointed out that the Confederate army was "defending a country with which it had become perfectly familiar by long occupation, and which was, more or less, of a kind with that in which all its soldiers had been reared." In contrast, the historian of the 146th New York asserted that the Federals "were in an enemy's country, unfamiliar both to ourselves and to our commanders." Adam Badeau, a member of Grant's staff, brought these two observations together, comparing "the ignorance of the country under which the national soldiers labored" with the fact that "the enemy was perfectly familiar" with the Wilderness, "having held it in constant military occupation for nearly two years, and moved over it in actual campaigning three separate times."[4]

Not long after the battle was over, some Union soldiers concluded that the Confederates had a greater familiarity with the Wilderness, from which the Rebels benefited.[5] Theodore Lyman conceded that "the Rebels had a very superior knowledge of the country." He was not alone in this opinion. A. Jackson Crossley, a soldier in the engineer battalion, explained that the Wilderness "is all woods and heavy undergrowth," with "very few cleared places which give the enemy a great advantage, we being the attacking party and they knowing the country so well they do good execution with their artillery while our own artillery have done but very little." He concluded, "our infantry have had to do this fighting under great disadvantages."[6]

Some former Confederates writing after the war agreed with their Union counterparts that they, or at least General Lee, had a superior knowledge of the Wilderness. Evander Law, a brigadier general in Longstreet's First Corps, claimed that Lee "knew this tangled wilderness well, and appreciated fully the advantages such a field afforded for concealing his great inferiority of force and for neutralizing the superior strength of his antagonist." Armistead Long, an artillery officer in the Army of Northern Virginia, agreed that "Lee had already tried the woods of the Wilderness as a battlefield, and knew its advantages." Perhaps more importantly, he remarked, "its intricacies, which were familiar to [Lee] and his generals, were unknown ground to Grant."[7]

Other observers, however, expressed doubts on this score, arguing that the Union and Rebel forces had comparable knowledge of the region. Even though Edward Porter Alexander called the Wilderness the Confederates' "favorite fighting ground," he still believed that because the Army of the Potomac had fought there previously, it "knew" the "geography & physical features & could form a very fair estimate of the difficulties [it] had to meet & the best ways of overcoming them." Maj. Gen. Cadmus Wilcox, who led a division in Lt. Gen. A. P. Hill's Third Corps, drew a similar conclusion. He noted that the Army of the

Potomac had spent nearly a week in the Wilderness near Mine Run and suggested that "the country about and near [Mine Run] was as well known to [the Federal] army as to that commanded by General Lee." Major General Humphreys, Meade's chief of staff, corroborated these statements to some degree, confessing that "the Army of the Potomac was well acquainted with the chief roads passing through that region," although he made no such claim about the "numerous wood-roads" that crisscrossed the Wilderness.[8]

By May 1864, both armies were already well acquainted with the region as a whole, although only portions of the Confederate army had passed through the Wilderness battlefield, with its reportedly thicker vegetation, while most of the Union soldiers had done so. Alexander noted as much, explaining that the Union advance of May 1864 "was the 3rd campaign which the enemy had tried in the Wilderness within 13 months."[9] In May 1863, the two armies had fought to a standstill near Chancellorsville, immediately east of what was to become the 1864 battlefield. During this campaign, Stonewall Jackson's Confederates had marched along the Brock Road, which according to Theodore Lyman boasted the densest vegetation in the Wilderness, while the remainder of the Confederates were either in the open areas beyond the Wilderness or in what Union veterans claimed were the thinner parts of forest. The Union army, meanwhile, operated in one of the more open parts of the Wilderness around Chancellorsville. In November and December 1863, the Federals had mounted a second campaign in the area, which came to grief along Mine Run, just to the west of the 1864 battleground. During this campaign, the Union troops marched along the Orange Turnpike and the Orange Plank Road, covering much of the same thickly wooded ground that they would pass through in May 1864. The Confederates, in contrast, spent much of the campaign in the more open areas west of the 1864 battlefield. In short, portions of both armies had spent time in the thicker and thinner parts of the Wilderness. Neither side monopolized knowledge about the region, but if either had an edge, it should have been with the Union soldiers, as a greater number of them actually spent time in what was to become the Wilderness battlefield.

If many soldiers in the two armies shared a basic familiarity with the Wilderness from past campaigns, there were others who were unacquainted with its peculiarities. For example, in the Army of Northern Virginia, General Longstreet, Lee's senior corps commander, had not been at Chancellorsville or Mine Run. In addition, portions of his corps had missed these actions.[10] Martin L. Smith, the Army of Northern Virginia's chief engineer who would figure prominently in Longstreet's famous flank attack on May 6, was also new to the Wilderness. In the Army of the Potomac, Maj. Gen. Ambrose Burnside's IX Corps and, more importantly, Ulysses S. Grant were unfamiliar with the area.[11]

Although the Wilderness lay on the Confederate side of the Rapidan River, it does not follow that the Rebels were any more familiar with it than were the Federals. Lee's infantry was stationed west of the Wilderness, which, besides cavalry patrols, saw few Confederates. Even the supposed advantage that might come from having native Virginians in the ranks proved negligible. Of Lee's thirty-four brigades at the Battle of the Wilderness, only six, or about 18 percent, contained Virginians.[12] But of these troops, how many were sufficiently familiar with the Wilderness to give them a material advantage over their foes? Even when certain Confederates, such as Brig. Gen. William Mahone, who had worked as an engineer laying out the Orange Plank Road, were familiar with the area, there is no evidence that Lee was able to take advantage of this knowledge. In fact, Mahone himself had trouble controlling and coordinating his forces in the Wilderness's thickets, a fact that ultimately resulted in the accidental shooting of Longstreet. Meanwhile, Chief Engineer Smith, who had never before set eyes on the Wilderness, provided crucial intelligence that allowed Longstreet to plan and execute his powerful flank attack on the sixth.[13]

While it is true that the Confederates could easily obtain local guides during the Battle of the Wilderness, it is unclear whether these guides provided a substantial advantage to Lee's army. The Confederate chief had certainly benefited at Chancellorsville when one of the locals had pointed out the route Jackson subsequently used to execute his famed flank march. Perhaps it was assumed that if Lee had benefited from a local's greater familiarity with the Wilderness in the past, then he would do so again. Union officers, however, were adept at drawing on the "reports of spies and of negroes" and had in the past found locals who were willing to act as guides, even if they were not always up to the task.[14]

For those who had fought in the Wilderness previously, the benefit of this experience is questionable. While the soldiers might be acquainted with its general qualities—dense trees, narrow roads, et cetera—this knowledge did not prepare those in either army to fight more effectively on terrain that was far from uniform, especially if assigned to areas with which they were unfamiliar. At best troops might enjoy a local advantage over the enemy in a specific location. Regardless if certain individuals knew the Wilderness better, it seems unlikely to have offered their army much of an advantage.

According to the traditional interpretation, another of the supposed advantages the Wilderness afforded the Confederates was hindering the ability of Union forces to make use of their superior numbers, especially in artillery and infantry. Even a superficial survey of both Union and Confederate accounts confirms the conspicuous absence of artillery during the Battle of the Wilderness. A chaplain with the 10th Massachusetts found that "from the nature of the country no artillery could be employed to advantage," while Charles Mills of the 56th Pennsylvania commented that "there was scarcely a piece of artillery fired in the whole action, owing to the ground." Confederates largely echoed their Union counterparts. One explained that "the thicket that lay, along the whole face of the Confederate array is so impenetrable as to have excluded the use of artillery by the enemy, save only for the breadth of those openings where it is penetrated . . . by the old turnpike, and . . . by the plank road." Likewise, Jacob Raymer of the 4th North Carolina remarked that "very little artillery was used" because of the thick vegetation, while Philip Pendleton, a Confederate artilleryman, made similar observations, blaming the topography and vegetation for the Rebels' inability to employ their artillery. Suffice it to say that there was consensus on the matter.[15]

Despite the challenges posed by the Wilderness, a small number of Union cannons did come into play and, on the whole, provided valuable service. These guns generally acted on the defensive, protecting fixed positions from enemy attacks, usually in clearings or along the roads, where they had a better field of fire. For instance, on May 5 a small detachment of Union artillery made the Confederates pay dearly as they advanced up the Orange Plank Road. One artilleryman recounted that when the Rebel column entered the road, he had his guns fire canister into it, "and well was it used." He discovered that "the plank road was well suited for it, as the splinters did as much damage as the shot," while the Confederates "learned that they could not advance down a narrow road in the face of two guns capable of throwing into their midst *a peck of bullets a minute.*"[16]

Likewise, on May 6 Union artillery played an important role in repelling the Confederate attack on the Brock Road. The Rebels had penetrated the outer Union breastworks, a section of which were on fire, and at that precarious moment Union artillery "opened with shell and case-shot." Later, when a Confederate "line advancing through the woods on" the "right and front" came into view, the guns "opened upon it with double-shotted canister," which "checked the enemy's advance until Carroll's brigade charged the enemy with such fury as to utterly rout them." Some Federals recognized the effectiveness and importance of this artillery support. Francis B. Harris of the 12th New Jersey recalled, "our masked brass battery opened with canister and mowed them down like grass." Another Union soldier simply concluded, "a few of our Batteries did good service, firing best at the most critical moment."[17]

Confederate gunners also had limited opportunities and made the most of them. William Pendleton's report noted that Lee's army used the few guns posted in the Orange Turnpike sector of the battlefield "several times . . . with good effect in repelling partial attacks of the enemy." Along the Orange Plank Road corridor on May 5, Lt. Col. William T. Poague's artillery "was effectively used in the bloody repulse . . . to a very heavy assault of the enemy." The next day these guns again came into play and provided immeasurable service to Lee's army. Hancock's morning assault had broken through the weak Confederate line, and Poague's guns opened fire on the "immense masses" of Union troops, an act that "checked [their] advance and enabled Longstreet's troops, just arriving on the field, to seize the favorable moment and compel them to recede with heavy loss."[18] In short, the little artillery used seems to have been put to good use by both sides. Even had the Federals been able to employ more guns, this would not have guaranteed them victory. One need only look to Chancellorsville for proof of this.

But what of the infantry? Did the Wilderness prevent the Army of the Potomac from bringing to bear its superior numbers? In order to address this important question, it is essential to understand how a Civil War army moved and how local circumstances affected that movement. As to the first point, when not in battle, armies moved in columns, like a long snake of men and wagons. Lyman witnessed this spectacle during the Mine Run Campaign, in which the Army of the Potomac used many of the same roads that it would later travel during the Battle of the Wilderness. "A division of 4000 men, closed up," explained Lyman, "would occupy some 1000 yards," assuming they were marching four abreast in a column. After "adding the space for pack horses, and the usual gaps and intervals, it would be nearer a mile." He concluded that "even with no artillery," which would take up even more space in the road, "an army would string out." Moreover, the winding column could only move as fast as its head.[19]

The speed at which troops could march obviously depended on the condition of the roads, and those that cut across the Wilderness were of varying quality.[20] The two main east–west routes were the Orange Turnpike and the Orange Plank Road. The former was originally a macadamized road made up of crushed stone but, by the time of the Civil War, the Turnpike had fallen into disrepair to become a plain dirt road. During the Mine Run Campaign, Lyman noted how troops "clattered along" what he called "the most infernal of pikes, in holes and over rocks." In a letter home he grumbled that "the road was horribly rough, full of great holes and big stones." Weather could also affect the road's condition. A Union surgeon described the Turnpike as "flinty" when it was dry but "quite muddy" if it rained.[21] The Orange Plank Road was of more recent construction. Completed sometime in the 1850s, only "the right-hand side coming eastward"—where "the more heavily loaded wagons" would travel—was actually planked. Nevertheless, like the Orange Turnpike, the Orange Plank Road had fallen into disrepair by the time war came to the Wilderness. Alpheus Williams, who encountered it during the Chancellorsville Campaign, called it "an old, worn-out plank road, full of holes and gullies and very slippery from the rain, the mud on what planks were left being a foot or so deep." During Mine Run, Lyman likewise complained of the "holes . . . among the broken boards." A Confederate observer during the Wilderness Campaign was equally critical of a road that "consists of one track of worn planking, and another of earth," while "its course, very irregular, vibrates in and out of the south side of the generally straight line, known as the turnpike." Another plank road, often called the Germanna Plank Road, ran from Culpeper across Germanna Ford to merge with the Orange Plank Road. It was also in poor shape by May 1864, according to Milton Myers of the 110th Ohio, who found it "much out of repair."[22]

Despite their sorry conditions, Lyman maintained that these three roads were among the handful "that can be counted on" in the Wilderness. In contrast were the "many narrow roads" that crisscrossed the region. "Winding and little known," Lyman thought that these routes "in good weather may serve for the slow passage of columns (though they are mere farmers' or woodcutters' thoroughfares)," but, he warned, "a day's rain will render them impassable for waggons and artillery."[23]

The Army of the Potomac could access two decent north–south roads leading from Germanna and Ely's Fords respectively, but even these could only handle so many soldiers at a time. When the Confederates arrived unexpectedly on May 5, the Federals altered their marching plans and had to rely upon the lesser routes running between the Orange Turnpike and Orange Plank Road. In contrast, two of Lee's corps could advance along two of the best roads in the Wilderness and arrive much faster than the Union high command had expected. Moreover, Lee did not have to rely on narrow backroads to reposition his forces once they arrived, as his men were already on the best east–west roads available. An exception was Longstreet's corps, which had to rely on a number of narrow backroads before it reached the Orange Plank Road.[24]

The narrow roadways and the thick woods of the Wilderness made it difficult for the four Federal corps—II, V, VI, and IX—to deploy during the battle. On making contact with the Confederates on May 5, the army was badly strung out. The V Corps was partly on the Orange Turnpike and partly between it and the Orange Plank Road. The VI Corps was farther back and had yet to reach the Orange Turnpike, while the II Corps was spread along backroads south of the Orange Plank Road. In order to fight the Confederates effectively, the Army of the Potomac needed to concentrate its strength. The V Corps had to pivot into line while reeling in its scattered units. The VI Corps was stuck behind the V Corps and consequently had to make its way along a narrow trail in an effort to engage the enemy and protect the dangling flank of the V Corps. Yet as Meade reported, "the Sixth Corps had not been able to get into position" to assist in the morning attack "owing to the dense thicket and want of roads." Meanwhile, the II Corps was held up as well. Hancock, the corps commander, blamed the delay on "the Brock road being very narrow and heavily wooded on both sides," which caused "the formation of the infantry in line of battle [to be] extremely slow," a problem aggravated "by the artillery occupying the road" that "greatly retarded . . . their march."[25] These delays nearly allowed the Confederates to seize the crucial intersection of the Orange Plank and Brock Roads, but a division of the VI Corps arrived just in time to prevent this. The next day Burnside found deploying his IX Corps in the gap between the Orange Turnpike and Plank Road to be a real struggle, noting that "a dense and almost impenetrable undergrowth caused considerable confusion, irregularity, and delay." Although Burnside's subsequent attack made some headway, Lyman observed that "it was too late and [Burnside] had not enough force to follow on."[26]

While the Wilderness admittedly hampered the deployment of Union forces, it is crucial to recognize that the Federals did not have to be in this predicament. As Gordon Rhea has pointed out, the Union cavalry did not properly screen Grant's columns, which allowed the Confederates to approach the Federals more or less undetected. Had the cavalry done its job, the Union army might have avoided being strung out, a dangerous situation that the Wilderness only exacerbated. Moreover, Rhea concludes that had Grant known the Confederates' whereabouts, he "would have had opportunity to concentrate his forces and wage an offensive—and quite likely successful—battle" instead of "wasting May 5 reacting to rebel thrusts and scrambling to reassemble his army."[27] In the end it was not the Wilderness that hamstrung the Army of the Potomac so much as the army's spread-out condition and the cavalry's failure to act its part.

The Confederates deployed their troops more easily than the Federals because of their smaller numbers, the better roads to which they had access, and the superior handling of their forces on the march. On May 5 Lt. Gen. Richard S. Ewell's Second Corps moved along the Orange Turnpike and Hill's corps along the Orange Plank Road. Their deployment was relatively easy, as they moved along two wide roads with smaller bodies of troops. The following day Longstreet's corps arrived on the Orange Plank Road, but its deployment proved troublesome. By the time his troops had arrived, Hancock's attack had sent Hill's corps reeling. Thus, while Longstreet's men were "forming line of battle in a dense thicket under a severe fire of the enemy the line was constantly broken through by men hurrying to the rear."[28] These conditions, Longstreet concluded, "were most unfavorable," nevertheless, his troops "not only held their own, but formed their line, and in turn, charging the enemy, drove him back in confusion over half a mile."[29] Longstreet's deployment epitomized the deft hand and pugnacious spirit that often characterized the Army of Northern Virginia's operations in the Wilderness. Once these initial deployments were completed, however, the Wilderness and its road system did not necessarily hamper one side more than the other.

As Earl Hess has argued, once battle actually commenced, the Wilderness played no favorites, frustrating both sides. One of the landscape's most pronounced effects was that it limited the soldiers' ability to maneuver. A chaplain with the 10th Massachusetts observed that the "thick growth of small oak trees from one to three inches in diameter and with the branches so interlaced" made "passage through them extremely difficult." Lemuel Abbot of Vermont experienced this firsthand with the VI Corps. He recalled that "there was no double quick about it—for a mile or more into the woods . . . stumbling over logs, ditches, brush, etc., till our faces, hands and shins smarted from bruises and scratches." Not only was marching in the Wilderness painful, but the inability to move quickly in the woods also proved perilous once the shooting started. Thomas Galwey of the II Corps concluded as much, noting that "it was no easy matter to work one's way through the wild and formidable thicket, so dense that even at noonday the sun's light scarcely penetrated it." Even though he and his comrades "could see the Confederates advancing almost at a run on our rear," they found themselves unable to shift their lines as "the stiff and crooked hazel brush that surrounded [them] prevented any sort of a regular formation at all."[30]

But Confederates also had difficulty moving through the woodlands. Alexander Boteler, a Confederate staff officer, claimed that the "tangled mass of undergrowth" was "so densely intricate that it would be difficult for a dog to get through it." Another Rebel observed that "the undergrowth of bushes and briars [was] so matted and tangled that it is very difficult to force a way through it." Lewis Leon of the 1st North Carolina also griped, "it is almost impossible for a man to walk, as the woods are thick with an underbrush growth and all kinds of shrubbery, old logs, grapevines, and goodness knows what."[31]

Predictably, the thick vegetation disrupted linear formations in both armies. The Federals recounted many a tale of woe on this score. A soldier from the 5th New Jersey found "it was impossible to keep a battalion or even company front, so dense was the growth of young saplings." The experience of the 5th Wisconsin's James Anderson confirmed this assessment. He explained that his unit fought "in a dense thicket and our ranks were broken at every step." Galwey similarly described the men of his unit "pushing [their] way through infernal thickets that flew up and struck [them] in the face at every step," noting that "the struggle up to this point had been over ground so rough and through a thicket so dense that when a halt was called to re-form, only a small part of any one command could be assembled."[32]

The Confederates faced similar challenges and offered the same sort of complaints. James Armstrong of the 1st South Carolina thought that the "dense thicket" ahead of his unit was "almost impassible for advancing in line." Others testified to this effect. During Gordon's May 6 flank attack, Henry Wingfield, a member of the 58th Virginia, discovered that "owing to the thick branches and undergrowth in the woods through which we passed our line was in considerable disorder." In a similar vein the 6th Alabama's John W. Roberts recalled that, after driving some Federal soldiers, his unit too was soon "advancing in considerable disorder."[33]

Another important impediment for both armies was limited visibility caused by a combination of thick vegetation and dense musketry smoke. While it is safe to say that visibility was generally poor in the Wilderness, the vegetation was a patchwork of different types of growth, and visibility varied accordingly, as evidenced in the soldiers' accounts. Stationed north of the Orange Turnpike, Abbot described how "the brush . . . kept each from seeing the other," although the enemy was "hardly a hundred yards away." Lyman, who saw several parts of the battlefield, gave a more conservative estimate. He explained that "there were many places where a line of troops could with difficulty be seen at fifty yards." Others claimed the visibility was even worse. In the Orange Plank Road corridor Galwey found that "in most parts of the thicket one could not see twenty feet plainly in any direction." Washington Roebling made an estimate on the V Corps's front, commenting that the soldiers there "had to advance through an exceedingly thick growth of small pines and underbrush where a man could not be seen 20 feet off." Charles Mills, an adjutant with the 56th Massachusetts in Burnside's IX Corps, must have found an especially thick patch in the Wilderness. He griped that "it was all blind work" as "the woods were intolerably thick, and composed of young trees, so that it was impossible to see half a rod [a little over eight feet] in front." Given the thick woods, Daniel Holt thought it "no wonder [that] we cannot find or see a reb until we get right upon them."[34]

The Wilderness caused similar problems for the Confederates, who also experienced varying levels of visibility. Armstrong of the 1st South Carolina pointed out that "in the Wilderness you could not see the left of your own regiment," while another Confederate remarked that "at a distance of forty or fifty yards the form of a man could scarcely be distinguished by any but a quick-sighted observer." Peter Alexander, a Confederate news correspondent, also complained of bad visibility. "So thick are the woods in some places," he concluded, "that it is impossible to distinguish a man, even in the absence of verdure, at a distance of fifty paces." Others could see even less. One Rebel recalled, "the woods in front were so thick that it was impossible to see more than 20 steps from our line." Worse off still was Maj. Gen. Henry Heth, one of Lee's division commanders, who complained that "the dense wood, on our right, left, and in our front obstructed all view."[35]

Under such conditions, soldiers had to rely on senses other than sight.[36] At the Battle of the Wilderness, hearing came to the forefront, and many soldiers noted how loud and intense the musketry was, often overwhelming the other senses. A good example of this is provided by A. M. Stewart, a Union chaplain, who discovered that "suddenly these hitherto quiet woods seemed to be lifted up, shook, rent and torn asunder" as "thousands and thousands of minie-rifles united their sharp crack and ear-piercing sound, rendering the tumult one of terrible grandeur." Later, he explained how the fire "along the whole line, often extending for miles, rolls an ever recurring crash, crash, roar, roar," and while "occasionally, and without any seeming concert, a momentary cessation occurs, yet like the lull in a hurricane, but to increase its strength." For him, the battle was fought "beneath a canopy of Sulphur and a bedlam of sounds, like confusion confounded." It is not surprising, then, that men often claimed that the musketry at the Battle of the Wilderness was the loudest they had ever heard.[37]

Soldiers on both sides often relied upon sound to direct their efforts in combat. Lyman had plenty of practice at this. In one instance he explained that the "sudden sound of heavy firing told of some new attack." In another, he used musketry to measure the progress of Union forces, at one moment learning that their advance "was quite apparent from the distance of the receding firing and the absense of those infernal minié balls." Later, as the Union forces were driven back, "the musketry . . . drew nearer," and soon "stragglers began to come back, and, in a little while, a crowd of men emerged from the thicket in full retreat." Galwey reported an instance when the Confederates used noise to find the position of troops they could not see. "The enemy," he wrote, "could see us no better than we could see them. But they could hear us as the brake crackled around us, and they could very well guess at what course to direct their fire." Galwey could also tell "from the heavy volleys" that his unit was "in action against fresh troops with plenty of ammunition." Similarly, a member of the 5th New Jersey remarked that his regiment "commenced a rapid and steady fire upon the enemy, whose direction and strength we could only judge by the storm of bullets whistling about us."[38]

Confederates had comparable experiences. General Ewell, who was in charge at the Orange Turnpike sector, relied on sound to measure the progress of fellow Confederates, specifically Hill's corps to the south along the Orange Plank Road.[39] Col. James Hagood, commanding the 1st South Carolina Infantry, used sound to determine the enemy's strength. For instance, he judged by "the timid firing of the enemy . . . that he was not in heavy force," though he still confirmed this by sending out skirmishers to feel for the Federals.[40]

As Hess has contended, the various limitations soldiers in both armies experienced combined to produce deadly, close-range shootouts. A signal officer in the II Corps reported that "in a place like this neither army could see the other until meeting almost face to face, necessarily making the fighting the closest and most desperate." For instance, Washington Roebling found "large crowds of soldiers pouring out of the woods in great confusion and almost panic-stricken; some said they were flanked, others that they had suddenly come upon the Rebs. lying concealed in two lines of battle in the thick underbrush, and that our men had broke and run after the first volley." In like manner the soldiers in Wilbur Fisk's outfit "saw nothing of the enemy, and heard nothing of them until . . . [their] column unexpectedly came up on a column of rebel troops coming this way." These Vermont soldiers were "under . . . fire over three hours," and Fisk found that the Union line was "close on to them, and [the rebel] fire was terribly effective." Several Union chaplains also provided excellent descriptions of the type of battle fought in the Wilderness. One remarked that his unit "suddenly encountered [the Rebels] without any previous admonition of their near proximity" and found themselves "within direct and deadly range" of the enemy's musketry. Another chaplain named Perkins noted that the battle "was simply a stand up fight of the most desperate and deadly nature," while John N. Brown, chaplain of the 111th New York, labeled it "a pure musketry fight of the severest kind with heavy loss on both sides."[41]

The Confederates endured the same kind of close-range, deadly combat. A member of the 15th Georgia concluded, "we had necessarily to fight at close quarters with muskets" since there was little chance for artillery support. In one instance Charles T. Bowen of the 12th US Infantry recalled waiting to fire on the advancing Confederates "[until] just as they raised above the hill." At that point the regulars "poured in our volley with deadly aim & raising to our feet charged," although they only found "the dead & wounded" in front of them. He concluded that "a regiment never got a more deadly volley than they & no wonder for we were within 20 yards of them." In another example, a Confederate remembered that Union forces "advanced to within fifty yards of our line, but were repulsed . . . leaving one hundred dead on the field." Roberts of the 6th Alabama provided an especially good account of the haphazard process of closing with the enemy and then fighting blindly at close quarters. He observed that "the contending forces were about eighty yards apart and the contest becoming warmer each minute." His line continued advancing until it was within "forty paces of the Yankees . . . standing erect and firing deliberately enough." But "the woods were fortunately very thick and they had not discovered our true position." Once the Confederates "commenced pouring into their ranks [their] well directed storm of lead," the Yankees found that "it was more than they could stand and in less than three minutes their line broke." Although trees could provide some protection in these close-range firefights, this sort of cover benefited both sides. General Heth explained that, on his part of the battlefield, "the men had no protection other than that afforded by the growth of timber in their front, which, of course afforded the enemy equal protection."[42]

Often the fighting was described as a sort of back-and-forth affair, with no clear winner except the angel of death. A Federal signal officer claimed that "the fighting was little more than charging and recharging, our men leaving their entrenchments, charging on the enemy, they repulsing us and driving us out, following us back, and we driving them back in turn." Elisha Hunt Rhodes similarly commented that "the line surged backwards and forwards, now advancing and now retreating until darkness put an end to the carnage." The price of this sort of fighting was terrible to behold. Lyman observed that "a great battle in America" consisted of little more than advancing and "then *wrang, wr-r-rang,* for three or four hours, or for all day, and the poor, bleeding wounded streaming to the rear." Hess was correct, then, that the Wilderness made it difficult for either side to gain a decisive advantage.[43]

While these examples might suggest that the Wilderness prevented the armies from functioning at all, it is important to realize that, despite such conditions, the armies continued to operate, albeit not at peak efficiency. Hess has noted that many historians "imply that the linear system was inadequate to meet the cluttered nature of the battlefield." Yet he maintained that "nothing could be further from the truth." Hess observed that unit commanders "normally overcame the difficulties and maintained forward movement or restored cohesion." The same could be said for the soldiers who fought in the Wilderness. They advanced despite the vegetation, although at a slower rate and in a less orderly manner than might be expected on an open battlefield. Moreover, when the lines became disordered, unit commanders did their best to dress them by calling a halt or reforming in an open area after a chaotic march through the woods. A soldier in the 5th New Jersey provided an excellent account of this pattern during the Battle of the Wilderness. He discovered that in advancing, "it was impossible to keep a battalion or even company front, so dense was the growth of young saplings; but the men soon found their places when the line came to be established, and lying flat upon the ground, commenced a rapid and steady fire upon the enemy." Later, his unit charged the Rebels, and the men "advanced as rapidly as possible under the circumstances for 50 or 75 yards." Then, realizing that only part of the line had charged, they "halted and again commenced our fire lying down," and "the line soon became readjusted." It was not parade-ground standards, but the soldiers made their tactics work and were still able to fight despite being in the Wilderness's tricky thickets.[44]

The Wilderness's woods not only disrupted formations and limited visibility but also provided fuel for fires. One could certainly argue that the fires that raged during the Battle of the Wilderness proved advantageous to the Confederates. This is especially the case in the oft-cited May 6 blaze along the Orange Plank Road corridor that engulfed the Federals' Brock Road breastworks, forcing the soldiers manning it to evacuate and allowing the Confederates to take possession for a time before being expelled by a Union counterattack. While many veterans simply stated that the woods were aflame or had caught fire, some Federals were quick to argue that the Confederates had not only benefited from these forest fires but also intentionally started them to alter the course of battle in their favor.[45] For instance, Emory Upton, a brigadier general in the VI Corps, thought that "the woods in front and around our position had been set on fire by the enemy to prevent our advance." Robert Robertson, a member of the 93rd New York, likewise claimed that "the Rebels [had] set the woods on fire to drive us out of our position."[46]

Many also thought that the Confederates used the fires to create smoke screens for their attacks. Josiah F. Murphey, a sergeant in the 20th Massachusetts, was unsure whether "the enemy [had] set the underbrush on fire or [if] it [had] caught fire," but he was certain that "under cover of the smoke they charged on us." A soldier in the 5th New Jersey noted how the Confederates located the unprotected Union flank along the Orange Plank Road and then proceeded to "set fire to the woods, advancing under cover of the smoke upon our flank." The Federals became aware of the advance only when they received "a volley . . . from about 300 yards in our rear." Similarly, James Freeman of the 11th New Jersey concluded that the Confederates had "got upon our left flank . . . by setting the leaves on fire in front of us, and drove us entirely out of the woods."[47]

Despite these assertions, there is no evidence that the Confederates intentionally started these fires. None ever claimed to do so, and—revealingly—they never accused Union soldiers of having done so. If anything, these assertions are just one more example of Federals accusing the Confederates of being up to something, a conspiratorial mindset that also led them to conclude that the Rebels had benefited from a superior knowledge of the Wilderness and had tried to trap the Union army there to neutralize its numerical advantage in infantry and artillery.[48]

Furthermore, the effect the fires actually had on the battle's outcome is debatable. Traditionally, historians have argued that the Brock Road works catching fire was the reason the Confederates were able to penetrate the Union position on May 6. Yet General Hancock, whose soldiers manned these breastworks, hinted that the flames may have merely aggravated an already deteriorating situation. The II Corps commander reported that Confederate musketry "was very heavy," although not very effective at first. "Some of the troops began to waver" after about half an hour of this firing, and some of the men stationed at the breastworks "gave way, retiring in disorder toward Chancellorsville." Hancock claimed that the "confusion and disorganization among a portion of the troops . . . on this occasion was greatly increased, if not originated, by the front line of breast-works having taken fire a short time before the enemy made his attack." The soldiers stationed there faced "the intense heat and the smoke, which was driven by the wind directly into" their faces, which "prevented them on portions of the line from firing over the parapet, and at some points compelled them to abandon the line." Hancock's account then suggests that, in one way or another, the blazing entrenchments influenced the Federal soldiers' actions. Whether the fires acted as a catalyst, speeding a process already under way, or whether they were chiefly responsible for the Union soldiers' retreat is unclear.[49]

Some, though, have argued that these fires have received too much credit. William Swan, a Union V Corps veteran, acknowledged that the blazing entrenchments were usually blamed for "the temporary loss of the works," but he argued "that too much importance has been given to this fire." While he did not explain his reasoning, there were other circumstances beside the fires that might have influenced the Federals' behavior. For instance, Francis Walker, in his history of the II Corps, judged that "some of Mott's troops in the second line gave way, [during the Confederate assault,] without the slightest cause other than excitement and the strain, the labors and the losses of the morning." These same types of strains no doubt affected the troops in the front line as well. Perhaps the fires just pushed the soldiers—already exhausted and demoralized to some degree—too far. How they would have reacted to the fires had they been fresh is unclear, but unquestionably an issue worth considering. Then again, perhaps the flaming entrenchments simply served as a convenient excuse to explain away the actions of unsteady troops. Regardless of the fires' role, had the wind simply blown in the other direction, they might have hindered, or even prevented, the Confederate assault rather than aiding it. Suffice it to say that even had the Confederates set the fires, there was no way for them to control the blaze afterward. Ultimately, the fact that the Union breastworks caught fire was pure luck—as was any benefit that the Confederates derived from this event.[50]

But did Lee's choice of battlefield hamstring his offensive tactics, especially the flank attacks that his army had so profitably employed in the past? To answer this, we must consider two events from May 6: Longstreet's morning assault on the Army of the Potomac's left flank and Gordon's evening attack against its right flank. In each case the general commanding the assault scouted the position to find a way around the Union flank, which, although hidden by the forest, remained vulnerable to being turned. In both cases the Confederates took the initiative to find their opponent's unprotected flank, which the

Federals might have done just as easily. On Longstreet's end, Maj. Gen. M. L. Smith, along with others, reconnoitered Hancock's position and "reported that the left of the enemy's line extended but a short distance beyond the plank road," which presented an inviting target to be sure. Moreover, the Confederates could get at this dangling flank undetected by means of an unfinished railroad that ran more-or-less parallel with the Orange Plank Road. On Gordon's front, the Confederates found that the Union position was "resting in a dense woodland," with its flank given no protection or support save a few lookouts. Gordon also had a convenient staging ground in a field that lay some four hundred yards from the Union flank. Here he could assemble "a line out of view and at right angles" to the Federal line.[51]

Longstreet's and Gordon's flank attacks were initially successful because the thick forest in each sector screened the movement of their forces and concealed the number of troops in their assault columns. Longstreet's soldiers, noted one Confederate, "rushed forward with overwhelming impetuosity, driving the enemy panic stricken and in . . . confusion from all his strongholds." The Rebels relished the chase, and as "the enemy continued to rush pell mell through the dense thicket of undergrowth on the left of the road," the Southerners hounded them, "pursuing rapidly and pouring a destructive fire into their scattered ranks." Another Confederate contended that "the flank movement was completely successful" as "the enemy was taken by surprise and driven back . . . with heavy loss," while nearby Federals were "retreating rapidly down the plank road." Later that day, on the other end of the Confederate line, Gordon's men found the Union troops of the VI Corps unprepared to meet their attack. Gordon himself reported that the Federals were "surprised by this sudden and vigorous attack," and they "deserted their trenches and fled" while "repeated efforts were made by [Union] brigade commanders to change front and check" the Rebel advance. These efforts were in vain, though, as the Federal units "were rapidly broken and scattered." Gordon concluded that "of the entire force which my brigade encountered not an organized regiment was left." In his words, "the rout was complete."[52]

The Union soldiers who witnessed or experienced these flank attacks offered similar accounts. One caught sight of a "perfect stampede" of troops "pouring down from the front" in the wake of Longstreet's attack and did the best he could just to rally the jittery men at the Brock Road, "which they were beginning to leave in panic." Union soldiers found Longstreet's attack particularly galling because they lost ground they had won at great cost earlier that morning.[53] Confusion, panic, and retreat reigned on Gordon's front as well. Roebling, a staff officer with the V Corps, witnessed "an excited crowd of soldiers apparently scared to death" in the wake of Gordon's attack. He claimed that "they amounted . . . to almost a division, and not a single one could tell why he was running." A soldier in the 110th Ohio, found himself caught up in the rout. He complained that "new troops broke and ran, coming down on us like a whirlwind." Despite his unit's readiness to repel the attackers, he and his comrades were reluctant to fire in the growing blackness, lest they mow down their own men. Such being the case, the Ohioan felt that "we could do no better than to go with the crowd."[54]

Yet the obstacles presented by the Wilderness, as well as other factors, limited the success of each flank attack. Longstreet's assault petered out as the "dense thicket of undergrowth" through which his soldiers were passing disordered their ranks. Brig. Gen. William T. Wofford, whose unit was involved in the flank attack, was obliged to call "a halt, in order that his line might be reformed," while also giving his exhausted troops a breather. Worse still, converging Confederate forces fired into each other, badly wounding Longstreet. Mahone's Brigade, which had been part of the attack, "was drawn up in the dense woods parallel to the [plank] road, and not more than seventy five paces from it." Even at such close range, they were "unable to distinguish one man from another through the woods" and fired on their supposed enemies.[55] One Confederate lamented that since there was "no one present to take charge of and make a proper disposition of our forces" after Longstreet's wounding, "we failed to follow up our glorious success, and thus permitted the enemy to escape an overwhelming and decisive defeat."[56]

Gordon's flank attack ran into similar problems. One Confederate explained how Brig. Gen. John Pegram's command met disaster during the attack. "A misconception of orders" led to the brigade breaking into two pieces, each following different trajectories. Darkness, combined with "the nature of the ground, which was a bog, covered with a thick and scrubby undergrowth," only increased the muddle, "breaking the line and throwing the men into huddles sometimes twenty deep picking their way through." What was left of the line then came "suddenly upon a portion of the enemy's works," and, to top things off, other Confederates involved in the attack fired into Pegram's flank.[57]

In the case of both Longstreet's and Gordon's flank attacks, the Wilderness proved a double-edged sword. On the one hand, the woods screened the Confederates, which made it possible for them to surprise the Federals on their vulnerable flanks—an opportunity that Lee's army might not have had in the open. It also amplified the effect of the relatively small attacking forces because the Union soldiers could not determine their opponents' strength. On the other hand, the Wilderness inevitably disordered the Confederate assaults, although other factors such as Longstreet's wounding and the oncoming darkness no doubt added to the confusion. Hess, then, was correct in that the Wilderness foiled some aspects of the Confederate offensive capability, but he failed to recognize the opportunities that it offered and to give the Confederates credit for taking advantage of those chances. It is also important to recognize that conditions on May 6 allowed for either army to mount a flank attack. Both sides were aware of the routes the Confederates used, but only the Rebels were bold enough to exploit them.[58] Furthermore, despite the problems with Longstreet's and Gordon's assaults, they were still among the most effective mounted during the battle. These attacks turned the thick forest—which was in most offensive operations a major liability—into a substantial asset that allowed the Confederates to turn the enemy's flanks undetected and to magnify the panic and confusion caused by a relatively small attacking force. While the Wilderness ultimately limited the success any offensive movement might have, one should not lose sight of what the Confederate flank attacks did achieve with so little force in such a difficult environment.

Although these operations were impressive, any account of Confederate tactical superiority must acknowledge that the Rebels did not always put in a good showing, with the Union army nearly achieving victory at one point. Lee's May 6 frontal assault on the Brock Road position was a bloody failure that certainly marred the Rebels' record. Long after the war, Porter Alexander argued that "this attack ought never, never to have been made," for it only resulted in "wasting good soldiers" and "discouraging pluck & spirit by setting it an impossible task." Perhaps the most telling example, though, was on the morning of May 6, when Hancock's men along the Orange Plank Road combined with Maj. Gen. James S. Wadsworth's force coming from the north to rout Hill's corps. When the Union attack began, the Confederate lines were in a sorry state. Neither entrenched nor aligned nor prepared, the Rebels were soon in flight. Unsurprisingly, however, the assault columns "had become terribly mixed and disordered," and the Federals lost momentum as they were forced to realign, allowing Longstreet time to counterattack and ultimately drive them back to the Brock Road.[59]

In this case, then, the Wilderness only acted to hinder the Union attack, though certainly not in a unique way—it would disorder the Confederate flank attacks later that day in a similar manner. The difference was that the power of this Union assault—and it was powerful and initially very successful—came not from any environmental advantage offered to the Federals by the Wilderness. Rather, Union success stemmed from sloppy Confederate preparation and from the immense weight of a finally concentrated force on both the front and flank of Hill's line. While the Confederate attacks also benefited from a lack of Union preparation, a key difference is that the Rebels took advantage of the Wilderness to conceal their movements and cloak their small numbers. There is nothing to suggest that this tactic was premeditated or that the Federals could not have gained the same advantages had they sought them. Admittedly, the Battle of the Wilderness was a tactical draw, though strategically Union forces were able to continue their march south because they held key roads. Nevertheless, the question is not who won the battle, but who took better advantage of the Wilderness. Clearly in this regard, the Confederates outperformed their Federal opponents.

Ultimately, the Wilderness was not a good place for the Confederates to fight due to any natural advantages it afforded to them alone. By and large, the landscape gave the Confederates as much grief as it did the Federals. Lee's men enjoyed no special familiarity with the region. They could see through the undergrowth no better than the Federals, nor move through its thickets with greater ease. Lee certainly did not start a fight in the Wilderness for the sake of obtaining some tactical edge from the ground itself. Yet despite this, the Confederates made it a good place to fight. Lee and his generals saw opportunities in the otherwise inhospitable Wilderness and boldly seized the initiative. Their aggressive advance on May 5, the skillful deployment of Longstreet's corps on May 6, and the flank attacks that same day demonstrate as much. As Lyman noted, the Confederates proved to be "more daring and sudden in their movements," even in such a challenging landscape. In short, the Army of Northern Virginia followed the advice of Lee to "live in the world you inhabit. Look upon things as they are. Take them as you find them. Make the best of them. Turn them to your advantage."[60] And that is what made all the difference.

5

THE WILDERNESS, MILITARY OPERATIONS, AND MEMORY

Historians from the Civil War to the present have drawn conclusions about how the Wilderness affected, or should have affected, Union and Confederate military operations. Two ideas are especially prevalent. One is the view that Maj. Gen. Joseph Hooker should have extricated the Army of the Potomac from the Wilderness during the Chancellorsville Campaign. In this interpretation, the Union defeat is blamed in large part on his decision to turn back and station his army around Chancellorsville instead of boldly pushing out of the Wilderness to attack the Army of Northern Virginia. The other is that in 1864 General Robert E. Lee, remembering his victory at Chancellorsville, intentionally sought to bring on a fight in the Wilderness at the start of the Overland Campaign in order to trap Union forces in an environment where the Confederates held the advantage.

To determine what, if any, role the Wilderness played in military operations in 1863–64 requires a careful examination of the Chancellorsville, Mine Run, and Wilderness Campaigns. Union forces initiated each of these operations, while the Confederates reacted to their movements. This being the case, it is of great importance to understand how the Wilderness figured into initial Union plans and actions as well as how the forest influenced the Confederate response. After the war the memory of the Wilderness's effects upon military operations solidified into familiar narratives as certain interpretations took hold, while others fell from favor. But a close analysis of the commanders' campaign reports suggests that the positions these early historians took were incorrect, mistaken conclusions that nevertheless formed a part of the larger Wilderness myth. Like the myth's other components, these errors were children of hindsight that have survived into the present as a consequence of historians' reliance on memoirs and early histories as well as their failure to question many of the assumptions and conclusions that these initial works promoted.

One must recognize that postwar writers often used the Wilderness as either a handy club for bludgeoning their enemies' reputations or a ready shield for defending their own—at times it was used for both. Examples of this pattern abound. Hooker's critics used the Wilderness to blame him for the defeat at Chancellorsville, while his supporters used it to defend his controversial actions. Confederates, meanwhile, emphasized the natural difficulties they had to overcome to win their great victory at Chancellorsville. In their accounts of the Battle of the Wilderness, Union writers used the region to excuse the Federal army's shortcomings and to either criticize or defend Grant's performance. In contrast, Confederate historians used it to highlight their own deeds and particularly to glorify Lee's generalship, which was standard fare in Lost Cause writings.[1] Suffice it to say that the way the Wilderness was remembered became entwined with the reputations of important generals and the explanations of vital campaigns.

A careful study of the three Wilderness campaigns provides little evidence that the Federals were trying to avoid this region or to move through it quickly for the sake of avoiding a fight amid the forest. The Union high command either did not take the Wilderness into account when crafting its strategies or allowed other factors to take precedence. The question is, then, what drove strategic decision making in these three operations if not the Wilderness itself? During the Chancellorsville, Mine Run, and Wilderness Campaigns, Federal commanders consistently sought to avoid Confederate entrenchments and steer clear of a fight while crossing the Rappahannock or Rapidan Rivers. Keeping the army supplied was also a major factor in the Mine Run and Wilderness Campaigns. These concerns led Union commanders to enter the Wilderness three times of their own free will.

For the Confederates, there is little to suggest that they would have wanted to bring on a battle in the Wilderness. Lee's reports on Chancellorsville and Mine Run recount in detail the problems that the landscape caused Rebel forces. Moreover, his actions in these two campaigns offer scant evidence that he was wedded to the idea of fighting in the region's thickets. At Chancellorsville, Hooker chose the Wilderness for the battlefield, while at Mine Run, when Lee had the chance to fight the Federals in the thick woods, he chose to withdraw to his entrenchments along that creek. Finally, Lee's wartime and postwar commentary about the Battle of the Wilderness suggests that he wanted to bring on a battle with Grant as soon as possible, although not necessarily in the Wilderness.

While many postwar sources castigated Hooker for his retreat into the Wilderness on May 1, 1863, contemporary accounts suggest that the general did not take the Wilderness into account when forming his initial plans. When Hooker sat down to decide what policy he would pursue in the spring of 1863, certain options were already closed to him. The failure of McClellan's Peninsula Campaign in June 1862 eliminated that line of advance against Richmond, and Burnside's disastrous attacks on Lee's army along the Fredericksburg heights the following December certainly did not recommend that route as a viable option.[2] This left Hooker with an overland route that presented two significant obstacles. First, his army would have to engage the Confederates at a site where they were not entrenched. Second, his forces would have to cross over a river or rivers and avoid a fight while in transit. Compared to these major obstacles, the Wilderness was a trifling concern.

The first obstacle the commanding general had to take into account when selecting locations for crossing the Rappahannock and Rapidan

Rivers was Confederate defenses. Brig. Gen. Gouverneur K. Warren, the Army of the Potomac's chief of topographical engineers, explained the difficulties the Federals faced in trying to find a way around some twenty miles of Confederate entrenchments. "The enemy," noted Warren, "occupied in strong force the heights south of the Rappahannock river from Skinker's Neck to Banks' Ford, having continuous lines of infantry parapets throughout . . . , his troops being so disposed as to be readily concentrated on any threatened point." In addition to these impediments, Lee had placed artillery "for sweeping the hill slopes and bottom lands on which our troops would have to march to the assault" and had erected abatis, which, along with "impassable swamps in places, still further strengthened his lines and reduced the number of assailable points."[3] Suffice it to say that crossing a river in front of such a formidable defensive array promised the kind of bloodbath that any sensible army commander sought to avoid.

Hooker instead looked to outflank the Confederate positions while avoiding a battle in midcrossing. In his testimony before the Joint Committee on the Conduct of the War, given in March 1865, he described his plan for forcing Lee out of his strong defenses along the Rappahannock. He first intended to send a flanking column across the river at Kelly's Ford and then proceed south to cross the Rapidan at Germanna and Ely's Fords. These sites were not well protected and were remote from the main body of Lee's army, which would ensure that the Federals could cross more or less unmolested. This maneuver also would "knock away the enemy's forces holding the United States and Banks's fords," which lay on the left flank of the Confederate line, "by attacking them in rear." Once this was done, Hooker then planned to "re-enforce the marching column sufficiently for them to continue the march upon the flank of the rebel army until his whole force was routed, and, if successful, his retreat intercepted." While this flanking movement was underway, another part of the army would "cross the Rappahannock below Fredericksburg and threaten the enemy in that quarter, including his depot of supplies, to prevent his dispatching an overwhelming force to his left."[4] This demonstration would further ensure that the flanking column could ford the rivers safely. Although crossing in the immediate vicinity of Lee's army, this decoy force would be protected by Union artillery on the heights across the Rappahannock. Clearly, Hooker's initial planning paid little attention to the Wilderness. The Union commander instead focused on avoiding the Confederate entrenchments and a battle at the river crossings.

The first part of Hooker's plan worked like a charm. The V, XI, and XII Corps crossed the Rappahannock and Rapidan and regrouped in the vicinity of Chancellorsville. Meanwhile, the rest of the army demonstrated in front of Fredericksburg. May 1 seemed a day of great promise. The Union forces around Chancellorsville advanced in the direction of Fredericksburg, but a portion of Lee's army, in turn, had marched out to intercept them. Hooker still had the opportunity to push his troops into the open country east of the Wilderness, but when he was confronted by this Rebel force, he chose to halt the advance and then march his men back to their former position in the woods around Chancellorsville.

Hooker later testified that "the passage-way through the forest was narrow," and he was "satisfied that [he] could not throw troops through it fast enough to resist the advance of General Lee," confessing that he "was apprehensive of being whipped in detail." Hooker thus explained his decision to remain in the Wilderness by blaming the forest for his inability to deploy his troops effectively. After the war he wrote to Samuel P. Bates, who was working on a history of the Chancellorsville Campaign, and again explained his chosen course. "I soon discovered that I was hazarding too much to continue the movement," contended Hooker, as "it was impossible to maneuver, on which I had largely depended on for success." These circumstances led him to withdraw. He concluded that "if situated in like manner again, I do not hesitate to declare . . . I should repeat the order," admitting also that at the time he "had no adequate conception" of the Wilderness. Bates in turn took up this line of argument when writing his history, emphasizing the importance of the Wilderness in Union decision making. When explaining Hooker's crucial choice on May 1 to return to the old lines around Chancellorsville, Bates parroted the army commander's explanation, pointing to the disadvantage the Union forces operated under "hemmed in on three narrow roads leading through an almost impenetrable forest, where it was impossible for him to manoeuvre them," while the Confederates worked to flank the right end of his position.[5]

While Hooker's testimony seems to indicate that he did take the Wilderness into account once his operations began, it is crucial to consider the context in which he was making these claims. Previous to Hooker's testimony before the Joint Committee on the Conduct of the War, others had decried the May 1 withdrawal and asserted that this move had interrupted a promising advance. Among these was Maj. Gen. Winfield Scott Hancock, at the time a division commander in the II Corps. Hancock certainly acknowledged "that the position of Chancellorsville was not a good one," that the area "was a flat country" and lacked any "local military advantages." He contended, however, that "if we had not stopped at Chancellorsville, but had marched right down to Banks's ford, the whole movement would have been a perfect success." For him "the mistake was, that when we had started an offensive fight, we stopped and fought a defensive one before the concentration was complete."[6] Andrew Humphreys, at the time a brigadier general and division commander in the Army of the Potomac, criticized the May 1 halt for similar reasons. "We had advanced along the road to Fredericksburg to attack the enemy," and "the troops were in fine spirits, and we wanted to fight a battle." Humphreys thought that "it was a mistake to fight a defensive battle after we had surprised the enemy," contending that the army ought to "have attacked the enemy immediately."[7]

General Warren offered an alternative explanation, stating that the need to get out of the Wilderness was the main reason that Hooker should have kept advancing. Given his training and position as chief of engineers, it is no surprise that in testimony before the joint committee on March 9, 1864, he dwelt at length upon the disadvantages that the Army of the Potomac faced because of the Wilderness's vegetation and topography. "All around [the Chancellor house] in every direction," noted Warren, "were very dense woods, not very large trees, but very difficult to get through, mainly of scrubby oak . . . , so that a man could hardly ride through it, and a man could not march through it very well with a musket in hand, unless he trailed it." In addition to the challenges posed by the vegetation, "a further disadvantage about it was that the highest ground was in the possession of the enemy, especially towards . . . the left of the line." Warren believed that Hooker had not looked over the ground but had only ordered the army there because it had occupied the site the previous day. Under the circumstances Warren thought it "was about the best that could be designated." He did admit, however, that the position "was probably not the best that might have been taken if [Hooker] had had more time to select it."[8]

Later in his testimony Warren concluded that, had he been in Hooker's place, "I never should have stopped at Chancellorsville; I should have kept advancing, and fought the enemy, instead of waiting for him to attack me." He argued that "the character of the country was the great reason for advancing, because as we advanced we kept getting out into more open country." This reasoning had been strikingly absent from the engineer's official report on the campaign, written in May 1863, which had only noted that the Union position was a poor one because the Confederates held the higher ground along parts of the line. While Warren would have been freer to criticize Hooker before the joint committee than as a member of the general's staff, he had not shied away from criticizing the line adopted by his commander on May 1 in his report—he had just criticized it for different reasons. This position, Warren concluded in his report, "was a bad line, and had several commanding positions in its front for the enemy to occupy." Yet despite his critical attitude, Warren did not disparage the position because it was in the Wilderness, as he would later in his testimony before the joint committee.[9]

When Federal observers writing immediately after the Chancellorsville Campaign lamented Hooker's halt on May 1, it was not necessarily because it meant returning to the Wilderness per se. In part, they expressed bafflement over the fact that they held the initiative and were just about to get Lee where they wanted him when Hooker inexplicably called off the advance. Some officers and soldiers found this very demoralizing, but the Wilderness had little to do with it. For example, Maj. Gen. George Meade, one of Hooker's corps commanders, reported that his troops "had a very handsome little affair, in which

[they] behaved very well and gained decided advantages, driving the enemy before them; but [they were] *recalled* just as [their] advance was successful." In a similar vein Brig. Gen. Alpheus Williams, a division commander in the XII Corps, described how "the men were eager and cheerful to joking, when up came an order to countermarch and go back to my original position." After this withdrawal, the feeling among Williams's troops changed dramatically. He found that "the men went back disappointed, not without grumbling," noting that "it really required some policy to satisfy them that there was not mismanagement somewhere."[10]

After the war, in contrast, there was a tendency to parrot Warren's joint-committee remarks and criticize Hooker's retreat on May 1, not only because it interrupted the advance and killed the army's momentum but also because it meant having to fight in the Wilderness. For instance, William Swinton condemned the commanding general for giving up "the fine position then gained" by which "he might have pushed out beyond the woods" and connected with the other wing of the army. Instead, Hooker "stood on the defensive in the Wilderness," in what to Swinton's mind "was absolutely a bad position" since higher ground commanded the army's position, while the thick woods prevented the use of cavalry or artillery, impeded the use of infantry, left the army's flank in the air, and provided a screen for Rebel movements. Theodore A. Dodge likewise argued that "there was every reason why the army should be got out of the Wilderness, in the midst of which lies Chancellorsville," for that region was "the least fit for an engagement . . . to secure the best tactical results." In contrast, moving in the direction of Fredericksburg "the ground opens, showing a large number of clearings, woods of less density, and a field suited to the operations of all arms." If getting out of the Wilderness was not motivation enough, the need to unite the two parts of the army ought to have impelled Hooker forward.[11]

Maj. Gen. Darius Couch, one of the Army of the Potomac's corps commanders, elaborated on Warren's conclusion in an oft-quoted piece he wrote after the war. After explaining Hooker's order to withdraw, he declared that the officers around him "all agreed with me that the ground [approaching Fredericksburg] should not be abandoned, because of the open country in front and the commanding position." Couch contrasted this with the area around Chancellorsville, which "for a defensive position was bad." There, he argued, "were no commanding positions for artillery, and but little open country to operate over." He concluded that "the advantage of ground for this arm was mainly with the attacking party." The Confederates would command the position at Chancellorsville, and the Union forces would not be able to gain access to Banks's Ford. "To hear from [Hooker's] own lips that the advantages gained by the successful marches of his lieutenants were to culminate in fighting a defensive battle in that nest of thickets was too much," Couch recounted. "I retired from his presence with the belief that my commanding general was a whipped man."[12]

John Bigelow, in his mammoth study of the Chancellorsville Campaign, was also critical of Hooker for not advancing out of the Wilderness on April 30 and for his withdrawal back to Chancellorsville on May 1. For Bigelow, however, the retreat into the Wilderness was not the key turning point that many postwar writers made it out to be. No doubt this was because he had a great appreciation for the many other flaws that marred the general's performance, such as sending his cavalry away, expecting Maj. Gen. John Sedgwick's VI Corps to save the rest of the army, and withdrawing the Army of the Potomac on the night of May 5 instead of awaiting Lee's attack.[13]

Although the conclusion that the Wilderness was a bad place for the Union army to fight eventually became more-or-less standard in histories of Chancellorsville, originally there were alternate interpretations. Lee's report dwelt on the disadvantages the Confederates faced in fighting in the Wilderness. After Hooker's forces retreated to the area around Chancellorsville, Lee gained the initiative. The Rebel chief, however, explained that the Federals "had assumed a position of great natural strength" because their forces were "surrounded on all sides by dense forest filled with a tangled undergrowth, in the midst of which breastworks of logs had been constructed in front as to form an almost impenetrable abatis." It was clear to Lee "that a direct attack upon the enemy would be attended with great difficulty and loss, in view of the strength of his position and his superiority of numbers." He and Stonewall Jackson subsequently "resolved . . . to turn [Hooker's] right flank and gain his rear, leaving a force in front to hold him in check and conceal the movement."[14] Jackson's famous flanking movement, then, was an attempt to bypass the obstacles the Wilderness placed in front of the Confederates, particularly the thick forest, as well as the Union field fortifications.

Once the Confederates went on the offensive, the Wilderness presented additional problems. Lee noted that during Jackson's flank attack, "in the ardor of pursuit through the thick and tangled woods the first and second lines . . . became mingled and moved on together as one." He later complained about Jackson having to realign his troops, as they "were completely blended and in such disorder from their rapid advance through intricate woods and over broken ground." Despite these impediments, the strike was successful and routed the XI Corps. Darkness, additional Union forces, the disordered Confederate lines, and Jackson's wounding all combined to bring the attack to a halt, but the next day Lee had his men renew their assaults. When describing the May 3 actions, Lee observed that "the troops having become somewhat scattered by the difficulties of the ground and the ardor of the contest were immediately reformed preparatory to renewing the attack." Later, when Lee intended to batter the final Union position, he again lamented the delay "in getting the troops into position, owing to the broken and irregular nature of the ground and the difficulty of ascertaining the disposition of the enemy's forces."[15] Clearly, the Confederate commander viewed the Wilderness as a hindrance to his army.

Some sympathetic postwar writers chose to follow Lee's interpretation of viewing the Wilderness as a place that hampered the Confederates. Most noteworthy among these were William Allan and Jedediah Hotchkiss, two former officers in the Army of Northern Virginia who together wrote about Chancellorsville shortly after the war. In their conventional description, the authors listed numerous obstacles that the Wilderness posed for any attacking force. To the usual complaints of limited visibility and disordered lines they added that the "avenues of approach were few and could be easily commanded by artillery" and that "the timber and brushwood afforded the amplest materials for fortifications to protect the attacked and delay the advance of the attacking force." While the two admitted that the left wing of the Federal line "in several places was commanded by the opposite heights," they claimed that the enemy's right "occupied a fine commanding position, running parallel to the Plank Road." Allan and Hotchkiss also argued that the ravines around Chancellorsville cut up the battlefield and provided good places from which Union soldiers could repel Confederate attacks. That the Rebels sought a way to flank the Union line rather than attack it head on suggests that they thought conditions in the Wilderness favored the Federals. Edward Porter Alexander, an artillery officer under Lee, also subscribed to this view in his published memoir, arguing that an army on the defensive held an advantage in the Wilderness. "No better field fortification can be desired," contended Alexander, "than what it was the quickest to build in the Wilderness." He concluded that "any charging line is brought to a halt by the entanglement, and held under close fire of musketry and canister, while the surrounding forest prevents the [attacking] enemy from finding positions to use his own artillery."[16]

Yet this Confederate interpretation effectively died out with time as the traditional view—that the Wilderness was disadvantageous for the Union army—took hold. Dodge, for example, acknowledged Lee's points about the Wilderness but found them unpersuasive. "While it is true," explained Dodge, "that the position was difficult to carry by direct assault, full compensation existed in other tactical advantages to the army taking the offensive." He contended that had Lee's and Hooker's roles been reversed, "it is not probable that Lee . . . would have selected such ground." After quoting Allan and Hotchkiss's description of how the Wilderness limited visibility and disordered linear formations, Dodge concluded that despite these drawbacks, "the density of these very woods was the main cause of Lee's success," pointing to how the trees limited Hooker's ability to maneuver and screened Rebel movements. Even Alexander questioned the Confederate interpretation in his other, longer memoir (published only in 1989). He straddled the line between the Federal view that Hooker was mistaken to retreat into the Wilderness and the Confederate view that the region offered the Army of the Potomac some substantial defensive benefits, but he ultimately sided with the Federals. "Defensive lines," explained Alexander, "were quick & easy to make, & hold, &, by cutting a little abattis in front of them, an entanglement would result which only rabbits could get through. But Hooker's move, clearly, should have been to get his men through the Wilderness country & out into the more open fields beyond, where his superior artillery could be deployed, & to push his advance as rapidly as possible towards Sedgewick."[17]

While the Confederate interpretation has fallen from favor, Hooker's and Bates's interpretation—which justified Hooker's decision to retreat by emphasizing the danger of the army being beaten in detail as it extricated itself from the Wilderness—has recently made a comeback of sorts. Stephen Sears, in his history of the Chancellorsville Campaign, largely repeated their arguments justifying the withdrawal into the Wilderness. He acknowledged criticism of the retreat on May 1 but argued that Hooker had a very definite idea of how many Confederates were in front of him. These forces outnumbered his troops and were concentrated along the Orange Turnpike and Orange Plank Road, giving them a considerable advantage. Sears contended, moreover, that "the ground where [the Union forces] were then engaged was hardly worth fighting for" and that the chances of pushing the Rebels back far enough to allow the Federals to deploy beyond the Wilderness were slim, so "there was little profit in continuing the battle where it was being fought." He concluded that despite the withdrawal, Hooker had actually "achieved his two primary aims—to get his army in good position south of the Rappahannock, and to draw General Lee out from behind his Fredericksburg fortifications."[18]

While various interpretations have come and gone, it remains clear that the Wilderness had little to do with Hooker's initial planning and actions during the campaign. Enemy entrenchments and crossing the Rappahannock and Rapidan Rivers safely shaped his preparations. Nevertheless, Hooker elected to fight in the Wilderness because he claimed, long after the fact, that he could not deploy his army fast enough along the narrow forest roads to avoid being overwhelmed by the oncoming Confederates. Yet this explanation was meant to defend his reputation from the damning testimony offered by other Union generals before the Joint Committee on the Conduct of the War. Such being the case, it merits critical scrutiny. Contemporary testimony shows that the main criticism of the retreat was that it interrupted a successful offensive movement, not that it meant returning to the Wilderness. It is also plain that far from a favorite battlefield, the region was a challenge and a seemingly constant headache for Lee and his army. The Wilderness thus became one of the chief scapegoats of the Chancellorsville Campaign.[19] For Hooker's critics, the Wilderness explained the Union army's defeat; for his defenders, it justified his actions; and for the Confederates, it glorified their victory.

The strategies both sides pursued during the Mine Run Campaign shared many similarities with those of the Chancellorsville Campaign. The Union high command again had to contend with factors that narrowed the lines of advance. In the fall of 1863, the Army of the Potomac, with George Meade now in command, had taken a position north of the Rappahannock along the Orange and Alexandria Railroad. Meade was—as was nearly always the case—under pressure to advance, but the Lincoln administration had a particular route in mind. On November 2, the general had written to Washington proposing to move "the whole army rapidly and secretly across the Rappahannock at Banks' Ford and Fredericksburg," with the hope of "taking [a] position on the heights beyond the town." By doing so, Meade hoped to station his army in a formidable location and then invite Lee to attack him. The next day Maj. Gen. Henry Halleck, the Union general in chief, torpedoed this plan. Lincoln had not found the proposed move very promising, so Halleck replied that "any tactical movement to turn a flank or threaten a communication is left to your own judgment; but an entire change of base under existing circumstances, I can neither advise nor approve." Meade was stuck. One can only imagine that past Union failures around Fredericksburg, as well as Meade's failure to bring Lee to battle in the months since Gettysburg, left Lincoln and Halleck feeling frustrated and led them to veto the proposal. Later that month Meade took the army across the Rappahannock along the Orange and Alexandria Railroad and forced the Confederates to retreat across the Rapidan.[20] As a result, at the outset of the Mine Run Campaign, Meade's army lay north of the Rapidan, relying on the Orange and Alexandria Railroad as a supply line, while Lee's army lay south of the river around Orange Court House.

Once more, Union planning revolved around the factors of avoiding entrenchments and crossing a river without coming under fire. Like Hooker at Chancellorsville, Meade sought to avoid a network of Confederate defenses. Lee's "strong intrenchments on the Rapidan" extended from "west of Orange Court-House" to Morton's Ford. Assaulting these works "had long been impracticable," and Meade reported to Halleck that he intended to turn one of the Confederates' flanks. After weighing all the factors, including how to keep his army supplied, he concluded that he should move to the east on Lee's right, which would require marching a shorter distance, cover his communications, and allow the army to safely retreat if necessary. His objections to moving to the west against Lee's left flank were that it would require a longer march, force him to abandon his communications, and make withdrawing in the face of the enemy more hazardous. He then added that "examinations are being made with a view of determining the practicability of turning the right by Germanna and Ely's" Fords, the same ones the Army of the Potomac had used in the Chancellorsville Campaign.[21] Another factor in selecting this route was that Meade had learned "that the enemy had abandoned the design of guarding the lower fords, but relied for the protection of his right flank on an intrenched line he had constructed perpendicular to the Rapidan" at Morton's Ford. This refused flank, however, did not extend far enough south to cover the Orange Turnpike or Orange Plank Road.[22] After taking all of these circumstances into consideration, Meade finally determined to cross his army east of the Confederate entrenchments at Germanna, Culpeper Mine, and Jacob's Fords, a line of march that would lead his troops into the Wilderness.

Once the route was determined, Meade had to figure out how to get his army across the Rapidan without having to fight the Confederates. Unlike Hooker at Chancellorsville, his troops were not stationed near Fredericksburg but farther to the north and west along the Orange and Alexandria Railroad. Meade made no plans to pin Lee's army in place, like Hooker had done, but rather intended to shift his entire army in a quick flanking movement. He hoped "to cross the Rapidan at the lower fords . . . and by a prompt movement seize the plank road and turnpike, advancing rapidly toward Orange Court-House, thus turning the enemy's works, and compelling him to give battle on ground not previously selected or prepared." Meade not only wanted to bring the Confederates to battle outside their entrenchments but also hoped to catch a section of the Army of Northern Virginia, which was strung out on a long defensive line, and badly damage it before the rest of Lee's command could be reunited so "as to render more certain the success of the final struggle."[23]

Nowhere in Meade's deliberations does the Wilderness appear as a factor in determining his operations. Instead, river crossings, entrenchments, and logistics occupied the general's mind. If the Union high command was so determined to avoid the Wilderness, they certainly could have hazarded the other, longer line of advance, but Meade decided to cross the Rapidan at the fords that would lead his army straight into its woodlands. His efforts to advance toward the west were aimed at getting around Lee's line of entrenchments, which petered out at the headwaters of Mine Run, and then engaging the Confederate army before it could concentrate.

At Mine Run, as at Chancellorsville, Lee simply reacted to the Federals' movements. Once learning that Meade was marching toward the lower fords that led into the Wilderness, he moved to intercept. Initially, he was unsure of the Federals' intended route because "the country in that vicinity," namely the Wilderness, "was unfavorable for observation, being almost an unbroken forest." With this thick curtain of vegetation blocking his view, Lee could not tell "whether it was the design of the Federal commander to advance toward Richmond or move up the Rapidan upon our right flank." Without knowing his enemy's destination, Lee concluded that he would attack the enemy army in the flank or in its rear if it moved toward the Confederate capital. If the Federals turned toward his army, then Lee fully intended to bring them to battle. Rebel cavalry later discovered the Federals marching up the Orange Turnpike and Orange Plank Road on November 27, but even then it was not clear if this was "only a force thrown out to cover the movement of the main body toward Fredericksburg." As a result, Lee continued to advance his men eastward until he was satisfied that a substantial Union force was in front of him.[24]

Since he found "it impossible to ascertain" the Federals' strength, Lee had his forward troops stall the enemy and skirmish in the Wilderness while his army concentrated. The only fight of consequence—a sharp little engagement at Payne's farm—was brought on by Union forces firing into Lee's men. While this engagement ended in a draw, it benefited the Rebels by preventing the Union army from concentrating and by contributing to the ruin of Meade's cherished timetable. Yet that night, Lee chose to leave the Wilderness's thick forests and take up a defensive position in the more open Mine Run valley.[25] Here he entrenched his forces on the far side of the valley on high ground and awaited the Union attack. When Meade's forces failed to deliver, he sought to make a flank attack, but a timely Union withdrawal foiled his plans.[26]

Nowhere in Lee's report does he give the impression that the Wilderness was a good place for his army to fight or that he hoped to trap the Army of the Potomac in its woodlands. Had the Wilderness been such an advantageous place for Lee to fight, why did he not attack Meade in the forest when he had him there? Why retreat to Mine Run instead of taking the initiative and striking when the Federals were stumbling about in the thickets? He certainly wanted to bring Meade to battle if possible, but nothing he wrote suggests that Lee was bent on engaging the Union army in the Wilderness. To the contrary, when his own army was in the Wilderness, he complained about how the Union position was stronger and how the forest prevented him from knowing his opponent's strength. Not unexpectedly, when a lull presented itself, Lee took advantage of it and moved his army out of the

Wilderness to high ground, where he had his men construct entrenchments. While the Confederates were outnumbered, that certainly had not deterred Lee from attacking Hooker at Chancellorsville. Ironically, Meade found himself in the very situation in which he had hoped to place the Confederates had Washington allowed him to seize the Fredericksburg heights.

Postwar writers made no connections between the Wilderness and military operations during the Mine Run Campaign, an omission that lies in stark contrast to the interpretations surrounding Chancellorsville and the Battle of the Wilderness. If the Wilderness affected Union and Confederate operational planning in those campaigns, then why would it not do so at Mine Run? When it came time to report on the movement's failure, Meade blamed the Army of the Potomac's disappointing performance on factors such as the weather, the failure of the III Corps to keep to its schedule, the steep banks at the fords, and the invulnerability of the Confederate entrenchments—in short, on everything but the Wilderness. The campaign's historians generally have followed his lead.[27] In this sense, the postwar studies of Mine Run give a better feel for how commanders would have approached operating in the Wilderness than do the histories of Chancellorsville and the Battle of the Wilderness.

The strategic considerations influencing the Army of the Potomac's high command at the outset of the Overland Campaign were very similar to those they grappled with during the Mine Run operation. Certain considerations, particularly the need to protect Washington, limited the possible lines of advance to an overland route. In January 1864, Lieutenant General Grant had written Halleck about the possibility of abandoning "all previously attempted lines to Richmond" in favor of moving inland from Suffolk, in southeastern Virginia, toward Raleigh, North Carolina. The purpose of this movement would be to destroy or threaten all the railroads south of Richmond, which "would virtually force an evacuation of Virginia" by the Confederates.[28] Halleck's response emphasized the military and political constraints under which the Army of the Potomac operated. He explained to Grant that the army simply did not have enough men to protect Washington and mount the proposed expedition. If the Federals moved troops to North Carolina, Lee would simply bolt northward to cause a panic, and "the popular sentiment [would] compel the Government to bring back the army in North Carolina to defend Washington, Baltimore, Harrisburg, and Philadelphia."[29]

Halleck then argued that the best plan was to place the army so as to cover Washington while marching against Richmond. This would allow the Federals to gather all their strength into this main army by not having to divide their forces between protecting the capital and operating against the enemy. Although Halleck conceded the past failure of McClellan on the Peninsula route and of Burnside, Hooker, and Meade along the overland route, he concluded that the best option was to fight the Rebels as near to Washington as possible. An overland route would allow Grant to "concentrate against [Lee] more men than anywhere else," and Halleck reasoned that if the troops could not achieve a victory there "with [their] combined force, [they] cannot hope to do so elsewhere with a divided army."[30] In short, it had to be an overland campaign, and the farther away from Richmond that Grant could bring the Confederates to battle, the better. It is also worth noting that McClellan at this time was persona non grata with the Republican administration, which made anything resembling his 1862 Peninsula Campaign unacceptable, while a successful overland advance would justify the route preferred by Lincoln's government.

Grant's postcampaign report explained that the Union high command considered two possible lines of advance, making no mention of the Wilderness in weighing the two options. It did, however, reveal a determination that Lee would not head north like he had done in the past, that Union forces might have continuous access to supplies, that Grant and Meade could cooperate with Maj. Gen. Benjamin Butler's army on the Peninsula, and that the army could cross over the Rapidan safely. Grant's only observation on the Wilderness was that "the whole army [was] brought into the fight as fast as the corps could be got upon the field, which considering the density of the forest and narrowness of the road, was done with commendable promptness." This suggests that the general in chief acknowledged the problems the Wilderness caused in retrospect, but even then he viewed the forest as just another obstacle his soldiers had overcome. More telling still is his comment that "the most serious apprehensions" he had were "of crossing the river in the face of an active, large, well appointed, and ably-commanded army, and how so large a train was to be carried through a hostile country." Meade's report, too, has little to say about the Wilderness. When explaining why the Army of the Potomac crossed opposite the Wilderness, its commanding general simply explained that it was done "to avoid the intrenchments of Mine Run." There is no indication that the Wilderness entered into his thinking one way or another. Beyond this, Meade, like Grant, had little to say about the Wilderness, merely noting that at several points it impeded Union maneuvering.[31]

Union dispatches from May 5, 1864, confirm that the Wilderness was far from the center of Federal concerns. When Meade reported to Grant that the Confederates were positioning themselves in a line of battle opposite his forces in the Wilderness, his first reaction was to attack them while halting the army's march "until this movement of the enemy is developed." He did not think the Confederates intended to fight there but instead were "trying to delay our movement." Meade betrayed no concern about stopping the Union advance in the middle of the Wilderness. Grant's response to him was simple: "If any opportunity presents itself for pitching into a part of Lee's army, do so without giving time for disposition." Again, there are no worries here about the Wilderness, only an injunction to attack the Rebels, to bring them to battle as soon as possible. Later Meade sent word to Grant that he thought "Lee is simply making a demonstration to gain time," in which case he meant to "punish him." In particular he boasted that if Lee was "disposed to fight this side of Mine Run at once, he shall be accommodated."[32] Once more, there is no evidence in this dispatch that the Union army commanders were concerned about fighting in the Wilderness. If they had been so troubled about such a possibility, they surely would have expressed it or acted in some way to avoid such a fate. Of more concern to them was the fact that at least a portion of Lee's army had left its formidable Mine Run defenses and consequently appeared vulnerable. Even if the Federals had unexpressed desires to avoid a fight in the Wilderness, the allure of engaging the Confederates away from their entrenchments was enough to make them jettison such worries.

Judging Confederate intentions is more difficult because no official report by Lee on the Battle of the Wilderness has survived. While he did send some brief dispatches to Richmond during the engagement, these tell us little.[33] Past reports from the Chancellorsville and Mine Run Campaigns, however, reveal some of his thinking about the Wilderness. These demonstrate that the Confederate commander understood the character of the region well. Nevertheless, the conclusion that Lee intentionally engaged the Federal army there to take advantage of its environmental characteristics seems fanciful, given that he constantly complained about how these put himself and his army at a disadvantage. Assuming that Lee was not using the Wilderness as an excuse to cover his own or his army's shortcomings, then his reports show that he did not find the area a very appealing battleground. His reports do not show that he had gone out of his way to fight there in the 1863 campaigns, and despite the claims that he actively sought to catch the Union army there in 1864, there is nothing to suggest that Lee would have had any desire to do so. During the Chancellorsville Campaign, he attacked Hooker in the Wilderness because his opponent chose the field and Lee wanted to take the initiative. At Mine Run, the general could have engaged the Union army in the woods but instead chose to withdraw to a good defensive position in an open stretch along the edge of the Wilderness.

The limited contemporary evidence from the Battle of the Wilderness suggests that Lee was committed to bringing on an engagement as soon as his army was ready, although he was flexible as to where it would be fought. A May 4 order to Ewell provides a window into the Confederate commander's thoughts. The order explained that "if the enemy moves down the river, [General Lee] wishes to push on after him," but "if he comes this way, we will take our old line," most likely meaning the Mine Run entrenchments. The order concluded that

Lee wanted "to bring [the enemy] to battle as soon now as possible."[34] Clearly, Lee was open to various options, depending on the Federals' movements, but battle was the end goal, although not necessarily in the Wilderness. The next day Ewell reported receiving orders from his commander explaining that the latter "preferred not to bring on a general engagement before General Longstreet came up," suggesting that Lee wanted to unite his army before committing to a decisive battle. Yet there is no mention of trying to trap the Federals in the Wilderness. Ewell in turn told several of his brigade commanders that they were "not to allow themselves to become involved [in sustained combat], but to fall back slowly if pressed." Lee's postwar testimony also suggests that he wanted to engage the Federals but was not particular about the location of the upcoming battle. An 1868 letter explained that "notwithstanding the demonstrations made against our front and left at the opening of the campaign of '64, I believed that Genl. Grant would cross the Rapidan on our right, and resolved to attack him whenever he presented himself."[35] Again, there is no mention here of trapping the Union army in the Wilderness.

Some authors have claimed that Chancellorsville was the model Lee looked to in May 1864. They argue that he intended to pin or trap Grant and Meade in the Wilderness with part of his army in order to attack them in the flank with the other, just as he had done at Chancellorsville.[36] While this is possible, the actions of both sides suggest that their experience at Mine Run is what truly guided them at the Battle of the Wilderness. Meade and Grant were willing to fight Lee in the Wilderness because they wanted to prevent his army, or at least a part of it, from getting back to the Mine Run entrenchments. In effect, they sought to avoid the stalemate and potential bloodbath the Army of the Potomac had faced in 1863, their actions suggesting that they saw Lee's army being away from Mine Run as an opportunity, even if it meant fighting in the Wilderness's thick woods. This bellicosity forced a battle that neither Lee nor the Federals were prepared to fight.

If anything, one gets the sense that the fight that developed in the Wilderness escalated in a way that Lee had neither planned nor desired, as the Confederates were unable to avoid the general engagement that

Lee had sought to postpone until after concentrating his army. Despite his reputation for aggression, his orders and Ewell's report suggest that Lee wanted to repeat what he had done during the Mine Run Campaign: namely, locate the Union army's position and delay a full-scale battle until he could concentrate his own forces. Then, if the Federals turned toward him, he would withdraw to Mine Run with the hopes of forcing Meade and Grant to attack him there. While he did want to bring on a battle as soon as possible, nothing suggests that the Rebel commander was wedded to the idea of trapping the Army of the Potomac in the Wilderness. After all, at Mine Run Lee had also reported that he had intended to give battle. Yet this desire to engage the enemy did not necessarily mean fighting in the Wilderness and certainly did not preclude him from retreating to Mine Run.[37] If indeed the Mine Run experience was informing operational decisions, then bringing on a fight in the Wilderness would have been seen as a boon for the Union army and a misfortune for Lee's. Perhaps, it was the Army of Northern Virginia rather than the Army of the Potomac that ended up trapped in the Wilderness.

In stark contrast to these contemporary accounts, claims that the Wilderness affected military planning became standard fare in the postwar histories of the Overland Campaign. William Swinton, a Grant critic writing in the immediate aftermath of the war, provided an early example of this tendency and set the tone for those who would follow. Swinton argued that the Wilderness played a primary role in determining Confederate military operations during the first stage of the campaign. In particular, he claimed that Lee took the offensive and sought to engage the Army of the Potomac in the Wilderness in order to trap it in "tangled labyrinths of confusion and disaster" that minimized its numerical advantage.[38]

The musings of Union soldiers after the battle reveal the seeds from which Swinton's interpretation grew. These men sought to make sense of what they had experienced at the Battle of the Wilderness. Some focused on what a difficult landscape the Wilderness was. James L. Van Buren, a staff member in Burnside's IX Corps, judged the "tangled, dense low growth" to be "terrible for fighting through," while Charles

Mills, an adjutant in the 56th Massachusetts, claimed that "the extraordinarily dense woods . . . made [the Wilderness battlefield] the worst battleground . . . of the war." Other soldiers sought to explain why they had fought in such a dreadful place. One Federal thought that "Lee hopes to draw us off and defeat us in the *'Wilderness.'*" Another agreed, remarking that "the rebels were bound to fight us in the dense wilderness."[39]

A letter by a Pennsylvania artilleryman to the *Columbia Democrat* provided one of the richest contemporary accounts explaining why some Federals thought the Confederates had chosen to fight them in the Wilderness. The writer first recounted some of the difficulties he and his comrades faced there: the dense vegetation "not only pre[v]ents the ordinary manoeuvres of troops, but conceals the enemy," moreover, "success or disasters at the different points cannot be noted, commands cannot be rapidly communicated, and in fact the only way to get along is to bush-whack on a grand scale." To this assessment the soldier added that "in this [bushwhacking], the enemy are evidently our superiors." He then remarked how Confederate infantry was thought to be better than Union infantry, while the reverse was true when it came to artillery. From these assumptions, he concluded, "this probably induced Lee to select the Wilderness as a battle ground, thereby depriving us of the use of our most efficient weapon."[40]

It is easy to see how the fact that the Confederates intercepted the Federals' march, combined with the problems the Union soldiers faced and the assumptions the men harbored about each army's relative strengths and weaknesses, could persuade Union soldiers to think that the Rebels had chosen to fight in the Wilderness. James Carter, a member of the 45th Georgia, saw things very differently. For him, the Battle of the Wilderness "was a hard fought battle and a fair test of the courage and prowess of the contending armies neither party having the advantage of breastwork or fortifications." As for the Confederates deliberately trapping the Federals in the Wilderness, Carter thought "the two armies ran together apparently by chance in the woods or forest."[41]

Nevertheless, many subsequent historians have echoed Swinton's arguments in one form or another. Most of those who espoused this interpretation were former Confederates who had every reason to use the Wilderness to glorify Lee's generalship and attack Grant's.[42] Armistead Long, an artillery commander in the Army of Northern Virginia, asserted that Lee, "perceiving that Grant was making the mistake that had proved so disastrous to Hooker, by plunging with his army into that dense and sombre thicket well named 'The Wilderness,' . . . took care to do nothing to obstruct so desirable a result." Furthermore, he contended that "there was much reason to believe that [Lee's] antagonist would be at his mercy while entangled in these pathless and entangled thickets." Evander Law, one of Lee's brigadier generals, likewise claimed that "General Lee had deliberately chosen this as his battle-ground," for "he knew this tangled wilderness well, and appreciated fully the advantages such a field afforded for concealing his great inferiority of force and for neutralizing the superior strength of his antagonist." Moreover, Law maintained that the Federal route "offered the expected opportunity of striking a blow upon [Grant's] flank while his troops were stretched out on the line of march." William Dame, a lowly private in the Rebel army, similarly observed that Lee "was far too deep a file, to stop his enemy from getting himself into 'a fix.' He knew that when Grant's great army got over there, they would be 'entangled in the land, the wilderness would shut them in.'" He concluded that "Lee wouldn't lift a finger to keep Grant from getting *into* the wilderness, but quick as a flash he was, to keep him from getting out."[43]

Some Federal writers who were hostile to Grant argued that the Union army had either actively avoided fighting in the woods or had regretted the choice of battlefield.[44] For instance, Andrew Humphreys, Meade's chief of staff during the Wilderness Campaign, commented that "the objection to moving by our left consisted in the character of the country south of the Rapidan, through which [the Union troops] must pass . . . after crossing the river, and in which [they] might be obliged to fight the first battle." He suggested that the high command only chose to pass through the Wilderness because they thought they could clear the region before Lee's army arrived. Once in more open country, Humphreys thought that the army could then "turn, or partly turn, the right flank of Lee before a general engagement took place."

Some Federals lamented the army's halt on May 4 when it might have continued onward to the open country beyond the woodlands. Francis Walker of the II Corps believed that "there was nothing . . . to prevent the Army of the Potomac being established on any north or south line it might have chosen to take up between 'the Wilderness' and Mine Run." Looking back, he called the May 4 halt "the first misfortune of the campaign."[45]

Adam Badeau, a member of Grant's staff, disagreed with these interpretations and insisted that the general in chief meant to force a battle as quickly as possible regardless of the field. He, like other Union commentators, described the Wilderness as "the most impracticable country possible for the manoeuvres of an army." Yet Badeau, whose purpose in writing was to defend Grant's generalship, explained that "it was not [Grant's] object to avoid the enemy," nor did he "desire to out-flank the rebel army, in a purely strategic sense, so much as to bring it to speedy battle." Thus when "he decided to plunge direct into the Wilderness," Grant did so to force "either immediate battle or the immediate retreat of Lee." In this interpretation the Wilderness was far from the deciding factor when it came to Union operational plans, although Badeau claimed that "it was the forest, and not the enemy, that had thwarted Grant."[46]

Grant himself largely echoed his own wartime report in his celebrated memoirs, ignoring the Wilderness when explaining operational decisions but putting greater emphasis on how the forest hindered the Federals and aided the Confederates. He argued that "all the conditions [in the Wilderness] were favorable for defensive operations" and that the roads Lee had access to provided him "unusual facilities, for that country, for concentrating his forces." He also mentioned instances during the battle when the woods disrupted formations and allowed the Confederates to approach undetected. Moreover, Grant asserted that if the Federals had been able to see how much distress their opponents were in on the morning of May 6, they would have done Lee's army so much damage that it would not have fought again outside Richmond. After recounting the difficulties his army had faced and acknowledging the high casualties suffered, Grant contended that the battle was a Union victory. Their success, he asserted, "consisted in having successfully crossed a formidable stream, almost in the face of an enemy, and in getting the army together as a unit." This conclusion reveals the same concern about being attacked while crossing the Rapidan that he had voiced in his wartime report. But even with hindsight and a greater appreciation for the challenges it presented his army, Grant never claimed that the Wilderness shaped Union campaign planning.[47]

Gordon Rhea later challenged parts of the traditional interpretation of Lee trapping the Army of the Potomac in the Wilderness. Like many writers before him, Rhea argued that "from the rebel perspective, the Wilderness offered an ideal battlefield" and "was clearly the Confederates' most advantageous field of battle" due to all of the obstacles it supposedly presented the Union army. This was straight from the traditional telling. But then Rhea changed tack. If the Wilderness really was the best field, he questioned why "Lee [then] neglected to take any steps calculated to influence Meade's advance or to ensure that the Confederates would reach the Wilderness ahead of him." Only the decision to halt the Federal army's march early while still in the Wilderness on May 4 afforded "Lee the opportunity that he had neglected to achieve by his own planning." Rather than a craftily laid trap, the Confederate commander stumbled into good fortune, catching the Federals in the woods and managing to survive a battle against a stronger army while waiting for Longstreet's arrival. In other words, Rhea accepted the traditional idea that the Wilderness was an advantageous place for the Confederates to fight in, but he criticized Lee for not taking the trouble to actually attempt to trap the Union army there.[48]

Which of these interpretations, then, is most accurate? The contemporary reports made by Grant and Meade support Badeau's assertions that the Union commanders did not take the Wilderness landscape much into account when determining their operational plans. Their reports, for instance, suggest that political considerations, logistics, the dangers of crossing a river, and the location of Confederate entrenchments held greater sway over Union decision making than did the presence of a forest, even a very thick one. Their actions once the battle had begun suggest that they were more concerned with damaging Lee's army while it was unprotected by any defensive works than with avoiding the Wilderness. Furthermore, understanding Lee's true opinion of the Wilderness goes a long way toward explaining the contradiction that Rhea observed in the general's actions during the Wilderness Campaign. Lee took no steps to trap the Union army south of the Rapidan because it was not his intention to do so. As Rhea observed, the fact that he did so was a matter of happenstance, not a matter of calculation.

Having reviewed the three campaigns conducted in the Wilderness, it is clear that this area's distinct environmental characteristics played an inconsequential role in shaping Union military operations. In contrast, Lee did take the Wilderness into account, but not in the way that many writers have asserted. Rather, such considerations were largely postwar inventions, the product of hindsight and of desires to explain away Union failures, indict Hooker or Grant, and highlight Lee's generalship. As is the case with all scapegoats, the Wilderness was blamed for that which it was blameless and has since come down in history as a stumbling block of a battlefield, foolishly selected by Hooker at Chancellorsville and craftily chosen by Lee during the Battle of the Wilderness. Whatever reservations the Union commanders felt about the region, they were not strong enough to override other concerns such as enemy entrenchments, logistics, and safe river crossings. The commanders' reports, moreover, reveal little in the way of anxiety about the forest interfering with their plans. Lee, in contrast, showed a marked awareness of the Wilderness and the problems it caused his army, which suggests that he would not intentionally fight there unless other circumstances compelled him to, as they did at the opening of the Overland Campaign.

CONCLUSION

The Wilderness was a region that lent itself to mythmaking, and William Swinton and those who followed his lead did not disappoint. Their creation—the Wilderness myth—had two components. First, the Wilderness was exceptional. It was unlike any other field of battle, and a mystique surrounded the place, associating it with woe, gloom, death, destruction, hell, fire, and the supernatural, among other things. This landscape in turn created a fight unlike any other at the Battle of the Wilderness. Second, the Wilderness was an asset to the Confederates. The battlefield conditions it created favored the Rebels, and for this reason, Lee tried to trap the Union army there in May 1864.

As the preceding chapters have shown, however, many components of this Wilderness myth were simply not true. Contemporary sources suggest that the Wilderness was not the continuous second-growth forest of legend, but instead a complex forest containing a variety of different types of vegetation, with a density ranging from near-impassable thickets to open fields. It was also not a unique landscape created by the local iron industry, for Wilderness-like forests could be found in other parts of Virginia where tobacco cultivation had taken place. Nor did the Wilderness create unique battlefield conditions. Chancellorsville, although it was fought in the same region, was a very different type of contest than the Battle of the Wilderness, while Chickamauga, despite being fought in a different forest in a different state, created many of the same tactical problems traditionally associated with combat in the Wilderness. Moreover, the Wilderness mystique grew over time as soldiers accumulated experiences in the region but hardened—after the Battle of the Wilderness—into the exaggerated aura that has characterized the Virginia forest to this day. Furthermore, conditions in the Wilderness did not favor the Confederates. The Rebels did not know the landscape any better than their Union opponents, they experienced the same tactical problems as the Federals, and any advantages they gained at the Battle of the Wilderness can be credited to their aggressive pursuit of the few opportunities this difficult battlefield offered. Such being the case, it should come as no surprise that Lee did not attempt to trap the Union army in the Wilderness, and that Union commanders, from Joseph Hooker to Ulysses Grant, made no effort to avoid the region. In the end, the only truly unique characteristic of the Wilderness was the myth that grew up around it.

This study suggests that the relationship between military campaigns and the environment can become distorted all too easily. Whenever the reputations of generals, armies, and units are at stake, there is ample incentive to twist the facts, including the influence of the environment upon a given campaign. In this case, desires to explain the outcome of certain campaigns, assumptions about Lee and his army, the agendas of certain historians and memoirists, and the simple passage of time all contributed to the misunderstandings surrounding the character of the Wilderness, the combat conditions it created, and its effect on military operations. While contemporary and postwar portrayals of combat conditions at the Battle of the Wilderness were largely in agreement, the meaning attributed to these conditions was not. Postwar memoirists and historians emphasized the supposedly unique nature of the Wilderness or how the Confederates held an advantage because of it, interpretations that were ultimately misleading. It is here, in the realm of interpretation, that distortions seem most likely to occur. What other battlefields and battles do we now misunderstand because of our uncritical reliance on postwar traditions? In other words, how have the vagaries of memory influenced our understanding of how historical environments and military campaigns interacted?

There is also the issue of how memory has shaped our interpretation of military campaigns.[1] In recent years questions about the larger meaning of the conflict have dominated studies of Civil War memory. Historians have investigated how memorial associations, veteran groups, and interested individuals shaped the legacies of generals, politicians, emancipation, Union victory, and Confederate defeat by writing memoirs and histories, observing memorial days, creating cemeteries, preserving battlefields, and erecting monuments.[2] One topic that has received less scrutiny, though, has been the details of military operations. Veterans and early historians came to blows as often over these particulars as they did over the larger issues of the war, and modern historians ignore these old quarrels at their peril. Understanding how interpretations of a battle or campaign originated and then evolved over time is a worthwhile exercise that can only help historians understand these events better, as the findings herein have demonstrated regarding the Wilderness.

This study also points to the danger of ignoring a campaign like Mine Run, which produced neither a large battle nor substantial casualties. The lack of scholarship on Mine Run suggests that historians have found it unworthy of any serious attention. Including Mine Run, however, has proved immensely beneficial to this study, for it likely served as a model for both armies' operations in 1864. A correct understanding of this campaign, then, helps explain the true intentions of both sides during the initial stages of the Battle of the Wilderness. Union soldiers also made many important observations about the Wilderness during the Mine Run operation that help us understand how interpretations of the region evolved over time. Finally, unlike the histories of Chancellorsville and the Battle of the Wilderness, the postwar accounts of Mine Run were not tainted by assumptions about how the Wilderness affected combat and military operations. As a result, the true role that its woodlands played in determining Federal and Confederate operations becomes apparent by looking at these sources.

Historians would do well to treat seemingly less-eventful campaigns with more care.

For now, there are many lingering questions. For example, did the physical landscape affect the operational plans of commanders in other Civil War campaigns? If so, in what ways? The findings here regarding the Wilderness suggest that logistics and the presence of entrenchments more than anything else drove Civil War military planning. Whether this is true in other cases as well is a topic worth investigating. Other questions also beckon to be answered, such as how assumptions about the enemy affected soldiers' interpretations of the environment during military operations. Did the Federals, for instance, think other battlefields were advantageous to the Confederates in the same way that they claimed the Wilderness battlefield was? Did the Federals always claim that Confederates fought better than themselves in forested terrain? One especially wonders if this was the case in the western theater, where Union forces dominated their Confederate counterparts and had less reason to attribute outstanding abilities to their adversaries.

There are also many questions about how soldiers remembered and interpreted battlefields outside of the Wilderness. How did other wooded battlefields—Shiloh or Chickamauga, for instance—figure into the narratives that soldiers created about their wartime service? What kind of reputations did other battlefields earn, and did postwar reputations differ from wartime ones? Did soldiers react more negatively toward other areas they fought in multiple times, places like Manassas or the Virginia Peninsula?

Finally, there are many questions about how disparate environments and varying places of origin affected soldiers' reactions. How did the experience of battle differ between engagements that were fought in open areas, wooded areas, swamps, deserts, beaches, and mountains? Did soldiers unfamiliar with a given environment find it more distressing to fight in such a place than those who were accustomed to it? For example, did soldiers from more settled areas find fighting in the woods more distressing than those from frontier regions, where untamed forests were more common?

This study of the Wilderness is just one piece of a much larger story that not only deserves to be told but also must be told in order to understand how environmental factors affected Civil War military operations as well as how soldiers chose to interpret and remember this interaction. Until we have a larger-scale investigation of the relationship between the generals, soldiers, and armies, on the one hand, and the landscape of war, on the other, our understanding of Civil War battle, battlefields, and memory will remain incomplete.

NOTES

PREFACE

1. For examples of some pioneering attempts at understanding various aspects of the Wilderness, see Kathryn S. Meier, "Fighting in 'Dante's Inferno': Changing Perceptions of Civil War Combat in the Spotsylvania Wilderness from 1863 to 1864," in *Militarized Landscapes: From Gettysburg to Salisbury Plain,* ed. Chris Pearson, Peter Coates, and Tim Cole (London: Continuum, 2010); Earl J. Hess, *Field Armies and Fortifications in the Civil War: The Eastern Campaigns, 1861–1864* (Chapel Hill: University of North Carolina Press, 2005), 175, 197; Hess, *Trench Warfare under Grant & Lee: Field Fortifications in the Overland Campaign* (Chapel Hill: University of North Carolina Press, 2007), 39–43; Sean Patrick Adams, *Iron from the Wilderness: The History of Virginia's Catharine Furnace* (Washington, DC: National Park Service, 2011); Aaron Sachs, "Stumps in the Wilderness," in *The Blue, the Gray, and the Green: Toward an Environmental History of the Civil War,* ed. Brian Allen Drake (Athens: University of Georgia Press, 2015); James Harrison Powell, "'Seven Year Locusts': The Deforestation of Spotsylvania County during the American Civil War," *Essays in History* 43 (2010). http://www.essaysinhistory.com/seven-year-locusts-the-deforestation-of-spotsylvania-county-during-the-american-civil-war/ (accessed June 28, 2017); and Stephen Cushman, *Bloody Promenade: Reflections on a Civil War Battle* (Charlottesville: University Press of Virginia, 1999).

2. "The Great Campaign," *New York Times,* May 13, 1864. See also J. Cutler Andrews, *The North Reports the Civil War* (Pittsburgh: University of Pittsburgh Press, 1955), 531, 731n23.

3. William Swinton, *Campaigns of the Army of the Potomac* (New York: Charles B. Richardson, 1866), 417–18, 428–29, 438–39.

4. James McPherson, *Battle Cry of Freedom: The Civil War Era* (New York: Oxford University Press, 1988), 724–25.

1. THE NATURE AND ORIGINS OF THE WILDERNESS

1. Armistead Long, *Memoirs of Robert E. Lee* (New York: J. M. Stoddart, 1886), 328; Edward Steere, *The Wilderness Campaign: The Meeting of Grant and Lee* (Mechanicsburg, PA: Stackpole Books, 1960), 1.

2. William Swinton, *Campaigns of the Army of the Potomac* (New York: Charles B. Richardson, 1866), 428; Adam Badeau, *Military History of Ulysses S. Grant from April, 1861, to April, 1865,* 3 vols. (New York: D. Appleton, 1881), 2:108; Stephen W. Sears, *Chancellorsville* (Boston: Houghton Mifflin, 1996), 193.

3. Andrew A. Humphreys, *The Virginia Campaign of '64 and '65* (New York: Charles Scribner's Sons, 1885), 55; Benson J. Lossing, *A History of the Civil War* (New York: War Memorial Association, 1912), 374.

4. Sean Patrick Adams, *Iron from the Wilderness: The History of Virginia's Catharine Furnace* (Washington, DC: National Park Service, 2011); Noel Harrison memo quoted in John Hennessy, "The Origins of the Wilderness: Part I—The Soil," July 15, 2010, *Mysteries & Conundrums: Exploring the Civil War–Era Landscape in the Fredericksburg & Spotsylvania Region,* https://npsfrsp.wordpress.com/2010/07/15/the-origins-of-the-wilderness-part-i-the-soil/ (accessed Sept. 26, 2016); Hennessy, "Wilderness Origins Part II: Clear-Cutting (or Not)," July 16, 2010, *Mysteries & Conundrums,* https://npsfrsp.wordpress.com/2010/07/16/wilderness-origins-part-ii-clear-cutting-or-not/ (accessed Sept. 26, 2016).

5. Albert J. Reid Diary, Dec. 1, 1863, Fredericksburg and Spotsylvania National Military Park, Fredericksburg, VA (hereafter cited as FSNMP), Bound Volume 284; "From the Army," *Brockport (NY) Republic,* June 16, 1864; William H. Randall Reminiscences, May 7, 1864, Michigan Historical Collections, University of Michigan, Bentley Historical Library, Ann Arbor; Edwin Groff to parents, May 20, 1864, FSNMP, Bound Volume 362.

6. Charles Trueheart and Henry Trueheart, *Rebel Brothers: The Civil War Letters of the Truehearts,* ed. Edward B. Williams (College Station: Texas A&M University Press, 1995), 90, 94; "Battle of the Wilderness," *Daily Constitutionalist* (Augusta, GA), May 31, 1864; Alexander Boteler Diary, May 4, 1864, William Elizabeth Brooks Collection, Library of Congress, Washington, DC.

7. I adopted this term from John Hennessy. See Hennessy, "Wilderness Origins Part II."

8. Wilbur Fisk, *Hard Marching Every Day: The Civil War Letters of Private Wilbur Fisk, 1861–1865,* ed. Emil Rosenblatt and Ruth Rosenblatt (Lawrence: University Press of Kansas, 1983), 166; Theodore Lyman, *Meade's Headquarters, 1863–1865: Letters of Colonel Theodore Lyman from the Wilderness to Appomattox,* ed. George R. Agassiz (Boston: Atlantic Monthly Press, 1922), 89.

9. Milton Myers Diary, May 6, 1864, FSNMP, Bound Volume 153; John R. Adams, *Memorial and Letters of Rev. John R. Adams, D.D., Chaplain of the Fifth Maine and One Hundred and Twenty-First New York Regiments during the War of the Rebellion, Serving from the Beginning to Its Close* (Cambridge, MA: University Press, Privately Printed, 1890), 149, 151; "Report of the Operations of the 5th Corps, A. P. in Genl. Grant's Campaign from Culpeper to Petersburg as Seen by W. A. Roebling, Maj. & A.D.C. 1864," May 5, 1864, Box 24, Vol. 7B, Gouverneur Kemble Warren Papers (SC 10668), New York State Library, Albany; Lewis Leon, *Diary of a Tar Heel Confederate Soldier* (Charlotte, NC: Stone, 1913), 60; Daniel M. Holt, *A Surgeon's Civil War: The Letters and Diary of Daniel M. Holt, M.D.*, ed. James M. Greiner, Janet L. Coryell, and James R. Smither (Kent, OH: Kent State University Press, 1994), 182–83.

10. Philip H. Powers to his wife, May 5 1864, FSNMP, Bound Volume 245; "Chaplain Stewarts Letter," *American Presbyterian* (Philadelphia), May 19, 1864; Daniel Handy to his wife, May 13, 1864, FSNMP, Bound Volume 119; "Letter from Chaplain Perkins," *Boston Recorder*, May 27, 1864; "From General Lee's Army," *Daily South Carolinian* (Columbia), May 28, 1864.

11. Fisk, *Hard Marching Every Day*, 166; Boteler Diary, May 5, 1864, Brooks Collection, Library of Congress; Alpheus S. Williams, *From the Cannon's Mouth: The Civil War Letters of General Alpheus S. Williams*, ed. Milo M. Quaife (Detroit: Wayne State University Press, 1959), 184.

12. Jerome N. Bonaparte Jr., "Journey to the Springs, 1846," ed. William D. Hoyt, *Virginia Magazine of History and Biography* 54, no. 2 (Apr. 1946): 121; Ralph Happel, "The Chancellors of Chancellorsville," *Virginia Magazine of History and Biography* 71, no. 3 (July 1963): 259.

13. Bonaparte, "Journey to the Springs, 1846," 121; Williams, *From the Cannon's Mouth*, 184; Charles Harvey Brewster, *When This Cruel War Is Over: The Civil War Letters of Charles Harvey Brewster*, ed. David W. Blight (Amherst: University of Massachusetts Press, 1992), 269; Lemuel Jeffries, "'The Excitement Had Begun!' The Civil War Diary of Lemuel Jeffries, 1862–1863," ed. Jason H. Silverman, *Manuscripts* 30 (Fall 1978): 272.

14. Lyman, *Meade's Headquarters*, 53, 58; Happel, "Chancellors of Chancellorsville," 261; Theodore Lyman, *Meade's Army: The Private Notebooks of Lt. Col. Theodore Lyman*, ed. David W. Lowe (Kent, OH: Kent State University Press, 2007), 76.

15. Happel, "Chancellors of Chancellorsville," 261; Williams, *From the Cannon's Mouth*, 184; Lyman, *Meade's Army*, 76; "Battle of the Wilderness," *Daily Constitutionalist* (Augusta, GA), May 31, 1864; Myers Diary, May 6, 1864, FSNMP; Thomas H. Mann, *Fighting with the Eighteenth Massachusetts: The Civil War Memoir of Thomas H. Mann*, ed. John J. Hennessy (Baton Rouge: Louisiana State University Press, 2000), 247. For a discussion of the nature of plank roads, their rise in popularity, and their fall from favor, see Daniel B. Klein and John Majewski, "Plank Road Fever in Antebellum America: New York State Origins," *New York History* 75, no. 1 (Jan. 1994): 42, 45, 62–63.

16. Swinton, *Campaigns of the Army of the Potomac,* 428; Badeau, *Military History of Ulysses S. Grant,* 2:105.

17. Morris Schaff, *The Battle of the Wilderness* (Boston: Houghton Mifflin, 1910), 57–62; George T. Stevens, *Three Years in the Sixth Corps* (New York: D. Van Nostrand, 1870), 308.

18. Francis A. Walker, *History of the Second Army Corps in the Army of the Potomac* (New York: Charles Scribner's Sons, 1887), 409; Humphreys, *Virginia Campaign,* 55n, 56; Sartell Prentice, "The Opening Hours in the Wilderness in 1864," in *Military Essays and Recollections: Papers Read before the Commandery of the State of Illinois, Military Order of the Loyal Legion of the United States,* vol. 2 (Chicago: A. C. McClurg, 1894), 102; Schaff, *Battle of the Wilderness,* 58.

19. Gordon C. Rhea, *The Battle of the Wilderness, May 5–6, 1864* (Baton Rouge: Louisiana State University Press, 1994), 27, 51.

20. Lyman, *Meade's Headquarters,* 89; Swinton, *Campaigns of the Army of the Potomac,* 417.

21. Lyman, *Meade's Headquarters,* 53; US War Department, *The War of the Rebellion: A Compilation of the Official Records of the Union and Confederate Armies,* 127 vols., index, and atlas (Washington, DC: Government Printing Office, 1880–1901), ser. 1, 25(1):197 (hereafter cited as *OR*).

22. Jacob Nathaniel Raymer, *Confederate Correspondent: The Civil War Reports of Jacob Nathaniel Raymer, Fourth North Carolina,* ed. E. B. Munson (Jefferson, NC: McFarland, 2008), 127; Myers Diary, May 6, 1864, FSNMP.

23. Edward Porter Alexander, *Military Memoirs of a Confederate* (New York: Charles Scribner's Sons, 1907), 325; Holman S. Melcher, "An Experience in the Battle of the Wilderness," in *War Papers, Read before the Commandery of the State of Maine, Military Order of the Loyal Legion of the United States,* vol. 1 (Portland, ME: Thurston Print, 1898), 73; Sears, *Chancellorsville,* 193; Daniel E. Sutherland, *Fredericksburg and Chancellorsville: The Dare Mark Campaign* (Lincoln: University of Nebraska Press, 1998), 141. My estimate is based on the following boundaries: the Rapidan on the north, Spotsylvania on the south, Mine Run to the west, and Mott's Run on the east. This measures roughly 12 miles north to south and 14 miles east to west. The low estimate of 132 square miles is based on an elliptical model, while 156 square miles is based on a rectangular one.

24. Avery O. Craven, *Soil Exhaustion as a Factor in the Agricultural History of Virginia and Maryland, 1606–1860* (Urbana: University of Illinois Press, 1925), 30; Adams, *Iron from the Wilderness,* 8.

25. Craven, *Soil Exhaustion,* 32–36.

26. William Byrd, "A Progress to the Mines in the Year 1732," in *The Westover Manuscripts: Containing the History of the Dividing Line Betwixt Virginia and North Carolina; A Journey to the Land of Eden, A.D. 1733; and A Progress to the Mines. Written from 1728 to 1736, and Now First Published* (Petersburg, VA: Edmund and Julian C.

Ruffin, 1841), available online at Documenting the American South, http://docsouth.unc.edu/nc/byrd/byrd.html (accessed Oct. 19, 2016), 132, 137; Frederick Law Olmsted, *A Journey in the Seaboard Slave States in the Years 1853–1854, with Remarks on Their Economy,* 2 vols. (New York: G. P. Putnam's Sons, 1904), 2:18, 72.

27. J. T. Trowbridge, *The South: A Tour of Its Battle-Fields and Ruined Cities, a Journey through the Desolated States, and Talks with the People* (Hartford, CT: L. Stebbins, 1866), 225; Robert Somers, *The Southern States since the War, 1870–1871* (New York: Macmillan, 1871), 11.

28. *OR* 25(1):196; AEOF to unknown, May 15, 1864, FSNMP, Bound Volume 325.

29. *OR* 36(1):77, 83; Lyman, *Meade's Headquarters,* 252; Ulysses S. Grant, *The Personal Memoirs of U. S. Grant,* 2 vols. (New York: Charles L. Webster, 1886), 2:178.

30. For more on how Union soldiers interpreted the Virginia landscape, see Reid Mitchell, *Civil War Soldiers* (New York: Viking, 1988), 95, 102.

31. Fisk, *Hard Marching Every Day,* 166; "Notes from the Battle-Field . . . ," *Xenia (OH) Torchlight,* June 1, 1864; "From General Lee's Army," *Daily South Carolinian* (Columbia), May 28, 1864.

32. Edwin C. Mason, "Recollections of the Mine Run Campaign," in *Glimpses of the Nation's Struggle: A Series of Papers Read before the Minnesota Commandery of the Military Order of the Loyal Legion of the United States,* vol. 1 (St. Paul: St. Paul Book and Stationary, 1897), 321; Prentice, "Opening Hours in the Wilderness," 102; "Getty's Hard Fight," *Philadelphia Weekly Times,* Oct. 15, 1881; Norton C. Shepard, *Out of the Wilderness: The Civil War Memoir of Cpl. Norton C. Shepard, 146th New York Volunteer Infantry,* ed. Raymond W. Smith (Hamilton, NY: Edmonston, 1998), 2; William P. Hopkins, *The Seventh Regiment Rhode Island Volunteers in the Civil War, 1862–1865* (Providence, RI: Snow & Farnham, 1903), 166.

33. Adams, *Iron from the Wilderness,* 1, 3, 9–11, 13–14, 46; Byrd, "Progress to the Mines," 132–33.

34. "Chaplain Stewarts Letter," *American Presbyterian* (Philadelphia), May 19, 1864; Swinton, *Campaigns of the Army of the Potomac,* 428–29; Schaff, *Battle of the Wilderness,* 62.

35. Sears, *Chancellorsville,* 193; Rhea, *Battle of the Wilderness,* 51; Aaron Sachs, "Stumps in the Wilderness," in *The Blue, the Gray, and the Green: Toward an Environmental History of the Civil War,* ed. Brian Allen Drake (Athens: University of Georgia Press, 2015), 100–101.

36. Hennessy, "Origins of the Wilderness: Part I"; Hennessy, "Wilderness Origins Part II"; Adams, *Iron from the Wilderness,* 40, 46–47; Sears, *Chancellorsville,* 193; Sutherland, *Fredericksburg and Chancellorsville,* 141.

37. Happel, "Chancellors of Chancellorsville," 263; Edward Perkins Preble Diary, Dec. 1, 1863, FSNMP, Bound Volume 34; William D. Landon, "Fourteenth Indiana Regiment, Letters to the Vincennes Western Sun," *Indiana Magazine of History* 34

(Mar. 1938): 77; Mann, *Fighting with the Eighteenth Massachusetts,* 247; "Army of the Potomac," *Mohawk Valley Register* (Fort Plain, NY), Dec. 17, 1863; "The 13th Regiment on the March," *Boston Evening Transcript,* Jan. 4, 1864.

38. Hennessy, "Wilderness Origins Part II."

39. Hennessy, "Wilderness Origins Part II."

40. McHenry Howard, "Notes and Recollections of Opening of the Campaign of 1864," in *Papers of the Military Historical Society of Massachusetts,* vol. 4 (Boston: Military Historical Society of Massachusetts, 1905), 97.

2. BATTLE IN THE WILDERNESS

1. William Swinton, *Campaigns of the Army of the Potomac* (New York: Charles B. Richardson, 1866), 438; Regis de Trobriand, *Four Years with the Army of the Potomac,* trans. George K. Dauchy (Boston: Ticknor, 1889), 571; Horace Porter, *Campaigning with Grant* (New York: Century, 1897), 72; Andrew A. Humphreys, *The Virginia Campaign of '64 and '65* (New York: Charles Scribner's Sons, 1885), 55; Fitzhugh Lee, *General Lee* (New York: Appleton, 1894), 333; Bruce Catton, *A Stillness at Appomattox* (Garden City, NY: Doubleday, 1953), 55–92. For an earlier version of Swinton's claim, see "The Great Campaign," *New York Times,* May 13, 1864.

2. Earl J. Hess, *Civil War Infantry Tactics: Training, Combat, and Small-Unit Effectiveness* (Baton Rouge: Louisiana State University Press, 2015), 89.

3. Swinton, *Campaigns of the Army of the Potomac,* 428–29; Humphreys, *Virginia Campaign,* 10–11; Robert Stiles, *Four Years under Marse Robert* (New York: Neale, 1904), 244.

4. J. F. J. Caldwell, *The History of a Brigade of South Carolinians, First Known as Gregg's, and Subsequently as McGowan's Brigade* (Philadelphia: King & Baird, 1866), 128, 131; G. Moxley Sorrel, *Recollections of a Confederate Staff Officer* (New York: Neale, 1905), 233; Francis A. Walker, *History of the Second Army Corps in the Army of the Potomac* (New York: Charles Scribner's Sons, 1887), 422.

5. William H. Powell, *The Fifth Army Corps* (New York: G. P. Putnam's Sons, 1896), 610; Hazard Stevens, "The Sixth Corps in the Wilderness," in *Papers of the Military Historical Society of Massachusetts,* vol. 4 (Boston: Military Historical Society of Massachusetts, 1905), 188; Porter, *Campaigning with Grant,* 72; Humphreys, *Virginia Campaign,* 55; Evander M. Law, "From the Wilderness to Cold Harbor," in *Battles and Leaders of the Civil War,* ed. Robert Underwood Johnson and Clarence Clough Buel, vol. 4 (New York: Century, 1884), 122.

6. Trobriand, *Four Years with the Army of the Potomac,* 571; Stevens, "Sixth Corps in the Wilderness," 192.

7. Gordon C. Rhea, *The Battle of the Wilderness, May 5–6, 1864* (Baton Rouge: Louisiana State University Press, 1994), 435, 440; Frank Wilkeson, *Recollections of a Private Soldier in the Army of the Potomac* (New York: G. P. Putnam's Sons, 1887), 60–61; Wil-

son W. Fay to Mrs. Griswold, Jan. 20, 1866, in Anna Griswold, *Col. Griswold* (Boston, 1867), 23; Andrew J. McBride to unknown, May 6, 1864, Andrew J. McBride Papers, Duke University, David M. Rubenstein Rare Book & Manuscript Library, Durham, NC; Isaac O. Best, "Through the Wilderness with Grant," James S. Schoff Civil War Collection, University of Michigan, William L. Clements Library, Ann Arbor.

8. Charles Trueheart and Henry Trueheart, *Rebel Brothers: The Civil War Letters of the Truehearts,* ed. Edward B. Williams (College Station: Texas A&M University Press, 1995), 94; "From the Army," *Brockport (NY) Republic,* June 16, 1864; "Grant's Virginia Campaign," *Columbia Democrat* (Bloomsburg, PA), June 18, 1864; Frederic Swift Diary, May 7, 1864, Coco Collection, US Army Heritage and Education Center, Carlisle Barracks, PA.

9. Alexander McNeil, a soldier in the 2nd South Carolina, wrote in late April 1864 that the "vegetation is just beginning to put forth, the trees are budding and in a few weeks everything will be clothed in green." He added that "last year at this season the woods were much greener than now." This suggests that at Chancellorsville the foliage might have been more mature than at the Battle of the Wilderness, which does not seem to match the fact that visibility was worse at the latter. Acknowledging variations in the density of vegetation helps resolve this issue. Alexander McNeil to his wife, Apr. 30, 1864, Fredericksburg and Spotsylvania National Military Park, Fredericksburg, VA, Bound Volume 242.

10. US War Department, *The War of the Rebellion: A Compilation of the Official Records of the Union and Confederate Armies,* 127 vols., index, and atlas (Washington, DC: Government Printing Office, 1880–1901), ser. 1, 25(1):651 (hereafter cited as *OR*).

11. *OR* 25(1):630.

12. *OR* 25(1):821, 998–99; "Gen. Doles' Brigade in the Chancellorsville Battle," *Chronicle and Sentinel* (Augusta, GA), June 6, 1863.

13. *OR* 25(1):941, 1004.

14. *OR* 25(1):1004–5.

15. *OR* 25(1):894, 986, 990.

16. *OR* 25(1):942.

17. *OR* 25(1):799–800, 902.

18. *OR* 25(1):871–72.

19. *OR* 25(1):954; C. W. Baker to his sister-in-law, May 14, 1863, in *Union (NY) News,* June 4, 1863; "From the Eleventh Regiment," *Centinel of Freedom* (Newark, NJ), May 26, 1863.

20. *OR* 25(1):943.

21. "Correspondence of the Register," *Mohawk Valley Register* (Fort Plains, NY), May 21, 1863; "Letter from Battery E.," *Providence (RI) Evening Press,* May 16, 1863; "A Full and Complete Description of the Battle of the Wilderness, Chancellorsville, Va.," *Chronicle and Sentinel* (Augusta, GA), May 26, 1863; Jacob Nathaniel Raymer, *Confederate Correspondent: The Civil War Reports of Jacob Nathaniel Raymer, Fourth North Carolina,* ed. E. B. Munson (Jefferson, NC: McFarland, 2008), 68.

22. Noah Collins Diary, May 3, 1863, Isaac S. London Collection, North Carolina State Archives, Raleigh.

23. *OR* 25(1):823; Robert McAllister, *The Civil War Letters of General Robert McAllister.* ed. James I. Robertson Jr. (New Brunswick, NJ: Rutgers University Press, 1965), 307; Alpheus S. Williams, *From the Cannon's Mouth: The Civil War Letters of General Alpheus S. Williams,* ed. Milo M. Quaife (Detroit: Wayne State University Press, 1959), 198.

24. Stephen W. Sears, *Chancellorsville* (Boston: Houghton Mifflin, 1996), 475–501. These figures exclude the units that only participated at the fighting at Fredericksburg. For units that fought in the Wilderness around Chancellorsville on May 1–3 and at Salem Church on May 3–4, 1863, it was impossible to distinguish how many casualties were suffered at any particular stage of the fighting, thus no attempt was made to do so.

25. McAllister, *Civil War Letters,* 302; Raymer, *Confederate Correspondent,* 67; Jedediah Hotchkiss, *Make Me a Map of the Valley: The Civil War Journal of Stonewall Jackson's Topographer,* ed. Archie P. McDonald (Dallas: Southern Methodist University Press, 1973), 140; Aaron L. DeArmond to his wife, May 7, 1863, Aaron L. DeArmond Letters, Civil War Documents Collection, US Army Heritage and Education Center, Carlisle Barracks, PA; Charles T. Bowen, *Dear Friends at Home: The Civil War Letters and Diaries of Sergeant Charles T. Bowen,* ed. Edward K. Cassedy (Baltimore: Butternut & Blue, 2001), 257.

26. *OR* 30(1):249; Henry Fales, *History of the Thirty-Eighth Regiment Indiana Volunteer Infantry* (Palo Alto, CA: F. A. Stuart, 1906), 90–91; Archer Anderson, *The Campaign and Battle of Chickamauga, an Address delivered before the Virginia Division of the Army of Northern Virginia Association, at Their Annual Meeting, in the Capitol at Richmond, Va., October 25, 1881* (Richmond: William Ellis Jones Steam Book and Job Printer, 1881), 22; Williams, *From the Cannon's Mouth,* 305.

27. Historians of Chickamauga have long recognized the less-than-ideal conditions that prevailed at that battlefield but have never claimed that these were unique. Instead, their comments have focused on the confusing nature of the fighting, the lack of visibility, and the inability of field officers to effectively control their troops. See John B. Turchin, *Chickamauga* (Chicago: Fergus Printing, 1888), 95; Glenn Tucker, *Chickamauga: Bloody Battle in the West* (Dayton, OH: Bobbs-Merrill, 1961), 8, 123–24; Peter Cozzens, *This Terrible Sound: The Battle of Chickamauga* (Urbana: University of Illinois Press, 1992), 90–91; Steven E. Woodworth, *Six Armies in Tennessee: The Chickamauga and Chattanooga Campaigns* (Lincoln: University of Nebraska Press, 1998), 86–87; and Earl J. Hess, *The Civil War in the West: Victory and Defeat from the Appalachians to the Mississippi* (Chapel Hill: University of North Carolina Press, 2012), 190–91.

28. Anderson, *Campaign and Battle of Chickamauga,* 27; J. B. Polley, *Hood's Texas Brigade: Its Marches, Its Battles, Its Achievements* (New York: Neale, 1910), 209; *OR* 30(2):370; N. J. Hampton, *An Eyewitness to the Dark Days of 1861–65* (Nashville, 1898), 31.

29. Arba N. Waterman, "The Battle of Chickamauga," in *Military Essays and Recollections: Papers Read before the Commandery of the State of Illinois, Military Order*

of the Loyal Legion of the United States, vol. 1 (Chicago: A. C. McClurg, 1891), 236; *OR* 30(1):335, 691; Fales, *History of the Thirty-Eighth Regiment,* 90. See Fales for the final quotation in the paragraph.

30. James Longstreet, *From Manassas to Appomattox: Memoirs of the Civil War in America* (Philadelphia: J. B. Lippincott, 1896), 449; Polley, *Hood's Texas Brigade,* 205.

31. Anderson, *Campaign and Battle of Chickamauga,* 27–28; Richard W. Johnson, *A Soldier's Reminiscences in Peace and War* (Philadelphia: J. R. Lippincott, 1886), 230; Waterman, "Battle of Chickamauga," 241.

32. Lyman G. Bennett and William M. Haigh, *History of the Thirty-Sixth Regiment Illinois Volunteers* (Aurora, IL: Knickerbocker & Hodder, 1876), 459; Johnson, *Soldier's Reminiscences,* 231; *OR* 30(1):691.

33. Fales, *History of the Thirty-Eighth Regiment,* 89; Bennett and Haigh, *History of the Thirty-Sixth Regiment,* 459; *OR* 30(1):279; Williams, *From the Cannon's Mouth,* 305.

34. Albion Winegar Tourgée, *The Story of a Thousand* (Buffalo, NY: S. McGerald & Son, 1896), 218–19; R. T. Coles, *From Huntsville to Appomattox: R. T. Coles's History of 4th Regiment, Alabama Volunteer Infantry, C.S.A., Army of Northern Virginia,* ed. Jeffrey D. Stocker (Knoxville: University of Tennessee Press, 1996), 135.

35. Longstreet, *From Manassas to Appomattox,* 440; *OR* 30(1):330, 693, 696.

36. *OR* 30(1):275, 426, 839.

37. *OR* 30(1):227, 713.

38. Coles, *From Huntsville to Appomattox,* 135; L. W. Day, *Story of the One Hundred and First Ohio Infantry: A Memorial Volume* (Cleveland, OH: W. M. Bayne Printing, 1894), 160.

39. Isaac Henry Clay Royse, *History of the 115th Regiment Illinois Volunteer Infantry* (Terre Haute, IN, 1900), 113, 115; Daniel H. Hill, "Chickamauga—The Great Battle of the West," in *Battles and Leaders of the Civil War,* ed. Robert Underwood Johnson and Clarence Clough Buel, vol. 3 (New York: Century, 1884), 654n.

40. Johnson, *Soldier's Reminiscences,* 230; Cozzens, *This Terrible Sound,* 534.

41. Quoted in Earl J. Hess, *The Union Soldier in Battle: Enduring the Ordeal of Combat* (Lawrence: University Press of Kansas, 1997), 49.

42. Fales, *History of the Thirty-Eighth Regiment,* 90; Williams, *From the Cannon's Mouth,* 305.

43. *OR* 30(1):876; Bennett and Haigh, *History of the Thirty-Sixth Regiment,* 469; Hampton, *Eyewitness to the Dark Days,* 34.

44. *OR* 30(2):418; Fales, *History of the Thirty-Eighth Regiment,* 93.

45. Theodore Lyman, *Meade's Headquarters, 1863–1865: Letters of Colonel Theodore Lyman from the Wilderness to Appomattox,* ed. George R. Agassiz (Boston: Atlantic Monthly Press, 1922), 173.

46. John Henry Otto, *Memoirs of a Dutch Mudsill: The "War Memories" of John Henry Otto, Captain, Company D, 21st Regiment Wisconsin Volunteer Infantry,* ed. David Gould and James B. Kennedy (Kent, OH: Kent State University Press, 2004), 371–72.

3. THE WILDERNESS MYSTIQUE

1. Roderick Frazier Nash, *Wilderness and the American Mind* (New Haven, CT: Yale University Press, 1967), 1–2.

2. Robert McAllister, *The Civil War Letters of General Robert McAllister*. ed. James I. Robertson Jr. (New Brunswick, NJ: Rutgers University Press, 1965), 372; Daniel Handy to his wife, May 13, 1864, Fredericksburg and Spotsylvania National Military Park, Fredericksburg, VA (hereafter cited as FSNMP), Bound Volume 119; Wilbur Fisk, *Hard Marching Every Day: The Civil War Letters of Private Wilbur Fisk, 1861–1865*, ed. Emil Rosenblatt and Ruth Rosenblatt (Lawrence: University Press of Kansas, 1983), 166; Philip H. Powers to his wife, May 5 1864, FSNMP, Bound Volume 245.

3. Nash, *Wilderness and the American Mind*, 28; A. M. Stewart, *Camp, March, and Battle-Field; or, Three Years and a Half with the Army of the Potomac* (Philadelphia: Jas. B. Rodgers, 1865), 380; Orlando B. Wilcox, *Forgotten Valor: The Memoirs, Journals, and Civil War Letters of Orlando B. Wilcox*, ed. Robert Garth Scott (Kent, OH: Kent State University Press, 1999), 511; Fitzhugh Lee, *General Lee* (New York: Appleton, 1894), 333; "The Wilderness: A Chapter in the History of the Second Day's Battle," *Cincinnati (OH) Commercial*, Sept. 24, 1881.

4. William Swinton, *Campaigns of the Army of the Potomac* (New York: Charles B. Richardson, 1866), 418, 429; Mason Whiting Tyler, *Recollections of the Civil War*, ed. William S. Tyler (New York: G. P. Putnam's Sons, 1912), 140.

5. Alpheus S. Williams, *From the Cannon's Mouth: The Civil War Letters of General Alpheus S. Williams*, ed. Milo M. Quaife (Detroit: Wayne State University Press, 1959), 186, 189, 197–98; Jacob Nathaniel Raymer, *Confederate Correspondent: The Civil War Reports of Jacob Nathaniel Raymer, Fourth North Carolina*, ed. E. B. Munson (Jefferson, NC: McFarland, 2008), 68; John Garibaldi to his wife Sarah, May 11, 1863, Virginia Military Institute Archives, Lexington; "Gen. Doles' Brigade in the Chancellorsville Battle," *Chronicle and Sentinel* (Augusta, GA), June 6, 1863; Lemuel Jeffries, "'The Excitement Had Begun!' The Civil War Diary of Lemuel Jeffries, 1862–1863," ed. Jason H. Silverman, *Manuscripts* 30 (Fall 1978): 272.

6. See US War Department, *The War of the Rebellion: A Compilation of the Official Records of the Union and Confederate Armies*, 127 vols., index, and atlas (Washington, DC: Government Printing Office, 1880–1901), ser. 1, 25(1):193, 196–97, 311, 315, 385, 386, 390, 394, 670 (hereafter cited as *OR*).

7. *OR* 25(1):888; Warren B. Persons to Daniel Dodge Persons, May 30, 1863, FSNMP, Bound Volume 147; *Mobile (AL) Advertiser & Register*, May 24, 1863.

8. *OR* 25(1):196–97.

9. "The 13th Regiment on the March," *Boston Evening Transcript*, Jan. 4, 1864; "Letter from the Potomac Army," *Columbia Democrat* (Bloomsburg, PA), Dec. 12, 1863; "Over the Rapidan," *Providence (RI) Evening Press*, Dec. 17, 1863.

10. *OR* 29(1):827; Oscar Hinrichs, *Stonewall's Prussian Mapmaker: The Journals of Captain Oscar Hinrichs,* ed. Richard Brady Williams (Chapel Hill: University of North Carolina Press, 2014), 98.

11. *OR* 29(1):900; Charles Frederic Bahnson, *Bright and Gloomy Days: The Civil War Correspondence of Captain Charles Frederic Bahnson, a Moravian Confederate,* ed. Sarah Bahnson Chapman (Knoxville: University of Tennessee Press, 2003), 97.

12. *OR* 29(1):847.

13. Edwin Groff to parents, May 20, 1864, FSNMP, Bound Volume 362; Henry Keiser Diary, May 5, 1864, FSNMP, Bound Volume 41; Daniel M. Holt, *A Surgeon's Civil War: The Letters and Diary of Daniel M. Holt, M.D.,* ed. James M. Greiner, Janet L. Coryell, and James R. Smither (Kent, OH: Kent State University Press, 1994), 182–83; Fisk, *Hard Marching Every Day,* 215; "From the 140th Regiment," *Washington (PA) Reporter,* June 1, 1864.

14. Charles Trueheart and Henry Trueheart, *Rebel Brothers: The Civil War Letters of the Truehearts,* ed. Edward B. Williams (College Station: Texas A&M University Press, 1995), 90; Raymer, *Confederate Correspondent,* 127; Alexander Boteler Diary, May 4, 1864, William Elizabeth Brooks Collection, Library of Congress, Washington, DC.

15. Fisk, *Hard Marching Every Day,* 215.

16. Norton C. Shepard, *Out of the Wilderness: The Civil War Memoir of Cpl. Norton C. Shepard, 146th New York Volunteer Infantry,* ed. Raymond W. Smith (Hamilton, NY: Edmonston, 1998), 2. For more on the reaction of Union soldiers to the southern landscape, see Reid Mitchell, *Civil War Soldiers* (New York: Viking, 1988), 95, 97, 98, 102.

17. See Carol Reardon, "Writing Battle History: The Challenge of Memory," *Civil War History* 53, no. 3 (Sept. 2007): 254–55; "Battle of the Wilderness," *Daily Dispatch* (Richmond, VA), May 13, 1863; "Gen. Meade's Army," *New York Times,* Nov. 30, 1863; "The Armies in Virginia," *New York Times,* Dec. 2 1863. For another Confederate example, see "The Battles on the Rappahannock," *Charleston (SC) Mercury,* May 13, 1863.

18. St. George Tucker Coalter Bryan, "Recollections of Experience in the Confederate Army in Virginia, 1861–1865," Mss5:1B8407:1, Virginia Historical Society, Richmond; Hazard Stevens, "The Sixth Corps in the Wilderness," in *Papers of the Military Historical Society of Massachusetts,* vol. 4 (Boston: Military Historical Society of Massachusetts, 1905), 187; Thomas W. Hyde, *Following the Greek Cross; or, Memories of the Sixth Army Corps* (Boston: Houghton, Mifflin, 1894), 185; *History of the Corn Exchange Regiment, 118th Pennsylvania Volunteers* (Philadelphia: J. L. Smith, 1888), 397.

19. Sartell Prentice, "The Opening Hours in the Wilderness in 1864," in *Military Essays and Recollections: Papers Read before the Commandery of the State of Illinois, Military Order of the Loyal Legion of the United States,* vol. 2 (Chicago: A. C. McClurg, 1894), 102; Mary Genevie Green Brainard, *Campaigns of the One Hundred and Forty-Sixth Regiment, New York State Volunteers* (New York: G. P. Putnam's Sons, 1915), 176; Morris Schaff, *The Battle of the Wilderness* (Boston: Houghton Mifflin, 1910), 58, 62, 110.

20. John D. Wells, "The Scars of War: Battlefields of Northern Virginia Forty-Five Years After," *Metropolitan Magazine* 25, no. 5 (Feb. 1907): 547; Howard R. Bayne and Peyton H. Hoge, *The Travels of Ego and Alter, an Epistolary Narrative of a Tramp through the Old Dominion* (Richmond, VA: West, Johnston, 1879), 9–10.

21. Bruce Catton, *A Stillness at Appomattox* (Garden City, NY: Doubleday, 1953), 56; Edward Steere, *The Wilderness Campaign: The Meeting of Grant and Lee* (Mechanicsburg, PA: Stackpole Books, 1960), 1; James M. McPherson, *Battle Cry of Freedom: The Civil War Era* (New York: Oxford University Press, 1988), 724; Mark Grimsley, *And Keep Moving On: The Virginia Campaign, May–June 1864* (Lincoln: University of Nebraska Press, 2002), 34.

22. For a wider discussion on the role that death played in Civil War America, see Drew Gilpin Faust, *This Republic of Suffering: Death and the American Civil War* (New York: Alfred A. Knopf, 2008); and Mark Schantz, *Awaiting the Heavenly Country: The Civil War and America's Culture of Death* (Ithaca, NY: Cornell University Press, 2008).

23. William D. Landon, "Fourteenth Indiana Regiment, Letters to the Vincennes Western Sun," *Indiana Magazine of History* 34 (Mar. 1938): 92; Cornelius Moore to Adeline, May 13, 1864, FSNMP, Bound Volume 147; Albert J. Reid Diary, May 8, 1864, FSNMP, Bound Volume 284; "Grant's Virginia Campaign," *Columbia Democrat* (Bloomsburg, PA), June 18, 1864; for "covered with" quotation from the 86th New York, see William Owen Diary, May 6, 1864, FSNMP, Bound Volume 318; for the longer quotations from the 86th New York, beginning with "slept among" and "the scenes," see "From the 86th Regiment," *Corning (NY) Journal*, May 19, 1864.

24. Orin G. Dority, "The Civil War Diary of Orin G. Dority," pt. 1, *Northwest Ohio Quarterly* 37, no. 1 (Winter 1964–65): 26; Cornelius Moore to Adeline, May 13, 1864, FSNMP, Bound Volume 147; Landon, "Fourteenth Indiana Regiment," 89; Charles Harvey Brewster, *When This Cruel War Is Over: The Civil War Letters of Charles Harvey Brewster*, ed. David W. Blight (Amherst: University of Massachusetts Press, 1992), 295.

25. Andrew J. McBride to unknown, May 6, 1864, Andrew J. McBride Papers, Duke University, David M. Rubenstein Rare Book & Manuscript Library, Durham, NC; "From the Army," *Brockport (NY) Republic*, June 16, 1864; Fisk, *Hard Marching Every Day*, 215–16; J. B. Polley, *A Soldier's Letters to Charming Nellie* (New York: Neale, 1908), 233; Theodore Lyman, *Meade's Headquarters, 1863–1865: Letters of Colonel Theodore Lyman from the Wilderness to Appomattox*, ed. George R. Agassiz (Boston: Atlantic Monthly Press, 1922), 92.

26. Landon, "Fourteenth Indiana Regiment," 90, 92–93; Fisk, *Hard Marching Every Day*, 215; John W. Roberts, "The Wilderness and Spotsylvania, May 4–12, 1864: Narrative of a Private Soldier, John W. Roberts." ed. Albert Hubbard Roberts, *Florida Historical Society Quarterly* 11 (Oct. 1932): 61; Raymer, *Confederate Correspondent*, 128.

27. Brewster, *When This Cruel War Is Over*, 295; "The Dead in the Wilderness," *Corning (NY) Journal*, July 21, 1864; "The Wounded in the Wilderness," *Boston Daily Advertiser*, June 22, 1864.

28. J. T. Trowbridge, *The South: A Tour of Its Battle-Fields and Ruined Cities, a Journey through the Desolated States, and Talks with the People* (Hartford, CT: L. Stebbins, 1866), 126; Faust, *This Republic of Suffering,* 213–19. For a more in-depth discussion of burial practices during the Civil War, see ibid., 61–81.

29. James M. Moore, report, July 3, 1865, in *Names of Officers and Soldiers Found on the Battle-fields of the Wilderness and Spottsylvania Court House, VA.* (Washington, DC: Government Printing Office, 1865), v; William D. Landon, "Prock's Last Letters to the Vincennes Western Sun," *Indiana Magazine of History* 35 (Mar. 1939): 77–78, 80–81; "An Ex-Campaigner in Virginia," in *Rifle Shots and Bugle Notes; or, The National Military Album of Sketches of the Principal Battles, Marches, Picket Duty, Camp Fires, Love Adventures, and Poems Connected with the Late War,* ed. Joseph A. Joel and Lewis R. Stegman (New York: Grand Army Gazette Publishing, 1884), 428.

30. Trowbridge, *The South,* 125; David Gregg McIntosh Manuscript, no. 1889, University of North Carolina at Chapel Hill, Southern Historical Collection, Wilson Library, p. 17.

31. Trowbridge, *The South,* 121–22; Theodore Lyman to his wife, Apr. 14, 17, 1866, Microfilm P374, Reel 28, Lyman Family Papers, Massachusetts Historical Society, Boston; "An Ex-Campaigner in Virginia," 428.

32. Swinton, *Campaigns of the Army of the Potomac,* 429; Frank Wilkeson, *Recollections of a Private Soldier in the Army of the Potomac* (New York: G. P. Putnam's Sons, 1887), 49–51; William J. Seymour, *The Civil War Memoirs of Captain William J. Seymour,* ed. Terry L. Jones (Baton Rouge: Louisiana State University Press, 1991), 118; Thomas Chamberlain, *History of the One Hundred and Fiftieth Regiment, Pennsylvania Volunteers, Second Regiment, Bucktail Brigade* (Philadelphia: J. B. Lippincott, 1895), 219.

33. Horace Porter, *Campaigning with Grant* (New York: Century, 1897), 72.

34. John Tiffany to his parents, May 8, 1863, FSNMP, Bound Volume 207; Francis S. Johnson to Emmie, May 9, 1863, University of Georgia, Special Collections, Hargrett Rare Books & Manuscript Library, Athens; McAllister, *Civil War Letters,* 307; Charles S. Wainwright, *A Diary of Battle: The Personal Journals of Colonel Charles S. Wainwright 1861–1865,* ed. Allan Nevins (New York: Harcourt, Brace, & World, 1962), 197.

35. Boteler Diary, May 4, 1864, Brooks Collection, Library of Congress; *Confederate Union* (Milledgeville, GA), June 7, 1864; Landon, "Fourteenth Indiana Regiment," 93.

36. *Confederate Union* (Milledgeville, GA), June 7, 1864; Raymer, *Confederate Correspondent,* 67.

37. George A. Bowen Diary, May 10, 1864, FSNMP, Bound Volume 228; *OR* 36(1):514; Josiah F. Murphey Reminiscences, Ms. "20th" Cab. 6.5, Boston Public Library.

38. Thomas F. Galwey, *The Valiant Hours: An Irishman in the Civil War,* ed. W. S. Nye (Harrisburg, PA: Stackpole, 1961), 200–201; Francis B. Harris Diary, May 6, 1864, FSNMP, Bound Volume 352; "Grant's Virginia Campaign," *Columbia Democrat* (Bloomsburg, PA), June 18, 1864.

39. Wilkeson, *Recollections of a Private,* 50, 66–67.

40. Abner R. Small, *The Road to Richmond: The Civil War Memoirs of Abner R. Small of the 16th Maine Volunteers* (Berkeley: University of California Press, 1939), 133.

41. Joseph R. C. Ward, *History of the 106th Regiment Pennsylvania Volunteers, 2d Brigade, 2d Division, 2d Corps, 1861–1865* (Philadelphia: F. McManus Jr., 1906), 242; Channing M. Smith, "In the Wilderness," *Confederate Veteran* 29, no. 6 (June 1921): 212; Porter, *Campaigning with Grant,* 72–73; Douglas Southall Freeman, *R. E. Lee: A Biography,* 4 vols. (New York: Charles Scribner's Sons, 1935), 3:297; Jeffry D. Wert, *The Sword of Lincoln: The Army of the Potomac* (New York: Simon & Schuster, 2005), 338.

42. Roderick Nash also points out the traditional connection between "wilderness," on the one hand, and the "supernatural and monstrous," on the other. Nash, *Wilderness and the American Mind,* 10.

43. J. E. Curran to unknown, Aug. 17, 1866, FSNMP, Bound Volume 342; Smith, "In the Wilderness," 212; Wells, "Scars of War," 546, 548.

44. Schaff, *Battle of the Wilderness,* 63–64, 108, 121–24, 273–74.

4. THE CONFEDERATE EDGE IN THE WILDERNESS

1. Frank Wilkeson, *Recollections of a Private Soldier in the Army of the Potomac* (New York: G. P. Putnam's Sons, 1887), 49–50.

2. William Swinton, *Campaigns of the Army of the Potomac* (New York: Charles B. Richardson, 1866), 418.

3. Earl J. Hess, *Trench Warfare under Grant & Lee: Field Fortifications in the Overland Campaign* (Chapel Hill: University of North Carolina Press, 2007), 39–41.

4. Swinton, *Campaigns of the Army of the Potomac,* 418; Wilkeson, *Recollections of a Private,* 48; Francis A. Walker, *History of the Second Army Corps in the Army of the Potomac* (New York: Charles Scribner's Sons, 1887), 409; Mary Genevie Green Brainard, *Campaigns of the One Hundred and Forty-Sixth Regiment, New York State Volunteers* (New York: G. P. Putnam's Sons, 1915), 176; Adam Badeau, *Military History of Ulysses S. Grant from April, 1861, to April, 1865,* 3 vols. (New York: D. Appleton, 1881), 2:113.

5. Northern newspaper correspondents often drew this same conclusion. See, for example, "The Great Campaign," *New York Times,* May 13, 1864; "The Great Conflict," *Chicago Tribune,* May 19, 1864; and "The Strategic Points," *Chicago Tribune,* May 24, 1864.

6. Theodore Lyman, *Meade's Headquarters, 1863–1865: Letters of Colonel Theodore Lyman from the Wilderness to Appomattox,* ed. George R. Agassiz (Boston: Atlantic Monthly Press, 1922), 99; A. Jackson Crossley to Sam, May 19, 1864, Fredericksburg and Spotsylvania National Military Park, Fredericksburg, VA (hereafter cited as FSNMP), Bound Volume 264.

7. Evander M. Law, "From the Wilderness to Cold Harbor," in *Battles and Leaders of the Civil War,* ed. Robert Underwood Johnson and Clarence Clough Buel, vol. 4 (New York: Century, 1884), 122; Armistead Long, *Memoirs of Robert E. Lee* (New York: J. M. Stoddart, 1886), 326.

8. Edward P. Alexander, *Fighting for the Confederacy: The Personal Recollections of General Edward Porter Alexander,* ed. Gary W. Gallagher (Chapel Hill: University of North Carolina Press, 1989), 351; Cadmus Wilcox, "Lee and Grant in the Wilderness," in *The Annals of the War Written by Leading Participants North and South* (Philadelphia: Times Publishing, 1879), 500; Andrew A. Humphreys, *The Virginia Campaign of '64 and '65* (New York: Charles Scribner's Sons, 1885), 10.

9. Alexander, *Fighting for the Confederacy,* 350–51.

10. Gordon C. Rhea, *The Battle of the Wilderness, May 5–6, 1864* (Baton Rouge: Louisiana State University Press, 1994), 354. Kershaw's division had missed Mine Run, while Field's division had missed both Chancellorsville and Mine Run. See Andrew A. Humphreys, *From Gettysburg to the Rapidan: The Army of the Potomac July, 1863, to April, 1864* (New York: Charles Scribner's Sons, 1883), chaps. 1, 3. See also the respective orders-of-battle appendices in Stephen W. Sears, *Chancellorsville* (Boston: Houghton Mifflin, 1996), and Rhea, *Battle of the Wilderness.*

11. Rhea, *Battle of the Wilderness,* 7, 34, 354.

12. Rhea, *Battle of the Wilderness,* 22–23. For the number of Virginia units during the Wilderness Campaign, see the Army of Northern Virginia order of battle in ibid., app.

13. Robert E. L. Krick, "Like a Duck on a June Bug: James Longstreet's Flank Attack, May 6, 1864," in *The Wilderness Campaign,* ed. Gary W. Gallagher (Chapel Hill: University of North Carolina Press, 1997), 238, 251–52.

14. Rhea, *Battle of the Wilderness,* 86; James Longstreet, *From Manassas to Appomattox: Memoirs of the Civil War in America* (Philadelphia: J. B. Lippincott, 1896), 557; Theodore Lyman, "Uselessness of the Maps Furnished to Staff of the Army of the Potomac Previous to the Campaign of May 1864," in *Papers of the Military Historical Society of Massachusetts,* vol. 4 (Boston: Military Historical Society of Massachusetts, 1905), 79. During the Mine Run Campaign, Meade employed a local Unionist as a guide, but he appeared to be of little use. See US War Department, *The War of the Rebellion: A Compilation of the Official Records of the Union and Confederate Armies,* 127 vols., index, and atlas (Washington, DC: Government Printing Office, 1880–1901), ser. 1, 29(2):493 (hereafter cited as *OR*). Another Union general apparently used a black man as a guide, also without great success. See ibid., 762.

15. "Letter from Chaplain Perkins," *Boston Recorder,* May 27, 1864; Charles Mills to his mother, May 10, 1864, Coco Collection, US Army Heritage and Education Center, Carlisle Barracks, PA; "Battle of the Wilderness," *Daily Constitutionalist* (Augusta, GA), May 31, 1864; Jacob Nathaniel Raymer, *Confederate Correspondent: The Civil War Reports of Jacob Nathaniel Raymer, Fourth North Carolina,* ed. E. B. Munson (Jefferson, NC: McFarland, 2008), 127; Philip H. Pendleton to his mother, May 5, 1864, Mss2 P3748 c 6–7, Pendleton Family Papers, 1861–64, Virginia Historical Society, Richmond.

16. "Grant's Virginia Campaign," *Columbia Democrat* (Bloomsburg, PA), June 18, 1864.

17. *OR* 36(1):514; Francis B. Harris Diary, May 6, 1864, FSNMP, Bound Volume 352; "Grant's Virginia Campaign," *Columbia Democrat* (Bloomsburg, PA), June 18, 1864.

18. *OR* 36(1):1038–40.

19. Lyman, *Meade's Headquarters,* 55. For other estimates for the length of columns, see Earl J. Hess, *Civil War Infantry Tactics: Training, Combat, and Small-Unit Effectiveness* (Baton Rouge: Louisiana State University Press, 2015), 56–57.

20. For a discussion of the speeds at which a Civil War army column could march, see Hess, *Civil War Infantry Tactics,* 56.

21. Ralph Happel, "The Chancellors of Chancellorsville," *Virginia Magazine of History and Biography* 71, no. 3 (July 1963): 261, 261n5; Theodore Lyman, *Meade's Army: The Private Notebooks of Lt. Col. Theodore Lyman,* ed. David W. Lowe (Kent, OH: Kent State University Press, 2007), 76; Lyman, *Meade's Headquarters,* 58; J. Franklin Dyer, *The Journal of a Civil War Surgeon,* ed. Michael B. Chesson (Lincoln: University of Nebraska Press, 2003), 133.

22. Happel, "Chancellors of Chancellorsville," 261; Alpheus S. Williams, *From the Cannon's Mouth: The Civil War Letters of General Alpheus S. Williams,* ed. Milo M. Quaife (Detroit: Wayne State University Press, 1959), 184; Lyman, *Meade's Army,* 76; "Battle of the Wilderness," *Daily Constitutionalist* (Augusta, GA), May 31, 1864; Milton Myers Diary, May 6, 1864, FSNMP, Bound Volume 153.

23. Lyman, *Meade's Headquarters,* 53.

24. Rhea, *Battle of the Wilderness,* 82–83.

25. Rhea, *Battle of the Wilderness,* 97–99, 104, 106, 109, 188; Mark Grimsley, *And Keep Moving On: The Virginia Campaign, May–June 1864* (Lincoln: University of Nebraska Press, 2002), 34–35, 42; *OR* 36(1):189, 320.

26. Grimsley, *And Keep Moving On,* 39; *OR* 36(1):906; Lyman, *Meade's Headquarters,* 96.

27. Gordon C. Rhea, "Union Cavalry in the Wilderness: The Education of Philip H. Sheridan and James H. Wilson," in *The Wilderness Campaign,* ed. Gary W. Gallagher (Chapel Hill: University of North Carolina Press, 1997), 124–25.

28. Rhea, *Battle of the Wilderness,* 82, 84–85, 120–27; *OR* 36(1):1063.

29. *OR* 36(1):1055.

30. "Letter from Chaplain Perkins," *Boston Recorder,* May 27, 1864; Lemuel Abijah Abbot, *Personal Recollections and Civil War Diary 1864* (Burlington, VT: Free Press Printing, 1908), 46; Thomas F. Galwey, *The Valiant Hours: An Irishman in the Civil War,* ed. W. S. Nye (Harrisburg, PA: Stackpole, 1961), 195, 199.

31. Alexander Boteler Diary, May 4, 1864, William Elizabeth Brooks Collection, Library of Congress, Washington, DC; "Gen. Longstreet and the Battle of the Wilderness, May 6, 1864," *Daily Constitutionalist* (Augusta, GA), Dec. 20, 1865; Lewis Leon, *Diary of a Tar Heel Confederate Soldier* (Charlotte, NC: Stone, 1913), 60.

32. "The 5th Regiment—One Month's Record," *Newark (NJ) Daily Advertiser,* June 17, 1864; James S. Anderson, *The Papers of James S. Anderson,* ed. Dennis R. Moore (Madison: Archives of the State Historical Society of Wisconsin, 1989), 313; Galwey, *Valiant Hours,* 197–98.

33. "Letter from Virginia," *Charleston (SC) Courier,* May 26, 1864; Henry W. Wingfield Diary, May 6, 1864, FSNMP, Bound Volume 167; John W. Roberts, "The Wilderness and Spotsylvania, May 4–12, 1864: Narrative of a Private Soldier, John W. Roberts," ed. Albert Hubbard Roberts, *Florida Historical Society Quarterly* 11 (Oct. 1932): 62.

34. Abbot, *Personal Recollections and Civil War Diary,* 44; Lyman, *Meade's Headquarters,* 89; Galwey, *Valiant Hours,* 197; "Report of the Operations of the 5th Corps, A. P. in Genl. Grant's Campaign from Culpeper to Petersburg as Seen by W. A. Roebling, Maj. & A.D.C. 1864," May 5, 1864, Box 24, Vol. 7B, Gouverneur Kemble Warren Papers (SC 10668), New York State Library, Albany; Charles Mills to his mother, May 10, 1864, Coco Collection; Daniel M. Holt, *A Surgeon's Civil War: The Letters and Diary of Daniel M. Holt, M.D.,* ed. James M. Greiner, Janet L. Coryell, and James R. Smither (Kent, OH: Kent State University Press, 1994), 182.

35. "Letter from Virginia," *Charleston (SC) Courier,* May 26, 1864; "Gen. Longstreet and the Battle of the Wilderness, May 6, 1864," *Daily Constitutionalist* (Augusta, GA), Dec. 20, 1865; "From General Lee's Army," *Daily South Carolinian* (Columbia), May 28, 1864; "Richmond Correspondence," *Mobile (AL) Advertiser and Register,* June 1, 1864; Henry Heth Report, Dec. 7, 1864, FSNMP, Bound Volume 178.

36. For an analysis of how senses affected the way people experienced certain events of the Civil War, see Mark Smith, *The Smell of Battle, the Taste of Siege: A Sensory History of the Civil War* (New York: Oxford University Press, 2015).

37. "Chaplain Stewarts Letter," *American Presbyterian* (Philadelphia), May 19, 1864. For examples of comments on the noise of the Wilderness combat, see William H. Morse Diary, May 5, 1864, Androscoggin Historical Society, Auburn, ME; William Owen Diary, May 6, 1864, FSNMP, Bound Volume 318; AEOF to unknown, May 15, 1864, FSNMP, Bound Volume 325; Alfred Apted Diary, May 6, 1864, FSNMP, Bound Volume 195.

38. Lyman, *Meade's Headquarters,* 94–95, 97; Galwey, *Valiant Hours,* 197–98; "The 5th Regiment—One Month's Record," *Newark (NJ) Daily Advertiser,* June 17, 1864.

39. *OR* 36(1):1070.

40. *OR* 36(1):1068.

41. "From the Army," *Brockport (NY) Republic,* June 16, 1864; "Report of the Operations of the 5th Corps," May 5, 1864, Warren Papers, New York State Library; Wilbur Fisk, *Hard Marching Every Day: The Civil War Letters of Private Wilbur Fisk, 1861–1865,* ed. Emil Rosenblatt and Ruth Rosenblatt (Lawrence: University Press of Kansas, 1983), 215; "Chaplain Stewarts Letter," *American Presbyterian* (Philadelphia), May 19, 1864; "Letter from Chaplain Perkins," *Boston Recorder,* May 27, 1864; John N. Brown Diary, May 5, 1864, FSNMP, Bound Volume 419.

42. "Benning's Brigade in the Virginia Battles," *Chronicle and Sentinel* (Augusta, GA), June 1, 1864; Charles T. Bowen, *Dear Friends at Home: The Civil War Letters and Diaries of Sergeant Charles T. Bowen,* ed. Edward K. Cassedy (Baltimore: Butternut & Blue, 2001), 459; "The Late Operations of Lee's Army—Battles in the Wilderness, Battle of Tuesday, the 10th, &c.," *Sentinel* (Richmond, VA), May 24, 1864; Roberts, "Wil-

derness and Spotsylvania," 59–60; Henry Heth Report, Dec. 7, 1864, FSNMP, Bound Volume 178.

43. "From the Army," *Brockport (NY) Republic,* June 16, 1864; Elisha Hunt Rhodes, *All for the Union: The Civil War Diary and Letters of Elisha Hunt Rhodes,* ed. Robert Hunt Rhodes (New York: Vintage, 1992), 136; Lyman, *Meade's Headquarters,* 101.

44. Hess, *Civil War Infantry Tactics,* 101; "The 5th Regiment—One Month's Record," *Newark (NJ) Daily Advertiser,* June 17, 1864.

45. For an example of a Union soldier simply stating that the woods were on fire or had caught fire without pointing an accusatory finger at the Confederates, see Rhodes, *All for the Union,* 138.

46. *OR* 36(1):665–66; Robert S. Robertson to his parents, May 14, 1864, FSNMP, Bound Volume 219.

47. Josiah F. Murphey Reminiscences, Ms. "20th" Cab. 6.5, Boston Public Library; "The 5th Regiment—One Month's Record," *Newark (NJ) Daily Advertiser,* June 17, 1864; James W. Freeman Diary, May 6, 1864, FSNMP, Bound Volume 480.

48. For more on the Federal inferiority complex in the Virginia theater, see Michael C. C. Adams, *Our Masters the Rebels: A Speculation on Union Military Failure in the East, 1861–1865* (Cambridge, MA: Harvard University Press, 1978).

49. *OR* 36(1):324

50. William W. Swan, "Battle of the Wilderness," in *Papers of the Military Historical Society of Massachusetts,* vol. 4 (Boston: Military Historical Society of Massachusetts, 1905), 161; Walker, *History of the Second Army Corps,* 432.

51. *OR* 36(1):1055, 1077.

52. "Wofford's Georgia Brigade," *Southern Confederacy* (Atlanta), June 15, 1864; "From General Lee's Army," *Daily South Carolinian* (Columbia), May 28, 1864; *OR* 36(1):1077.

53. Charles Mills to his mother, May 10, 1864, Coco Collection. For an example of a Union soldier's reaction, see Fisk, *Hard Marching Every Day,* 216.

54. "Report of the Operations of the 5th Corps," May 6, 1864, Warren Papers, New York State Library; "From the 110th—Letter from Fred. Larue," *Xenia (OH) Torchlight,* June 1, 1864.

55. "Wofford's Georgia Brigade," *Southern Confederacy* (Atlanta), June 15, 1864; "From General Lee's Army," *Daily South Carolinian* (Columbia), May 28, 1864.

56. "Wofford's Georgia Brigade," *Southern Confederacy* (Atlanta), June 15, 1864.

57. "The Late Operations of Lee's Army—Battles in the Wilderness," *Sentinel* (Richmond, VA), May 24, 1864.

58. Krick, "Like a Duck on a June Bug," 239–40; Rhea, *Battle of the Wilderness,* 353; Thomas W. Hyde, *Following the Greek Cross; or, Memories of the Sixth Army Corps* (Boston: Houghton, Mifflin, 1894), 186.

59. Alexander, *Fighting for the Confederacy,* 363; Galwey, *Valiant Hours,* 198.

60. Lyman, *Meade's Headquarters,* 99; Lee quoted in Emory Thomas, *Robert E. Lee: A Biography* (New York: W. W. Norton, 1995), 414.

5. THE WILDERNESS, MILITARY OPERATIONS, AND MEMORY

1. For a better understanding of the Lost Cause mythology and how it affected the interpretation of the Overland Campaign, see Mark Grimsley, *And Keep Moving On: The Virginia Campaign, May–June 1864* (Lincoln: University of Nebraska Press, 2002), 235–36; Thomas L. Connelly, *The Marble Man: Robert E. Lee and His Image in American Society* (New York: Knopf, 1977), 90–91; Joan Waugh, *U. S. Grant: American Hero, American Myth* (Chapel Hill: University of North Carolina Press, 2009), 185–86, 189; and Brooks D. Simpson, "Continuous Hammering and Mere Attrition: Lost Cause Critics and the Military Reputation of Ulysses S. Grant," in *The Myth of the Lost Cause and Civil War History,* ed. Gary W. Gallagher and Alan T. Nolan (Bloomington: Indiana University Press, 2000).

2. US War Department, *The War of the Rebellion: A Compilation of the Official Records of the Union and Confederate Armies,* 127 vols., index, and atlas (Washington, DC: Government Printing Office, 1880–1901), ser. 1, 25(1):195 (hereafter cited as *OR*).

3. *OR* 25(1):194.

4. *Report of the Joint Committee on the Conduct of the War, at the Second Session Thirty-Eighth Congress,* 3 vols. (Washington, DC: Government Printing Office, 1865), 1:116.

5. *Report of the Joint Committee on the Conduct of the War,* 1:120, 124–25; Joseph Hooker to Samuel Bates, Apr. 2, 1877, Samuel Penniman Bates Papers, 1853–95, Pennsylvania State Archives, Harrisburg; Samuel P. Bates, *The Battle of Chancellorsville* (Meadville, PA: Edward T. Bates, 1882), 67–68.

6. *Report of the Joint Committee on the Conduct of the War,* 1:66, 69.

7. *Report of the Joint Committee on the Conduct of the War,* 1:63.

8. *Report of the Joint Committee on the Conduct of the War,* 1:44.

9. *Report of the Joint Committee on the Conduct of the War,* 1:50; *OR* 25(1):193–204, 29(1):199. Warren appeared before the joint committee in March 1864, between the Mine Run Campaign and the Battle of the Wilderness. One wonders if a second exposure to the Wilderness had caused his understanding of the forest to evolve from the opinions he had expressed in his initial report. *Report of the Joint Committee on the Conduct of the War,* 1:43.

10. George Gordon Meade, *Life and Letters of George Gordon Meade,* ed. George Meade, 2 vols. (New York: Charles Scribner's Sons, 1913), 1:372; Alpheus S. Williams, *From the Cannon's Mouth: The Civil War Letters of General Alpheus S. Williams,* ed. Milo M. Quaife (Detroit: Wayne State University Press, 1959), 186–87.

11. William Swinton, *Campaigns of the Army of the Potomac* (New York: Charles B. Richardson, 1866), 280–81, 303–4; Theodore A. Dodge, *The Campaign of Chancellorsville* (Boston: J. R. Osgood, 1881), 49–50.

12. Darius N. Couch, "The Chancellorsville Campaign," in *Battles and Leaders of the Civil War,* ed. Robert Underwood Johnson and Clarence Clough Buel, vol. 3 (New York: Century, 1884), 159, 161.

13. John Bigelow Jr., *The Campaign of Chancellorsville* (New Haven, CT: Yale University Press, 1910), 235–36, 241, 248, 254–55, 269, 477, 481–82.

14. Robert E. Lee, *The Wartime Papers of R. E. Lee,* ed. Clifford Dowdey and Louis H. Manarin (Boston: Little, Brown, 1961), 462.

15. Lee, *Wartime Papers,* 463, 465, 468.

16. William Allan and Jedediah Hotchkiss, *The Battlefields of Virginia: Chancellorsville, Embracing the Operations of the Army of Northern Virginia, from the First Battle of Fredericksburg to the Death of Lieutenant-General Jackson* (New York: D. Van Nostrand, 1867), 40–42, 66; Edward Porter Alexander, *Military Memoirs of a Confederate* (New York: Charles Scribner's Sons, 1907), 327–28, 357.

17. Dodge, *Campaign of Chancellorsville,* 59–60; Edward Porter Alexander, *Fighting for the Confederacy: The Personal Recollections of General Edward Porter Alexander,* ed. Gary W. Gallagher (Chapel Hill: University of North Carolina Press, 1989), 197.

18. Stephen W. Sears, *Chancellorsville* (Boston: Houghton Mifflin, 1996), 212–13, 223–24.

19. In the immediate aftermath of Chancellorsville, many Union soldiers blamed their defeat on the XI Corps. See Cornelius Moore to Adeline, May 10, 1863, Fredericksburg and Spotsylvania National Military Park, Fredericksburg, VA (hereafter cited as FSNMP), Bound Volume 147; and Christian B. Keller, *Chancellorsville and the Germans: Nativism, Ethnicity and Civil War Memory* (New York: Fordham University Press, 2007).

20. *OR* 29(2):409, 412, 429, 449.

21. *OR* 29(1):13, 29(2):474.

22. *OR* 29(1):13; Meade, *Life and Letters,* 2:156–57.

23. *OR* 29(1):13; Meade, *Life and Letters,* 2:156–57.

24. *OR* 29(1):827.

25. Oscar Hinrichs, a Confederate staff officer, pointed to low ammunition as a reason for the Confederate withdrawal on the night of November 27. Hinrichs, *Stonewall's Prussian Mapmaker: The Journals of Captain Oscar Hinrichs,* ed. Richard Brady Williams (Chapel Hill: University of North Carolina Press, 2014), 98.

26. *OR* 29(1):828–29.

27. *OR* 29(1):14–18. For examples of how historians have interpreted the Mine Run Campaign, see Andrew A. Humphreys, *From Gettysburg to the Rapidan: The Army of the Potomac, July, 1863, to April, 1864* (New York: Charles Scribner's Sons, 1883), 49–70; Jay Luvaas and Wilbur S. Nye, "The Campaign That History Forgot," *Civil War Times Illustrated* 8 (Nov. 1969): 12–36; and Martin F. Graham and George F. Skoch, *Mine Run: A Campaign of Lost Opportunities, October 21, 1863–May 1, 1864* (Lynchburg, VA: H. E. Howard, 1987).

28. *OR* 33:394–95.

29. *OR* 32(2):411–12.

30. *OR* 32(2):412–13.

31. *OR* 36(1):15, 18, 189–90; Meade, *Life and Letters,* 2:194–95, 211.

32. *OR* 36(2):403–4. For other accounts of Meade's reaction, see Swinton, *Campaigns of the Army of the Potomac,* 420–21n; and Charles A. Page, *Letters of a War Correspondent* (Boston: L. C. Page, 1899), 47.

33. *OR* 36(1):1028.

34. *OR* 36(2):948.

35. *OR* 36(1):1070; Robert E. Lee to William L. Smith, July 27, 1868, Mss1 L51c 738, Lee Family Papers, Virginia Historical Society, Richmond.

36. Grimsley, *And Keep Moving On,* 30; Edward Steere, *The Wilderness Campaign: The Meeting of Grant and Lee* (Mechanicsburg, PA: Stackpole Books, 1960), 86–87; Gordon C. Rhea, *The Battle of the Wilderness, May 5–6, 1864* (Baton Rouge: Louisiana State University Press, 1994), 90.

37. *OR* 29(1):827–29.

38. Swinton, *Campaigns of the Army of the Potomac,* 418. For more on Swinton's criticisms of Grant and how Grant's critics used them, see Simpson, "Continuous Hammering and Mere Attrition," 156–59. For an earlier version of Swinton's interpretation, see "The Great Campaign," *New York Times,* May 13, 1864.

39. James L. Van Buren Diary, May 5, 1864, FSNMP, Bound Volume 466; Charles Mills to his mother, May 10, 1864, Coco Collection, US Army Heritage and Education Center; "From the 140th Regiment," *Washington (PA) Reporter,* June 1, 1864; "From the Seventeenth Regiment," *Lamoille Newsdealer* (Hyde Park, VT), June 8, 1864.

40. "Grant's Virginia Campaign," *Columbia Democrat* (Bloomsburg, PA), June 18, 1864.

41. James W. Carter to Mrs. Bell A. Montfort, May 29, 1864, Montfort-Pope-Spain Families Collection, Middle Georgia Archives, Washington Memorial Library, Macon.

42. See, for example, Waugh, *U. S. Grant,* 185–86, 189; Simpson, "Continuous Hammering and Mere Attrition," 148, 157.

43. Armistead Long, *Memoirs of Robert E. Lee* (New York: J. M. Stoddart, 1886), 325–27; Evander M. Law, "From the Wilderness to Cold Harbor," in *Battles and Leaders of the Civil War,* ed. Robert Underwood Johnson and Clarence Clough Buel, vol. 4 (New York: Century, 1884), 122; William M. Dame, *From the Rapidan to Richmond and the Spottsylvania Campaign* (Baltimore: Green-Lucas, 1920), 76.

44. See Simpson, "Continuous Hammering and Mere Attrition," 160–61, 166.

45. Andrew A. Humphreys, *The Virginia Campaign of '64 and '65* (New York: Charles Scribner's Sons, 1885), 10–11; Francis A. Walker, *History of the Second Army Corps in the Army of the Potomac* (New York: Charles Scribner's Sons, 1887), 409.

46. Adam Badeau, *Military History of Ulysses S. Grant from April, 1861, to April 1865,* 3 vols. (New York: D. Appleton, 1881), 2:96–97, 130.

47. Ulysses S. Grant, *The Personal Memoirs of U. S. Grant,* vol. 2 (New York: Charles L. Webster, 1886), 134–37, 178, 180, 185, 187–88, 194, 197–99, 204.

48. Rhea, *Battle of the Wilderness,* 27–28, 55.

CONCLUSION

1. For an excellent analysis of the various factors that distort the memory of combat or a given engagement, see Carol Reardon, "Writing Battle History: The Challenge of Memory," *Civil War History* 53, no. 3 (Sept. 2007).

2. Pertinent studies of Civil War memory are too numerous to mention here. For a brief and broad review of the literature, see Caroline E. Janney, "Memory," in *A Companion to the U.S. Civil War,* vol. 2, ed. Aaron Sheehan-Dean (Malden, MA: Wiley-Blackwell, 2014), 1139–54.

BIBLIOGRAPHY

MANUSCRIPTS

Androscoggin Historical Society, Auburn, ME
William H. Morse Diary

Boston Public Library
Josiah F. Murphey Reminiscences

Boston University, Howard Gotlieb Archival Research Center
Massachusetts Military History Society Collection

Duke University, David M. Rubenstein Rare Book & Manuscript Library, Durham, NC
Confederate Veteran Papers
F. L. Hudgins, "Civil War Battles Section" (1901)
John B. Evans Correspondence
Andrew J. McBride Papers

Emory University, Stuart A. Rose Manuscript, Archives, and Rare Book Library, Atlanta
Benjamin Wesley Justice Papers
David Read Evans Winn Papers
George L. Wren Diaries

Filson Historical Society, Louisville, KY
Rowley-Gifford-Clegg Papers
William Clegg Letter

Fredericksburg and Spotsylvania National Military Park, Fredericksburg, VA (largely copies from miscellaneous collections and descendants of soldiers)
AEOF Letter
Alfred Apted Diary
George A. Bowen Diary
John N. Brown Diary
James A. Carman Letters
T. A. Cooper Memoir
Frederick W. Cross Account
A. Jackson Crossley Letter
J. E. Curran Letter
James W. Freeman Diary
Graham Family Letters
Edwin Groff Letters
Daniel Handy Letter
Francis B. Harris Diary
Charles H. Haynes Diary
Henry Heth Report
George Hugunin Memoir
Henry Keiser Diary
Alexander McNeil Letters
James T. Miller Letters
Cornelius Moore Letters
Milton Myers Diary
William Owen Diary
Alexander S. Patten Diary
Hugh C. Perkins Letters
Warren B. Persons Letter
Philip H. Powers Letters
Edward Perkins Preble Diary
Albert J. Reid Diary
Robert S. Robertson Letters
John H. Shannon Letter

Cyrenus Stevens Diary
John Tiffany Letter
James M. Treichler History
Samuel Turner Letter
James L. Van Buren Diary
Henry W. Wingfield Diary
Thomas F. Wood Memoirs and Letters
George S. Young Diary

Georgia State Archives, Morrow
Civil War Miscellany Personal Papers
David Champion Reminiscences

Library of Congress, Manuscripts Division, Washington, DC
William Elizabeth Brooks Collection
Alexander Boteler Diary
Jedediah Hotchkiss Papers

Massachusetts Historical Society, Boston
Lyman Family Papers

Middle Georgia Archives, Washington Memorial Library, Macon
Montfort-Pope-Spain Families Collection

New Hampshire Historical Society Library, Concord
George E. Upton Letters

New York State Library, Albany
Gouverneur Kemble Warren Papers

North Carolina State Archives, Raleigh
Isaac S. London Collection
Noah Collins Diary

Pennsylvania State Archives, Harrisburg
Samuel Penniman Bates Papers, 1853–95

US Army Heritage and Education Center, Carlisle Barracks, PA
Civil War Documents Collection
Isaac McQueen Auld Letters
Aaron L. DeArmond Letters
William Kerns Diary
Civil War Times Illustrated Collection
Frederick W. Oesterle Memoir
Coco Collection
Charles Mills Letters
Frederick Swift Diary
William Howard Collection
George B. Wolcott Letters

University of Georgia, Special Collections, Hargrett Rare Books & Manuscript Library, Athens
Francis S. Johnson Letters

University of Michigan, Bentley Historical Library, Ann Arbor
Michigan Historical Collections
James Houghton Journal
William H. Randall Reminiscences
Lucis B. Shattuck Papers

University of Michigan, William L. Clements Library, Ann Arbor
James S. Schoff Civil War Collection
Isaac O. Best, "Through the Wilderness with Grant"
Nathaniel W. Bunker Memoir

University of North Carolina at Chapel Hill, Southern Historical Collection, Wilson Library
Charles William Dabney Papers
David Gregg McIntosh Manuscript

Virginia Historical Society, Richmond
St. George Tucker Coalter Bryan Memoir
Grinnan Family Papers
James Hays Papers

Lee Family Papers
James Eldred Phillips Papers
Pendleton Family Papers

Virginia Military Institute Archives, Lexington
John Garibaldi Letters

NEWSPAPERS

American Presbyterian (Philadelphia)
Boston Daily Advertiser
Boston Evening Transcript
Boston Recorder
Brockport (NY) Republic
Centinel of Freedom (Newark, NJ)
Charleston (SC) Courier
Charleston (SC) Mercury
Chronicle and Sentinel (Augusta, GA)
Columbia Democrat (Bloomsburg, PA)
Confederate Union (Milledgeville, GA)
Corning (NY) Journal
Daily Constitutionalist (Augusta, GA)
Daily Dispatch (Richmond, VA)
Daily Saratogian (Saratoga Springs, NY)
Daily South Carolinian (Columbia)
Fayetteville (NC) Observer
Hillsborough (NC) Recorder
Lamoille Newsdealer (Hyde Park, VT)
Mobile (AL) Advertiser and Register
Mohawk Valley Register (Fort Plain, NY)
National Tribune (Washington, DC)
Newark (NJ) Daily Advertiser
New York Times
Philadelphia Weekly Times
Providence (RI) Evening Press
Sentinel (Richmond, VA)
Southern Confederacy (Atlanta, GA)

Union (NY) News
Washington (PA) Reporter
Xenia (OH) Torchlight

PRIMARY SOURCES—BOOKS

Abbot, Lemuel Abijah. *Personal Recollections and Civil War Diary 1864*. Burlington, VT: Free Press Printing, 1908.

Adams, John R. *Memorial and Letters of Rev. John R. Adams, D.D., Chaplain of the Fifth Maine and One Hundred and Twenty-First New York Regiments during the War of the Rebellion, Serving from the Beginning to Its Close.* Cambridge, MA: University Press, Privately Printed, 1890.

Alexander, Edward P. *Fighting for the Confederacy: The Personal Recollections of General Edward Porter Alexander.* Edited by Gary W. Gallagher. Chapel Hill: University of North Carolina Press, 1989.

———. *Military Memoirs of a Confederate.* New York: Charles Scribner's Sons, 1907.

Anderson, James S. *The Papers of James S. Anderson.* Edited by Dennis R. Moore. Madison: Archives of the State Historical Society of Wisconsin, 1989.

Bahnson, Charles Frederic. *Bright and Gloomy Days: The Civil War Correspondence of Captain Charles Frederic Bahnson, a Moravian Confederate.* Edited by Sarah Bahnson Chapman. Knoxville: University of Tennessee Press, 2003.

Bayne, Howard R., and Peyton H. Hoge. *The Travels of Ego and Alter, an Epistolary Narrative of a Tramp through the Old Dominion.* Richmond, VA: West, Johnston, 1879.

Bowen, Charles T. *Dear Friends at Home: The Civil War Letters and Diaries of Sergeant Charles T. Bowen.* Edited by Edward K. Cassedy. Baltimore: Butternut & Blue, 2001.

Brewster, Charles Harvey. *When This Cruel War Is Over: The Civil War Letters of Charles Harvey Brewster.* Edited by David W. Blight. Amherst: University of Massachusetts Press, 1992.

Buell, Augustus C. *"The Cannoneer": Recollections of Service in the Army of the Potomac.* Washington, DC: National Tribune, 1890.

Caldwell, J. F. J. *The History of a Brigade of South Carolinians, First Known as Gregg's, and Subsequently as McGowan's Brigade.* Philadelphia: King & Baird, 1866.

Coles, R. T. *From Huntsville to Appomattox: R. T. Coles's History of 4th Regiment, Alabama Volunteer Infantry, C.S.A., Army of Northern Virginia.* Edited by Jeffrey D. Stocker. Knoxville: University of Tennessee Press, 1996.

Dame, William M. *From the Rapidan to Richmond and the Spottsylvania Campaign.* Baltimore: Green-Lucas, 1920.

Dyer, J. Franklin. *The Journal of a Civil War Surgeon.* Edited by Michael B. Chesson. Lincoln: University of Nebraska Press, 2003.

Fisk, Wilbur. *Hard Marching Every Day: The Civil War Letters of Private Wilbur Fisk, 1861–1865.* Edited by Emil Rosenblatt and Ruth Rosenblatt. Lawrence: University Press of Kansas, 1983.

Galwey, Thomas F. *The Valiant Hours: An Irishman in the Civil War.* Edited by W. S. Nye. Harrisburg, PA: Stackpole, 1961.

Grant, Ulysses S. *The Personal Memoirs of U. S. Grant.* 2 vols. New York: Charles L. Webster, 1886.

Griswold, Anna. *Col. Griswold.* Boston, 1867.

Hampton, N. J. *An Eyewitness to the Dark Days of 1861–65.* Nashville, 1898.

Hinrichs, Oscar. *Stonewall's Prussian Mapmaker: The Journals of Captain Oscar Hinrichs.* Edited by Richard Brady Williams. Chapel Hill: University of North Carolina Press, 2014.

Holt, Daniel M. *A Surgeon's Civil War: The Letters and Diary of Daniel M. Holt, M.D.* Edited by James M. Greiner, Janet L. Coryell, and James R. Smither. Kent, OH: Kent State University Press, 1994.

Hotchkiss, Jedediah. *Make Me a Map of the Valley: The Civil War Journal of Stonewall Jackson's Topographer.* Edited by Archie P. McDonald. Dallas: Southern Methodist University Press, 1973.

Hyde, Thomas W. *Following the Greek Cross; or, Memories of the Sixth Army Corps.* Boston: Houghton, Mifflin, 1894.

Johnson, Richard W. *A Soldier's Reminiscences in Peace and War.* Philadelphia: J. R. Lippincott, 1886.

Lee, Robert E. *The Wartime Papers of R. E. Lee.* Edited by Clifford Dowdey and Louis H. Manarin. Boston: Little, Brown, 1961.

Leon, L. *Diary of a Tar Heel Confederate Soldier.* Charlotte, NC: Stone, 1913.

Longstreet, James. *From Manassas to Appomattox: Memoirs of the Civil War in America.* Philadelphia: J. B. Lippincott, 1896.

Lyman, Theodore. *Meade's Army: The Private Notebooks of Lt. Col. Theodore Lyman.* Edited by David W. Lowe. Kent, OH: Kent State University Press, 2007.

———. *Meade's Headquarters, 1863–1865: Letters of Colonel Theodore Lyman from the Wilderness to Appomattox.* Edited by George R. Agassiz. Boston: Atlantic Monthly Press, 1922.

Mann, Thomas H. *Fighting with the Eighteenth Massachusetts: The Civil War Memoir of Thomas H. Mann.* Edited by John J. Hennessy. Baton Rouge: Louisiana State University Press, 2000.

Marshall, Jeffrey D. *A War of the People: Vermont Civil War Letters.* Hanover, NH: University Press of New England, 1999.

McAllister, Robert. *The Civil War Letters of General Robert McAllister.* Edited by James I. Robertson Jr. New Brunswick, NJ: Rutgers University Press, 1965.

Meade, George Gordon. *Life and Letters of George Gordon Meade.* 2 vols. Edited by George Meade. New York: Charles Scribner's Sons, 1913.

Names of Officers and Soldiers Found on the Battle-fields of the Wilderness and Spottsylvania Court House, VA. Washington, DC: Government Printing Office, 1865.

Olmsted, Frederick Law. *A Journey in the Seaboard Slave States in the Years 1853–1854, with Remarks on Their Economy.* 2 vols. New York: G. P. Putnam's Sons, 1904.

Otto, John Henry. *Memoirs of a Dutch Mudsill: The "War Memories" of John Henry Otto, Captain, Company D, 21st Regiment Wisconsin Volunteer Infantry.* Edited by David Gould and James B. Kennedy. Kent, OH: Kent State University Press, 2004.

Page, Charles A. *Letters of a War Correspondent.* Boston: L. C. Page, 1899.

Polley, J. B. *A Soldier's Letters to Charming Nellie.* New York: Neale, 1908.

Porter, Horace. *Campaigning with Grant.* New York: Century, 1897.

Raymer, Jacob Nathaniel. *Confederate Correspondent: The Civil War Reports of Jacob Nathaniel Raymer, Fourth North Carolina.* Edited by E. B. Munson. Jefferson, NC: McFarland, 2008.

Report of the Joint Committee on the Conduct of the War, at the Second Session Thirty-Eighth Congress. 3 vols. Washington, DC: Government Printing Office, 1865.

Rhodes, Elisha Hunt. *All for the Union: The Civil War Diary and Letters of Elisha Hunt Rhodes.* Edited by Robert Hunt Rhodes. New York: Vintage, 1992.

Seymour, William J. *The Civil War Memoirs of Captain William J. Seymour.* Edited by Terry L. Jones. Baton Rouge: Louisiana State University Press, 1991.

Shepard, Norton C. *Out of the Wilderness: The Civil War Memoir of Cpl. Norton C. Shepard, 146th New York Volunteer Infantry.* Edited by Raymond W. Smith. Hamilton, NY: Edmonston, 1998.

Small, Abner R. *The Road to Richmond: The Civil War Memoirs of Abner R. Small of the 16th Maine Volunteers.* Berkeley: University of California Press, 1939.

Smith, Thomas W. *We Have It Damn Hard Out Here: The Civil War Letters of Sergeant Thomas W. Smith, 6th Pennsylvania Cavalry.* Edited by Eric J. Wittenberg. Kent, OH: Kent State University Press, 1999.

Somers, Robert. *The Southern States since the War, 1870–1871.* New York: Macmillan, 1871.

Sorrel, G. Moxley. *Recollections of a Confederate Staff Officer.* New York: Neale, 1905.

Stevens, George T. *Three Years in the Sixth Corps.* New York: D. Van Nostrand, 1870.

Stewart, A. M. *Camp, March, and Battle-Field; or, Three Years and a Half with the Army of the Potomac.* Philadelphia: Jas. B. Rodgers, 1865.

Stiles, Robert. *Four Years under Marse Robert.* New York: Neale, 1904.

Trobriand, Regis de. *Four Years with the Army of the Potomac.* Translated by George K. Dauchy. Boston: Ticknor, 1889.

Trowbridge, J. T. *The South: A Tour of Its Battle-Fields and Ruined Cities, a Journey through the Desolated States, and Talks with the People.* Hartford, CT: L. Stebbins, 1866.

Trueheart, Charles, and Henry Trueheart. *Rebel Brothers: The Civil War Letters of the Truehearts.* Edited by Edward B. Williams. College Station: Texas A&M University Press, 1995.

Tyler, Mason Whiting. *Recollections of the Civil War.* Edited by William S. Tyler. New York: G. P. Putnam's Sons, 1912.

US War Department. *The War of the Rebellion: A Compilation of the Official Records of the Union and Confederate Armies.* 127 vols., index, and atlas. Washington, DC: Government Printing Office, 1880–1901.

Wainwright, Charles S. *A Diary of Battle: The Personal Journals of Colonel Charles S. Wainwright, 1861–1865.* Edited by Allan Nevins. New York: Harcourt, Brace, & World, 1962.

Wilcox, Orlando B. *Forgotten Valor: The Memoirs, Journals, and Civil War Letters of Orlando B. Wilcox.* Edited by Robert Garth Scott. Kent, OH: Kent State University Press, 1999.

Wilkeson, Frank. *Recollections of a Private Soldier in the Army of the Potomac.* New York: G. P. Putnam's Sons, 1887.

Williams, Alpheus S. *From the Cannon's Mouth: The Civil War Letters of General Alpheus S. Williams.* Edited by Milo M. Quaife. Detroit: Wayne State University Press, 1959.

PRIMARY SOURCES—ARTICLES

"An Ex-Campaigner in Virginia." In *Rifle Shots and Bugle Notes; or, The National Military Album of Sketches of the Principal Battles, Marches, Picket Duty, Camp Fires, Love Adventures, and Poems Connected with the Late War*, edited by Joseph A. Joel and Lewis R. Stegman, 423–28. New York: Grand Army Gazette Publishing, 1884.

Bates, Samuel P. "Hooker's Comments on Chancellorsville." In *Battles and Leaders of the Civil War*, edited by Robert Underwood Johnson and Clarence Clough Buel, 3:215–23. New York: Century, 1884.

Bonaparte, Jerome N., Jr. "Journey to the Springs, 1846." Edited by William D. Hoyt. *Virginia Magazine of History and Biography* 54, no. 2 (April 1946): 119–36.

Byrd, William. "A Progress to the Mines in the Year 1732." In *The Westover Manuscripts: Containing the History of the Dividing Line Betwixt Virginia and North Carolina; a Journey to the Land of Eden, A.D. 1733; and a Progress to the Mines. Written from 1728 to 1736, and Now First Published.* Petersburg, VA: Edmund and Julian C. Ruffin, 1841. Available online at Documenting the American South, http://docsouth.unc.edu/nc/byrd/byrd.html.

Couch, Darius N. "The Chancellorsville Campaign." In *Battles and Leaders of the Civil War*, edited by Robert Underwood Johnson and Clarence Clough Buel, 3:154–71. New York: Century, 1884.

Dority, Orin G. "The Civil War Diary of Orin G. Dority." Pt. 1. *Northwest Ohio Quarterly* 37, no. 1 (Winter 1964–65): 7–26.

Hill, Daniel H. "Chickamauga—The Great Battle of the West." In *Battles and Leaders of the Civil War*, edited by Robert Underwood Johnson and Clarence Clough Buel, 3:638–62. New York: Century, 1884.

Howard, McHenry. "Notes and Recollections of Opening of the Campaign of 1864." In *Papers of the Military Historical Society of Massachusetts.* Vol. 4:81–116. Boston: Military Historical Society of Massachusetts, 1905.

Jeffries, Lemuel. "'The Excitement Had Begun!': The Civil War Diary of Lemuel Jeffries, 1862–1863." Edited by Jason H. Silverman. *Manuscripts* 30 (Fall 1978): 265–78.

Landon, William D. "Fourteenth Indiana Regiment, Letters to the Vincennes Western Sun." *Indiana Magazine of History* 34 (March 1938): 71–98.

———. "Prock's Last Letters to the Vincennes Western Sun." *Indiana Magazine of History* 35 (March 1939): 76–94.

Law, Evander M. "From the Wilderness to Cold Harbor." In *Battles and Leaders of the Civil War*, edited by Robert Underwood Johnson and Clarence Clough Buel, 4:118–44. New York: Century, 1884.

Lyman, Theodore. "Uselessness of the Maps Furnished to Staff of the Army of the Potomac Previous to the Campaign of May 1864." In *Papers of the Military Historical Society of Massachusetts*, 4:77–80. Boston: Military Historical Society of Massachusetts, 1905.

Mason, Edwin C. "Recollections of the Mine Run Campaign." In *Glimpses of the Nation's Struggle: A Series of Papers Read before the Minnesota Commandery of the Military Order of the Loyal Legion of the United States*, 1:308–36. St. Paul: St. Paul Book and Stationary, 1887.

Melcher, Holman S. "An Experience in the Battle of the Wilderness." In *War Papers, Read before the Commandery of the State of Maine, Military Order of the Loyal Legion of the United States*, 1:73–84. Portland, ME: Thurston Print, 1898.

Oden, John Piney. "The End of Oden's War: A Confederate Captain's Diary." Edited by Michael Barton. *Alabama Historical Quarterly* 43, no. 2 (Summer 1981): 73–98.

Prentice, Sartell. "The Opening Hours in the Wilderness in 1864." In *Military Essays and Recollections: Papers Read before the Commandery of the State of Illinois, Military Order of the Loyal Legion of the United States*, 2:99–119. Chicago: A. C. McClurg, 1894.

Roberts, John W. "The Wilderness and Spotsylvania, May 4–12, 1864: Narrative of a Private Soldier, John W. Roberts." Edited by Albert Hubbard Roberts. *Florida Historical Society Quarterly* 11 (October 1932): 58–76.

Seiser, August. "August Seiser's Civil War Diary." Edited by Blake McKelvery. *Rochester Historical Society Publications* 22 (1944): 174–98.

Smith, Channing M. "In the Wilderness." *Confederate Veteran* 29, no. 6 (June 1921): 212.

Starr, Darius. "From Spotsylvania Courthouse to Andersonville: A Diary of Darius Starr." Edited by E. Merton Coulter. *Georgia Historical Quarterly* 41 (June 1957): 176–90.

Stevens, Hazard. "The Sixth Corps in the Wilderness." In *Papers of the Military Historical Society of Massachusetts*, 4:175–203. Boston: Military Historical Society of Massachusetts, 1905.

Swan, William W. "Battle of the Wilderness." In *Papers of the Military Historical Society of Massachusetts*, 4:117–63. Boston: Military Historical Society of Massachusetts, 1905.

Venable, Charles S. "General Lee in the Wilderness Campaign." In *Battles and Leaders of the Civil War.* Edited by Robert Underwood Johnson and Clarence Clough Buel, 4:240–46. New York: Century, 1884.

Waterman, Arba N. "The Battle of Chickamauga." In *Military Essays and Recollections: Papers Read before the Commandery of the State of Illinois, Military Order of the Loyal Legion of the United States,* 1:231–45. Chicago: A. C. McClurg, 1891.

Wells, John D. "The Scars of War: Battlefields of Northern Virginia Forty-Five Years After." *Metropolitan Magazine* 25, no. 5 (February 1907): 532–49.

Wilcox, Cadmus. "Lee and Grant in the Wilderness." In *The Annals of the War Written by Leading Participants North and South,* 485–501. Philadelphia: Times Publishing, 1879.

SECONDARY SOURCES—BOOKS

Adams, Michael C. C. *Our Masters the Rebels: A Speculation on Union Military Failure in the East, 1861–1865.* Cambridge, MA: Harvard University Press, 1978.

Adams, Sean Patrick. *Iron from the Wilderness: The History of Virginia's Catharine Furnace.* Washington, DC: National Park Service, 2011.

Allan, William, and Jedediah Hotchkiss. *The Battlefields of Virginia: Chancellorsville, Embracing the Operations of the Army of Northern Virginia, from the First Battle of Fredericksburg to the Death of Lieutenant General Jackson.* New York: D. Van Nostrand, 1867.

Anderson, Archer. *The Campaign and Battle of Chickamauga: An Address delivered before the Virginia Division of the Army of Northern Virginia Association, at Their Annual Meeting, in the Capitol at Richmond, Va., October 25, 1881.* Richmond: William Ellis Jones Steam Book and Job Printer, 1881.

Andrews, J. Cutler. *The North Reports the Civil War.* Pittsburgh: University of Pittsburgh Press, 1955.

Badeau, Adam. *Military History of Ulysses S. Grant from April, 1861, to April, 1865.* 3 vols. New York: D. Appleton, 1881.

Bates, Samuel P. *The Battle of Chancellorsville.* Meadville, PA: Edward T. Bates, 1882.

Battine, Cecil. *The Crisis of the Confederacy: A History of Gettysburg and the Wilderness.* London: Longmans, Green, 1905.

Bennett, Lyman G., and William M. Haigh. *History of the Thirty-Sixth Regiment Illinois Volunteers.* Aurora, IL: Knickerbocker & Hodder, 1876.

Bigelow, John, Jr. *The Campaign of Chancellorsville*. New Haven, CT: Yale University Press, 1910.

Brady, Lisa M. *War upon the Land: Military Strategy and the Transformation of Southern Landscapes during the American Civil War*. Athens: University of Georgia Press, 2012.

Brainard, Mary Genevie Green. *Campaigns of the One Hundred and Forty-Sixth Regiment, New York State Volunteers*. New York: G. P. Putnam's Sons, 1915.

Catton, Bruce. *A Stillness at Appomattox*. Garden City, NY: Doubleday, 1953.

Chamberlain, Thomas. *History of the One Hundred and Fiftieth Regiment, Pennsylvania Volunteers, Second Regiment, Bucktail Brigade*. Philadelphia: J. B. Lippincott, 1895.

Connelly, Thomas L. *The Marble Man: Robert E. Lee and His Image in American Society*. New York: Knopf, 1977.

Cowdrey, Albert E. *This Land, This South: An Environmental History*. Lexington: University Press of Kentucky, 1983.

Cozzens, Peter. *This Terrible Sound: The Battle of Chickamauga*. Urbana: University of Illinois Press, 1992.

Craven, Avery O. *Soil Exhaustion as a Factor in the Agricultural History of Virginia and Maryland, 1606–1860*. Urbana: University of Illinois Press, 1925.

Cudworth, Warren H. *History of the First Regiment (Massachusetts Infantry)*. Boston: Walker, Fuller, 1866.

Cushman, Stephen. *Bloody Promenade: Reflections on a Civil War Battle*. Charlottesville: University Press of Virginia, 1999.

Day, L. W. *Story of the One Hundred and First Ohio Infantry: A Memorial Volume*. Cleveland, OH: W. M. Bayne Printing, 1894.

Dodge, Theodore A. *The Campaign of Chancellorsville*. Boston: J. R. Osgood, 1881.

Fales, Henry. *History of the Thirty-Eighth Regiment Indiana Volunteer Infantry*. Palo Alto, CA: F. A. Stuart, 1906.

Faust, Drew. *This Republic of Suffering: Death and the American Civil War*. New York: Alfred A. Knopf, 2008.

Freeman, Douglas Southall. *R. E. Lee: A Biography*. 4 vols. New York: Charles Scribner's Sons, 1935.

Graham, Martin F., and George F. Skoch. *Mine Run: A Campaign of Lost Opportunities, October 21, 1863–May 1, 1864*. Lynchburg, VA: H. E. Howard, 1987.

Grimsley, Mark. *And Keep Moving On: The Virginia Campaign, May–June 1864*. Lincoln: University of Nebraska Press, 2002.

Hess, Earl J. *Civil War Infantry Tactics: Training, Combat, and Small-Unit Effectiveness*. Baton Rouge: Louisiana State University Press, 2015.
———. *The Civil War in the West: Victory and Defeat from the Appalachians to the Mississippi*. Chapel Hill: University of North Carolina Press, 2012.
———. *Field Armies and Fortifications in the Civil War: The Eastern Campaigns, 1861–1864*. Chapel Hill: University of North Carolina Press, 2005.
———. *Trench Warfare under Grant & Lee: Field Fortifications in the Overland Campaign*. Chapel Hill: University of North Carolina Press, 2007.
———. *The Union Soldier in Battle: Enduring the Ordeal of Combat*. Lawrence: University Press of Kansas, 1997.
History of the Corn Exchange Regiment, 118th Pennsylvania Volunteers. Philadelphia: J. L. Smith, 1888), 397.
Hopkins, William P. *The Seventh Regiment Rhode Island Volunteers in the Civil War, 1862–1865*. Providence, RI: Snow & Farnham, 1903.
Humphreys, Andrew A. *From Gettysburg to the Rapidan: The Army of the Potomac July, 1863, to April, 1864*. New York: Charles Scribner's Sons, 1883.
———. *The Virginia Campaign of '64 and '65*. New York: Charles Scribner's Sons, 1885.
Jackson, Harry F. "The Utica Turnpike Road Company." *New York History* 40, no. 1 (January 1959): 18–32.
Keller, Christian B. *Chancellorsville and the Germans: Nativism, Ethnicity and Civil War Memory*. New York: Fordham University Press, 2007.
Kirk, Hyland C. *Heavy Guns and Light: A History of the 4th New York Heavy Artillery*. New York: C. T. Dillingham, 1890.
Lee, Fitzhugh. *General Lee*. New York: D. Appleton, 1894.
Long, Armistead. *Memoirs of Robert E. Lee*. New York: J. M. Stoddart, 1886.
Lossing, Benson J. *A History of the Civil War*. New York: War Memorial Association, 1912.
McPherson, James M. *Battle Cry of Freedom: The Civil War Era*. New York: Oxford University Press, 1988.
Meier, Kathryn Shively. *Nature's Civil War: Common Soldiers and the Environment in 1862 Virginia*. Chapel Hill: University of North Carolina Press, 2015.
Mitchell, Reid. *Civil War Soldiers*. New York: Viking, 1988.
Nash, Roderick Frazier. *Wilderness and the American Mind*. New Haven, CT: Yale University Press, 1967.
Nelson, Megan Kate. *Ruin Nation: Destruction and the American Civil War*. Athens: University of Georgia Press, 2012.

Polley, J. B. *Hood's Texas Brigade: Its Marches, Its Battles, Its Achievements.* New York: Neale, 1910.

Powell, William H. *The Fifth Army Corps.* New York: G. P. Putnam's Sons, 1896.

Rhea, Gordon C. *The Battle of the Wilderness, May 5–6, 1864.* Baton Rouge: Louisiana State University Press, 1994.

Royse, Isaac Henry Clay. *History of the 115th Regiment Illinois Volunteer Infantry.* Terre Haute, IN, 1900.

Schaff, Morris. *The Battle of the Wilderness.* Boston: Houghton Mifflin, 1910.

Schantz, Mark. *Awaiting the Heavenly Country: The Civil War and America's Culture of Death.* Ithaca, NY: Cornell University Press, 2008.

Sears, Stephen W. *Chancellorsville.* Boston: Houghton Mifflin, 1996.

Smith, Mark. *The Smell of Battle, the Taste of Siege: A Sensory History of the Civil War.* New York: Oxford University Press, 2015,

Steere, Edward. *The Wilderness Campaign: The Meeting of Grant and Lee.* Mechanicsburg, PA: Stackpole Books, 1960.

Sutherland, Daniel E. *Fredericksburg and Chancellorsville: The Dare Mark Campaign.* Lincoln: University of Nebraska Press, 1998.

Swinton, William. *Campaigns of the Army of the Potomac.* New York: Charles B. Richardson, 1866.

Thomas, Emory. *Robert E. Lee: A Biography.* New York: W. W. Norton, 1995.

Tourgée, Albion Winegar. *The Story of a Thousand.* Buffalo, NY: S. McGerald & Son, 1896.

Tucker, Glenn. *Chickamauga: Bloody Battle in the West.* Dayton, OH: Bobbs-Merrill, 1961.

Turchin, John B. *Chickamauga.* Chicago: Fergus Printing, 1888.

Walker, Francis A. *History of the Second Army Corps in the Army of the Potomac.* New York: Charles Scribner's Sons, 1887.

Ward, Joseph R. C. *History of the 106th Regiment Pennsylvania Volunteers, 2d Brigade, 2d Division, 2d Corps, 1861–1865.* Philadelphia: F. McManus Jr., 1906.

Waugh, Joan. *U. S. Grant: American Hero, American Myth.* Chapel Hill: University of North Carolina Press, 2009.

Wert, Jeffry D. *The Sword of Lincoln: The Army of the Potomac.* New York: Simon & Schuster, 2005.

Winters, Harold A. *Battling the Elements: Weather and Terrain in the Conduct of War.* Baltimore: Johns Hopkins University Press, 1998.

Woodworth, Steven E. *Six Armies in Tennessee: The Chickamauga and Chattanooga Campaigns.* Lincoln: University of Nebraska Press, 1998.

SECONDARY SOURCES—ARTICLES

Happel, Ralph. "The Chancellors of Chancellorsville." *Virginia Magazine of History and Biography* 71, no. 3 (July 1963): 259–77.

Hennessy, John. "The Origins of the Wilderness: Part I—The Soil." July 15, 2010. *Mysteries & Conundrums: Exploring the Civil War–Era Landscape in the Fredericksburg & Spotsylvania Region.* https://npsfrsp.wordpress.com/2010/07/15/the-origins-of-the-wilderness-part-i-the-soil/.

———. "Wilderness Origins Part II: Clear-cutting (or not)." July 16, 2010. *Mysteries & Conundrums: Exploring the Civil War–Era Landscape in the Fredericksburg & Spotsylvania Region.* https://npsfrsp.wordpress.com/2010/07/16/wilderness-origins-part-ii-clear-cutting-or-not/.

Janney, Caroline E. "Memory." In *A Companion to the U.S. Civil War.* Edited by Aaron Sheehan-Dean, 2:1139–54. Malden, MA: Wiley-Blackwell, 2014.

Klein, Daniel B., and John Majewski. "Plank Road Fever in Antebellum America: New York State Origins." *New York History* 75, no. 1 (January 1994): 39–65.

Krick, Robert E. L. "Like a Duck on a June Bug: James Longstreet's Flank Attack, May 6, 1864." In *The Wilderness Campaign,* edited by Gary W. Gallagher, 236–64. Chapel Hill: University of North Carolina Press, 1997.

Luvaas, Jay, and Wilbur S. Nye. "The Campaign That History Forgot." *Civil War Times Illustrated* 8 (November 1969):11–37.

Meier, Kathryn S. "Fighting in 'Dante's Inferno': Changing Perceptions of Civil War Combat in the Spotsylvania Wilderness from 1863 to 1864." In *Militarized Landscapes: From Gettysburg to Salisbury Plain,* edited by Chris Pearson, Peter Coates, and Tim Cole, 39–56. London: Continuum, 2010.

Neely, Mark E., Jr. "Wilderness and the Cult of Manliness: Hooker, Lincoln, and Defeat." In *Lincoln's Generals,* edited by Gabor S. Boritt, 51–77. New York: Oxford University Press, 1995.

Powell, James Harrison. "'Seven Year Locusts': The Deforestation of Spotsylvania County during the American Civil War." *Essays in History* 43 (2010). http://www.essaysinhistory.com/seven-year-locusts-the-deforestation-of-spotsylvania-county-during-the-american-civil-war/.

Reardon, Carol. "Writing Battle History: The Challenge of Memory." *Civil War History* 53, no. 3 (September 2007): 252–63.

Rhea, Gordon C. "Union Cavalry in the Wilderness: The Education of Philip H. Sheridan and James H. Wilson." In *The Wilderness Campaign,* edited by Gary W. Gallagher, 106–35. Chapel Hill: University of North Carolina Press, 1997.

Sachs, Aaron. "Stumps in the Wilderness." In *The Blue, the Gray, and the Green: Toward an Environmental History of the Civil War*. Edited by Brian Allen Drake, 96–108. Athens: University of Georgia Press, 2015.

Simpson, Brooks D. "Continuous Hammering and Mere Attrition: Lost Cause Critics and the Military Reputation of Ulysses S. Grant." In *The Myth of the Lost Cause and Civil War History*. Edited by Gary W. Gallagher and Alan T. Nolan, 147–69. Bloomington: Indiana University Press, 2000.

INDEX

Note: Page numbers in italics signify illustrations.